D1066140

"Fear Was Not In Him"

Francis C. Barlow as a major general. (Library of Congress)

"Fear Was Not In Him"

The Civil War Letters of
Major General Francis C. Barlow, U.S.A.

Edited by
CHRISTIAN G. SAMITO

Fordham University Press
New York
2004

The North's Civil War, No. 28
ISSN 1089-8719

Library of Congress Cataloging-in-Publication Data

Barlow, Francis C. (Francis Channing), 1834-1896.
    Fear was not in him : the Civil War letters of Major General Francis C. Barlow, U.S.A. / edited by Christian G. Samito.
        p.   cm.— (The North's Civil War series)
    Includes bibliographical references and index.
    ISBN 0-8232-2323-X—ISBN 0-8232-2324-8 (pbk.)
    1. Barlow, Francis C. (Francis Channing), 1834–1896—Correspondence.   2. United States—History—Civil War, 1861–1865—Personal narratives.   3. United States—History—Civil War, 1861–1865—Campaigns.   4. Generals—United States—Correspondence.   5. United States. Army—Biography.
I. Samito, Christian G.   II. Title.   III. North's Civil War
E467.1.B25A4   2004
973.7′3′092—dc22   2003024283

Printed in the United States of America
08   07   08   05   04   5   4   3   2   1
First edition

For James V. Samito, who fought with the 88th "Blue Devil" Division in Italy, and Henry S. Kazmierski, who fought with the 688th Field Artillery Battalion in France during World War II

CONTENTS

PREFACE AND ACKNOWLEDGMENTS

The Civil War remains fresh in American memory, in part, because personal papers written by participants in that conflict are continually being discovered or published. In this way, modern readers can bridge the divide of time and gain fresh insights into the inner thoughts and experiences of those who witnessed and shaped events that occurred decades ago.

In June 1942, the children of Francis Channing Barlow donated their father's letters to the Massachusetts Historical Society in Boston. At present, the Massachusetts Historical Society holds most of the surviving letters written by Barlow, and all the letters used in this volume are located there unless otherwise noted. With this publication, the words and deeds of a remarkable Union general take on new immediacy.

Several people assisted me in this work and I would like to acknowledge their help. As usual, Peter Drummey, Ted Hutchinson, and the rest of the staff at the Massachusetts Historical Society proved invaluable during this project, and I am grateful for that institution's permission to publish these letters as well as for their cheerful support. The National Archives, New-York Historical Society, and the library staffs at Harvard University and Bowdoin College swiftly sent me necessary archival papers upon request. Andrew J. Martin, Director of Communications at the Association of the Bar of the City of New York assisted in my understanding of Barlow's role with that organization's founding, and Libby MacDonald Bischoff aided my interpretation of Barlow's relations with Winslow Homer. As the dean of Gettysburg historians, Harry W. Pfanz not only engaged in a friendly and encouraging correspondence with me concerning this project but also showed himself to be both a scholar and a gentleman. I am also grateful to Frank A. Boyle for his encouragement and for providing his typescript copy of the Thomas Smyth diary.

At Boston College, Professor David Quigley provided me with valuable ideas and considerations after reading and commenting on this manuscript. He has not only greatly aided in producing this volume but, along with Professors Alan Rogers and James O'Toole, been a true mentor. I not only appreciate their academic guidance but friendship as well. Professor Robin Fleming obtained a research grant for me from Boston College that helped defray some of my initial research costs. As they have done for years, the Interlibrary Loan Staff at O'Neill Library has cheerfully obtained for me all sorts of obscure sources and continually surprises me as to how they do it.

I would like to thank Professor Paul Cimbala and the staff at Fordham University Press both for their valuable comments and improvements on my manuscript as well as for agreeing to publish it in the first place.

I would like to thank all my friends, whose support and fellowship are more important to me than they might know. From those dating back to my days at Holy Cross to those friends met in Boston or through my various projects, to the History Department at Boston College, to Donovan Hatem—all of these individuals at times feel more like an extended family, and I am very lucky to know them. Finally, I would like to thank my parents and family for their continuous love and support, as well as their patience in enduring frequent digressions into the nineteenth century. This book is dedicated to my grandfathers, who taught me more than they probably realized.

Although Barlow's penmanship was less than stellar, few words turned out to be completely illegible and those have been noted as such in the text. I have preserved Barlow's spellings, grammar, and punctuation as they appear in the original letters unless they were clearly a mere slip of the pen, though in some areas, I have placed bracketed additions for the sake of clarity. Indentations have been standardized for the sake of clarity and appearance.

Where Barlow's quotations have been extracted in the explanatory text, I have sometimes changed the capitalization of the first word of the quote for a better syntactic fit within the sentence containing the quotation. Where a quoted sentence has been truncated for use within an explanatory sentence, I have added a bracketed period [.] to show that the original sentence is longer.

Finally, I have tried to identify all individuals with brief biographical information at their first mention, as well as provide other notes and context in footnotes.

INTRODUCTION

Among events that have transformed American life, government, and culture, few have wrought as many changes as the Civil War. In light of the magnitude and volume of these tremendous reorganizations, it is easy to lose sight of the personal and individual impact the Civil War had on the American populace. Oliver Wendell Holmes Jr.'s assertion that through the war, "our hearts were touched with fire," is oft quoted but little understood. One way to fill this gap is to examine the lives and thoughts of select individuals and, in so doing, better understand the personal journeys experienced during a cataclysmic event that left an indelible mark on nearly all it involved. An effective way of accomplishing this is to read the words and confidences of actual participants and feel these experiences through them. Through letters, we can witness the transformations they underwent as close to firsthand as possible.

In this respect, one of the most instructive collections of Civil War letters is that of Francis Channing Barlow. A young intellectual from Massachusetts, Barlow was a successful lawyer in New York City when the war erupted. When he went off to war, leaving his wife hours after their marriage, Barlow probably never contemplated the conversion he would undergo in the next several years. Originally commissioned a lieutenant, he ended the war as one of the North's premier combat generals, and though he entered the service with nascent leadership qualities, he resigned tempered and tested with a honed sense of his own authority. More importantly, Barlow had transformed from a contemplative, Harvard-educated man of society to a vigorous figure engaged with life and politics. Reading his letters, one can sense the wavering between the "delicate life of New York" and the rougher but more active existence lived in the field, and he chose the latter. Through the privations Barlow suffered, including two battlefield wounds and an exhaustive collapse following the death of his wife while she nursed Federal soldiers, Barlow's spirit grew energized. War acted as a portal through which he entered into a different, more involved life.

Francis C. Barlow was born in Brooklyn on October 19, 1834, where his father, David Hatch Barlow, preached as pastor of the First Unitarian Church. A farm boy from Vermont, David Barlow graduated first in his Harvard College class of 1824 and served as class poet. He continued on at Harvard Divinity School, where he finished in 1829, and took a parish in Lynn, Massachusetts. He wed Almira Penniman, the daughter of Elisha Penniman of Brookline, Massachusetts, and the couple enjoyed acclaim as a celebrated and popular Boston couple. An intimate of intellectual circles, David Barlow enjoyed a special friendship with the Emerson family and penned a special tribute to Ralph Waldo Emerson's brother Edward upon his death on October 1, 1834.[1]

While Francis was a young boy, David Barlow abandoned his family after suffering a descent into alcoholism and possibly other psychological problems. Initially, Almira Barlow took Francis and her two other sons, Edward and Richard, to her father's house before another option presented itself. In early April 1841, George Ripley, his wife and sister, and fifteen others set out for the Ellis Farm in West Roxbury, Massachusetts. There, they sought to create a utopian commune they named Brook Farm, where Nathaniel Hawthorne lived for a period and Ralph W. Emerson and Theodore Parker frequently visited. By late April 1841, Almira and the three young Barlow brothers sought to build a life at the experimental farm community.[2]

Brook Farm attracted mostly upper-class inhabitants who had abandoned, among other things, formal prayer and religious creed to reflect spiritually in their own way. By midsummer,

---

[1] Edwin H. Abbott, "Francis Channing Barlow," *Harvard Graduates' Magazine* 4, no. 16 (June 1896): 526–42: 526. Edith Roelker Curtis, *A Season in Utopia: The Story of Brook Farm* (1961; repr. New York: Russell & Russell, 1971), 564 (page citation is to repr. ed.). Ralph W. Emerson to David Hatch Barlow, New York, October 24, 1834, in *The Letters of Ralph Waldo Emerson*, ed. Ralph L. Rusk and Eleanor M. Tilton, 10 vols. (New York: Columbia University Press, 1939–95), 1:422.

[2] Gilman M. Ostrander, *Republic of Letters: The American Intellectual Community, 1776–1865* (Madison, Wis.: Madison House Publishers, 1999), 226. Curtis, *Season in Utopia*, 52, 54, 64.

those living at the farm had been organized into three companies to perform field, mechanical, and domestic tasks, while the children performed chores and household duties in addition to attending coed classes. George Ripley had graduated first in his Harvard class of 1823 and taught mathematics and philosophy to his pupils, while other members lectured in disciplines in which they had particular knowledge. By its second year, some thirty young men and women were in attendance, some from as far away as Manila, Havana, and Florida, and this Preparatory School soon caught Harvard's eye and served as a conduit of students for that institution—Francis Barlow among them.[3]

Almira immediately made an impression on the community's inhabitants. She had flowing dark hair, and Nathaniel Hawthorne, who possibly used her as a model for the character Zenobia in his *Blithedale Romance,* described her as "a most comfortable woman to behold, she looks as if her ample person was stuffed full of tenderness—indeed as if she were of one great kind heart." Many of the women at Brook Farm, however, held a different opinion of her. They resented her flirtatious nature and her practice of holding court in a parlor while they performed household chores and kept up the cooperative. Almira had a brief affair with one of the community's leaders, John S. Dwight, before she decided she wanted to maintain their friendship but eliminate its romantic component. She then met the future founder of the Paulist order of Roman Catholic priests, Isaac Hecker, and pursued him in a relationship destined to end in her heartbreak. Hecker converted to Roman Catholicism in 1844 and shortly thereafter, began studying for the priesthood, celebrating his ordination in 1849.[4]

Between Almira's flirtations and disdain for work, some of Brook Farm's residents wearied of her presence, and on April 27, 1843, the directors voted that her parlor be converted to public use. On May 27, they ordered her to leave the community by the first of June, though the family obtained a brief reprieve until mid-July, when it became clear that they should depart. George William Curtis swiftly found lodging for Almira and her three

---

[3] Curtis, *Season in Utopia,* 67, 69–71.
[4] Ibid., 65, 133–35.

sons in Concord, Massachusetts, but by early 1844, she had fallen into such a deep depression and cried so easily that Curtis felt horror at the tedium of spending an evening alone with her.[5] A major cause for Almira's sadness was her growing realization that she would never share more than friendship with Hecker, as he became more and more engaged in his spiritual pursuits. Within weeks of his conversion to Catholicism he wrote in his diary, "Almira has lost all, or, at least, so it seems, affinity with my life." Chillingly, he expressed, "We do not feel any loss."[6]

Barlow, however, most likely enjoyed his life in Concord, as he spent his formative years in a place that valued education and cherished its role in the American Revolution. The town not only had a public library but its famed Concord Lyceum, which admitted schoolboys to its meetings for free, hosted debates and lectures, and provided Barlow the opportunity to listen to intellectual luminaries of Boston and Concord discuss various issues. During his residence in the town, Barlow became acquainted with his father's friend, the great transcendentalist Ralph W. Emerson, as well as someone who would later promote his career both during and after the Civil War, future attorney general Ebenezer R. Hoar. Furthermore, as Concord was a great center of abolitionism, Barlow became thoroughly imbued with antislavery sentiment. And, while here, young Barlow undoubtedly continued developing the independent and headstrong nature for which he had already been dubbed "Crazy Barlow" at Brook Farm, for his propensity to make "headlong" rushes at "whatever object he had in view."[7]

Francis Barlow entered Harvard College in 1851, and although described as a "slight boy of seventeen," he quickly made

---

[5] See note 27 in chapter 2 for biographical information on Curtis.

[6] In 1844, Ripley transformed Brook Farm into a community following the ideas of utopian socialist François-Marie-Charles Fourier, with emphasis on phalanxes of the best of the human race and promoting collectivism as a way for individual humans, having but a partial soul, to achieve greater personal fulfillment. A massive and destructive fire in 1846 led the commune to disband the following year. Ostrander, *Republic of Letters*, 226. Curtis, *Season in Utopia*, 136, 140, 197, 203.

[7] Ruth R. Wheeler, *Concord: Climate for Freedom* (Concord, Mass.: Concord Antiquarian Society, 1967), 155, 161, 163, 180–84. John van der Zee Sears, *My Friends at Brook Farm* (New York: Desmond Fitz-Gerald, 1912), 39.

an impression on his fellow students with his scholarly ability as well as a "sardonic wit." Classmate James Kendall Hosmer admired Barlow as a young man who was well read in classical literature even before attending college and who possessed so keen a mind that it seemed "easy for him almost without study to take a leading place." Barlow held himself with "nonchalance" in the classroom and never appeared nervous or unsure during questions, displaying some of the characteristics that would serve him in good stead during the Civil War. As Hosmer observed, "I never saw him thrown off his poise in any emergency. The straits of course are not great in which a college boy is placed, but such as they were, Barlow was always cool, with his mind working at its best in the midst of them. He was never abashed, but had a resource and an apt one in every emergency. He was absolutely intrepid before the thrusts of our sharpest examiners and . . . could bluff it boldly and dexterously where his knowledge failed[.]" Another classmate recalled that nothing in Barlow's personal bearing during college indicated that he would earn military glory but, in retrospect, identified traits apparent even then which would enable him to excel as a leader on the battlefield:

> He always perceived existing facts and relations with singular precision and quickness. He prided himself in college upon having no illusions, and was resolved to see things as they really were. He then, and ever afterwards, spoke his thoughts without restraint, and with a singular and almost contemptuous disregard of consequence. He indulged throughout his life in a very unusual freedom, not to say license, of speech. He acted and spoke without paying any regard to what man could do, or say, or think about him.

While these qualities may have impaired Barlow's sense of the poetic, they ensured he would have "a certain honesty of thought and independence in action which is by no means common among men" and the combination of his keen skill at assessing a situation and "power of prompt decision and utter fearlessness" led to his reputation as a man who could seize "the right moment for daring act in the crisis of an event."[8]

---

[8] James Kendall Hosmer, *The Last Leaf: Observations, during Seventy-five Years, of Men and Events in America and Europe* (New York: G. P. Putnam's Sons, 1912), 57–58, 60. Abbott, "Francis Channing Barlow," 536–37.

While at Harvard, however, Barlow also betrayed a boyish sense of fun not revealed in his Civil War correspondence. For example, the freshmen of the class of 1855 formed a writing and debate society that held somber meetings in the lodge room of the "Glorious Apollers." During the proceedings of one such convocation, Barlow surprised those in attendance by appearing "from a side-door rigged out most fantastically in plumes and draperies. He had somehow got hold of the regalia of the order and drawlingly announced himself as the great panjandrum who had come to take part," and his antics threw everyone into hysterical laughter. During that same freshman year, Barlow fired, in the middle of the night, a cannon located in the arsenal in Cambridge that had lain quiet since the War of 1812. Hosmer noted that Barlow "was no respecter of conventions and sometimes trod ruthlessly upon proprieties. 'What will Barlow do next?' was always the question." Although Barlow may have relished this quality in his youth, he had no time for it in adulthood.[9]

These antics were typical of undergraduates at Harvard at this period. Although the school's strict curriculum emphasized recitation and markedly stressed the classics, students explored their intellectual curiosities during their free time, which was largely their own to do with as they wished. Private, extracurricular societies comprised their great social activity, where students met to eat, drink, collect books, discuss papers, and carry on literary or musical exercises—in all, a system of student education both more experimental and current than the traditional one followed by Harvard as an institution. These student organizations played a critical role in the social lives of boys maturing into men, as did the chance for freedom and an opportunity for misbehavior not available while living under the rules at home. In this freedom, however, professors tended to be aloof from the intellectual development of their charges. Although Harvard's faculty included some of the most eminent scholars of the day, few energetically tried to shape the individual minds of their students during their formative years. As such, a significant part of the growth experienced by Harvard students, including Barlow,

---

[9] Hosmer, *Last Leaf,* 57–59. Abbott, "Francis Channing Barlow," 536.

came within explorations and interactions carried out amongst themselves. As one scholar observed, "it was through their engagement in extracurricular activities that students, as peers, were most apt to acquire a sense of themselves as the emerging intellectual elite of the province or the nation."[10]

Barlow graduated first in his class in July 1855 but, to Emerson's chagrin, still had not found what he was looking for in Boston and resolved to relocate to New York. "I am resigned to your going to New York where so many high prizes glitter for your ambition but I am sorry you do not decide for Massachusetts, humbler but surer," urged the eminent thinker. "Perhaps you will after looking at Broadway." Nonetheless, Emerson also armed young Barlow with a letter of introduction to his brother William, taking care to mention the young Harvard graduate's high level of scholarship. By September 1855, Barlow lived in New York and tutored students, among them the young Robert Gould Shaw, who called him the "Crammer." The following year, Barlow entered the law office of William Curtis Noyes and earned admission to the New York bar in May 1858. Soon thereafter, he practiced law in partnership with George Bliss Jr. and occasionally reported on law cases and performed editorial duties for Horace Greeley's *New York Tribune* until the Civil War erupted with the bombardment of Fort Sumter.[11]

Barlow found easy access to the literary circles of New York, heavily influenced and populated by New England Yankees, and

[10] Ostrander, *Republic of Letters,* 16, 28–29. Bernard Bailyn, "Why Kirkland Failed," in *Glimpses of the Harvard Past,* ed. Bernard Bailyn, et al. (Cambridge, Mass.: Harvard University Press, 1986), 19–44: 24. Oscar Handlin, "Making Men of the Boys," in Bailyn, *Glimpses of the Harvard Past,* 53, 55, 56. Seymour Martin Lipset and David Riesman, *Education and Politics at Harvard* (New York: McGraw-Hill Book Company, 1975), 83, 85.

[11] A staunch Republican vehemently opposed to slavery and supportive of a wide range of moral reform movements, Greeley had played an important role in convincing Ripley to transform Brook Farm into a Fourierist community in 1844. Ralph W. Emerson to William Emerson, Concord, Mass., August 27, 1855; Ralph W. Emerson to Francis C. Barlow, Concord, Mass., August 27, 1855, in Rusk and Tilton, *Letters of Ralph Waldo Emerson,* 4:525. Abbott, "Francis Channing Barlow," 526. New York Monuments Commission, *In Memoriam: Francis Channing Barlow 1834–1896* (Albany: J. B. Lyon Company: 1923), 60. Russell Duncan, ed., *Blue-Eyed Child of Fortune: The Civil War Letters of Colonel Robert Gould Shaw* (Athens: University of Georgia Press, 1992), 11.

he no doubt felt comfortable in what turned out to be an outpost of Boston culture during this period. The young attorney also met and courted Arabella Wharton Griffith. Born on February 29, 1824, Arabella grew up in New Jersey before moving into New York City in late 1846. Her father was a merchant who developed a drinking problem—similar to Barlow's father—and lost his wealth. In New York, Arabella circulated among the city's lawyers and also contributed articles of "beauty and delicacy" to the paper for which her future husband also wrote, the *Tribune*. Despite the ten-year age difference, the couple had much in common, including mutual ambition and intelligence.[12]

Barlow married Arabella on April 20, 1861, the day before he departed as a member of the Twelfth New York State Militia Regiment deployed to defend the Federal capital. New York diarist Maria L. Daly noted the striking age difference between the couple, calling Francis "Arabella's boy-husband" and finding it strange and disrespectful to hear him affectionately refer to her as "Belle." She also recounted that on the evening of November 23, 1861, her servant opened the Daly residence's door to announce that "there was a young soldier and his mother in the parlor." Daly depicted Arabella Barlow as a vivacious woman with a strong personality, something borne out by her activities during the Civil War. Arabella "was more subdued than usual last evening," Daly wrote of one visit, "but there is always a want of refinement about her, even in the very motion of her hand in taking a cup of tea and in the tones of her voice. She is off to Washington on Monday for the winter. I wonder whether she would not rather be there as Miss Griffith. There is such a field for intriguing, clever women in Washington. . . . Arabella says that women rule everything and can get anything[.]"[13]

During his military service, Barlow sent home a long and informative series of letters; unfortunately none written to Arabella seem to have survived. In all likelihood, he did not write her

---

[12] Ostrander, *Republic of Letters*, 304–8. Don Richard Lauter, "'Once upon a Time in the East': Arabella Wharton Griffith Barlow," *Journal of Women's Civil War History* 1 (2001): 8–25: 8–9, 14.

[13] Abbott, "Francis Channing Barlow," 526. Maria L. Daly diary entry, November 24, 1861, in Harold Earl Hammond, *Diary of a Union Lady 1861–1865* (New York: Funk & Wagnalls Company, 1962), 80.

frequently as she was often not far from him, either visiting during winter quarters or in her service as a nurse to wounded Federal soldiers. Although Barlow's letters home therefore lack a romantic element, they are striking in that they preserve and illuminate their author's emotions and opinions over time. When the war began, Barlow was an educated and well-connected professional but one completely unused to the military life. Through his service, he not only adapted to the privations endured by a soldier, but he learned how to become an effective officer in command of men in battle. At times throughout the war, he expressed varying opinions that strike one examining the entire collection of his available writings as occasionally paradoxical. Yet in this, one consistency does become clear: that participation in the Civil War was, for Barlow, not only an affirmation of his manhood and abilities, but a growth experience that tempered and honed nascent leadership skills.

Through the war, Barlow enjoyed rapid promotion, entering as a junior officer in a regiment and ending as one of the North's high-level combat commanders. In part, this came from his skill and personal energy as a leader. For his service on the Peninsula, Barlow received praise for his "gallantry, coolness + good conduct" while several officers urged his promotion. Politics and personal friendships, however, with influential figures on the home front also played a critical role and ensured his success. Barlow's antislavery stance endeared him to influential Northern abolitionists who watched his career. Barlow's law partner, George Bliss, was a staunch Republican who joined the staff of New York Governor E. D. Morgan when war erupted, and in time Morgan wrote Lincoln personally to urge Barlow's promotion. Meanwhile, John M. Forbes championed Barlow's cause to Massachusetts' powerful Senator Charles Sumner, and Charles Russell Lowell Jr. contacted Solicitor William Whiting at the War Department. No less a figure than Ralph W. Emerson penned a letter praising Barlow's skills and supporting his appointment to brigadier general, and obtained the endorsements of such luminaries as Nathaniel Hawthorne and Oliver Wendell Holmes for his sentiments. Later, when illness and Barlow's grief for his dead wife in 1864 made his friends realize that he needed to take a vacation to recuperate, Sumner (and probably Governor

Andrew) intervened so that the War Department granted the unusual allowance during wartime.[14]

Almost immediately upon enlisting in the Twelfth New York
Militia, Barlow came to the realization that a soldier's life was
not one of continual action and glory. By June 19, 1861, Barlow
wrote his brother that that he found performing a captain's duties during his temporary company commander's absence to be
"arduous," and he vowed not to reenlist in the army when his
three-month term of service expired, as he had grown "sick of
this damned Regt." Yet, in a short time, pride in the Twelfth
New York welled up within Barlow, and when it paraded before
President Abraham Lincoln and Major General Winfield Scott
for a Fourth of July review, Barlow reported to his mother that
his unit "surpassed them all" and that Scott complimented them
as "really magnificent." Later, during "fatiguing" maneuvers in
the vicinity of Martinsburg, West Virginia, in mid-July, Barlow
noted how his unit marched better than did all the others in the
Federal column and how its camp proved superior in neatness
and military layout.[15]

Despite a lack of military training, Barlow learned quickly
about what was expected of a good officer. It helped that while

---

[14] Barlow to Richard Barlow, July 24, 1862. William H. French, Headquar-
ters French's Brigade, July 12, 1862; John C. Caldwell, Harrison's Landing,
Va., July 14, 1862; O. O. Howard to the Secretary of War, Tenallytown, Md.,
September 4, 1862; E. D. Morgan to Abraham Lincoln, Albany, N.Y., September 12, 1862; J. M. Forbes to Charles Sumner, Boston, February 19, 1863;
endorsement of Charles Sumner, February 21, 1863; Charles R. Lowell Jr. to
William Whiting, Boston, March 2, 1863; Letter of Charles Sumner, Boston,
October 29, 1864; telegram of E. D. Townsend to Francis C. Barlow, November
5, 1865; telegram of John A. Andrew to Colonel E. D. Townsend, November 7,
1864, all in Francis C. Barlow papers, M-1064 microfilm roll 241, National
Archives, Washington, D.C. (hereafter cited as Barlow Papers NA; also cited in
this book are Francis C. Barlow's Generals Papers, RG 94-9W4/6/10/A, Box 2
[Barlow's Generals Papers NA] and Francis C. Barlow File, Field and Staff Officers Papers, Sixty-first New York Volunteer Infantry [Barlow Field and Staff
Officers Papers NA]). Ralph W. Emerson to Ethan Allen Hitchcock Concord
and Boston, February 28, 1863; Ralph W. Emerson to Francis C. Barlow, Concord, Mass., c. March 10, 1863, all in Rusk and Tilton, *Letters of Ralph Waldo
Emerson*, 5:315–16, 318–19.

[15] Barlow to mother, May 2, 1861. Barlow to Edward Barlow, June 19, 1861.
Barlow to mother, July 5, 1861. Barlow to Edward Barlow, July 18, 1861. (All
letters from Barlow to his family members, including these, are from the Massachusetts Historical Society collection in Boston, unless noted otherwise.)

his regiment was camped in Washington, D.C., during the early days of war, Emory Upton, a young West Point graduate who later earned renown for his tactical skills, instructed the unit's officers. After only two months of service, Barlow believed himself to be "quite competent to be Capt.," and his observance of the strict military discipline that accompanied a march into hostile territory led him to grow accustomed to what he deemed "the realities of war." Regardless of this confidence, however, Barlow simultaneously expressed an ignorance of those same "realities of war" on the field of battle. Without experience in combat, he believed that "the evolutions, as far as the management of a company is concerned are the same in battle as on parade" and confessed, "I understand but little of the practical duties of an officer in battle + no one else here does. We ought to be instructed in it." December 1861 found Barlow still reviewing and analyzing military tactics, though he had to wait until the following spring and the Peninsula campaign for an opportunity to gain practical experience.[16]

Barlow had an uneven adjustment to the camaraderie of military life and sometimes became frustrated at a lack of intellectual stimulation. While serving with the Twelfth New York Militia in Washington, D.C., in early July, he noted that he had not encountered one person in the capital "who was above the ranks of commonplace," and he yearned to "get into the society of intelligent people" and make a long visit to Massachusetts when his term of service expired. Several times in 1861–62, he asked his mother to keep a diary and periodically send it to him in order to keep him informed about events at home, and he continually inquired into whom his brothers saw. Following a visit by his brother and the artist Winslow Homer, Barlow realized how much he missed the company of his intellectual friends, noting that "it is very tedious living so many months with men who are so little companions for me as our officers are. There is not one who I am at all intimate with or who is any companion to me." He also voraciously read newspapers and closely examined the

---

[16] Barlow to Edward Barlow, June 19, 1861. Barlow to Edward Barlow, July 18, 1861 ("parade," "practical duties"). Barlow to mother, December 24, 1861.

news reports and editorials in periodicals from New York City, especially the *Herald* and *Tribune*. Yet, occasionally Barlow could appreciate some of the simplicity of the men he commanded, and in time he made some friendships. During his regiment's maneuvers in mid-July 1861, Barlow enjoyed "several very amusing men in the ranks who make a good many amusing jokes &c. + have really a good deal of humor," though he disapproved of their extreme use of profanity. By summer 1862, the shared hardships of soldiering fostered in Barlow a sense of camaraderie that led him to mourn, after the casualties of the Peninsula, "almost every officer who started with us is gone. I miss them sadly[.]"[17]

One apparent theme within Barlow's letters was how proud he felt at bearing himself under the privations of military service. The educated and cultured urban attorney found the rough life a vehicle to tangibly demonstrate his manhood and physical worth. This was a common phenomena among members of Barlow's class and educational achievement, and his good friend Charles Russell Lowell similarly embarked on a personal quest to cultivate his inner self through an active life. Thus, some of high lineage eagerly joined the war in order to stiffen their sinews and test their mettle. Although some Brahmins felt anxious about their practical worth, their ability to look to the martyrdom of Robert Gould Shaw at the head of his Fifty-fourth Massachusetts Infantry or construct Memorial Hall at Harvard University, a tangible commemoration of their service as "gentlemen heroes," was a source of tremendous honor and pride.[18]

---

[17] Barlow to mother, July 5, 1861 ("commonplace," "intelligent people"). Barlow to Edward Barlow, July 18, 1861 ("amusing men"). Barlow to mother, December 3, 1861. Barlow to mother, December 17, 1861. Barlow to mother, December 24, 1861. Barlow to Edward Barlow, December 28, 1861. Barlow to mother, January 9, 1862. Barlow to mother, January 18, 1862. Barlow to mother, January 30, 1862. Barlow to mother, February 16, 1862. Barlow to mother, February 18, 1862. Barlow to Edward Barlow, April 18, 1862 ("tedious"). Barlow to mother, June 5, 1862. Barlow to mother and Edward Barlow, June 10, 1862. Barlow to mother and Edward Barlow, June 15, 1862. Barlow to Richard Barlow, June 18, 1862. Barlow to Edward and Richard Barlow, July 12, 1862. Barlow to mother and Edward Barlow, August 9, 1862 ("miss them sadly").

[18] George M. Frederickson, *The Inner Civil War: Northern Intellectuals and the Crisis of the Union* (1965; repr. Chicago: University of Illinois Press, 1993), 30, 72–73, 154–55 (page citations are to repr. ed).

Less than two weeks after leaving New York, Barlow wrote from Washington that soldiering was unpleasant but that he "did not come for pleasure + can endure anything for 3 months." Later that summer, while the regiment was relocating from Washington to northwestern Virginia, he assured his mother, "I am very well and bear the heat + fatigue as well as 'any other man' if not better." The maneuvers and long marches his regiment conducted during this period, often under the expectation of meeting the enemy, made for "a surprising change from the delicate life of New York," but Barlow noted that "we have all got used to it." The genteel son of Brook Farm and Harvard College found himself, by mid-July 1861, joining others in eating "like pigs" or going to a pump in the busiest section of Charlestown, Virginia, where he and a fellow officer stripped off their jackets and shirts and "stood entirely naked except trousers, stockings + shoes + washed + cleaned ourselves in the face of the multitude" of soldiers surrounding them nearby. Although he still complained, "If I had stayed at home + gone out + slept in a pig pen at night I should have had about the same experience that we have had here," Barlow had grown accustomed to it and glad that he bore it well.[19]

Barlow's letters that winter further express his acceptance of and, in some cases, enjoyment of this more strenuous life. In mid-December, he described sleeping comfortably on the ground, without a blanket though near a fire, after a three-mile night march. He happily characterized his log cabin in the winter quarters camp, nearly completed as of Christmas Eve, and how comfortable it would be with an open fire and the spaces between the logs plastered in with clay. And again, he proudly asserted, "I have been remarkably well. I always stand fatigue + exposure better than much stronger people." Soon he wanted his brothers Edward and Richard to visit, not only for their company but because he believed it would be a "fine opportunity" for them "to see Army life in the field" and experience some of this for themselves. In a letter urging Edward to come, he de-

---

[19] Barlow to mother, May 2, 1861 ("very well"). Barlow to mother, July 5, 1861 ("pig pen"). Barlow to mother, July 9, 1861. Barlow to Edward Barlow, July 18, 1861 ("surprising change," "like pigs," "entirely naked").

scribed the rough country and how they rode "across fields + through roads which would scare one at home," but assured that witnessing such a life would do his brother good. Barlow perceived military life as character building, though different from the education obtained in the halls at Harvard. By May 1862, he urged that his brothers participate in some way and assured that "their want of human knowledge need be no obstacle," because he felt military service not only benefited health but understanding as well. In this way, Barlow joined other young intellectuals in viewing the war as a way to be "rescued from an aimless literary or scholarly existence" and engage in a life where one applied professional skills as a vigorous actor within society.[20]

By spring 1862, Barlow reported confronting wood ticks, a horrible smell, and subsisting on meatless bean soup and rice for several days in a camp near Yorktown, Virginia. He was still "well + hearty in every respect," however, and stood "everything beautifully," even when suffering from a toothache that deprived him of several nights' sleep and required the regimental surgeon to repeatedly attempt an extraction, breaking off everything above the gum with "instruments . . . of a rude character," which "hurt like hell." After finishing a "sumptuous dinner" of "lemonade + heavy pancake made of flour + fat with a sauce" while suffering in extreme Virginia heat, Barlow could still assure, "I have got pretty well used to hard living by this time." Even sleeping outside in a pouring rain did not diminish his spirit.[21]

More emphatic proofs of manly worth came in courageous acts on the field of battle, though. After his first real action at Fair Oaks on June 1, 1862, Barlow's lengthy and detailed letters exude excitement at having seen combat, and his account of the fight demonstrates his eager and active sense of leadership. As a

---

[20] Barlow to mother, December 12, 1861. Barlow to mother and Edward Barlow, December 14, 1861 ("remarkably well," "fine opportunity"). Barlow to mother, December 24, 1861. Barlow to Edward Barlow, January 26, 1862 ("across fields"). Barlow to mother and Richard Barlow, May 17, 1862 ("human knowledge"). Barlow to mother, June 7, 1863. Frederickson, *Inner Civil War,* 175–76 ("rescued").

[21] Barlow to Edward Barlow, April 23, 1862. Barlow to Edward Barlow and Mother, May 15, 1862 ("well + hearty," "instruments," "lemonade," "hard living"). Barlow to mother, June 5, 1862. Barlow to mother and Edward Barlow, June 15, 1862.

colonel leading his Sixty-first New York Infantry into the fray, Barlow observed several skulkers crouching in the brush and pointed them out to his own men as examples of cowardice. Such behavior was unacceptable to Barlow, though he proudly recalled that his own regiment behaved admirably, "cool + obedient to orders," not breaking despite that the "singing of the balls was awful," with men "dying + groaning + running about with faces shot + arms shot" in "an awful sight." In this first battle, Barlow felt he had connected with his men, as a good Civil War officer should, and he reported that they "cheered [him] violently during the fight" and were "much pleased with [him] since the action." After its fine performance, he happily believed that his unit had won a reputation for being a "crack Regt."[22]

Nonetheless, in the gory aftermath of combat, Barlow reacted with a sense of disconnect at the sights that confronted him. On the one hand, he assured his family that he felt he "was not born to be killed in battle," though he simultaneously witnessed the "horrid scenes" of comrades less lucky than he felt. He reported that all had grown quickly and completely "accustomed to dead, wounded, + decayed men," hospitals full of soldiers with "shocking wounds," and corpses decaying in Virginia's June sun.[23]

The rigors of military life and the labor involved in disciplining his men could be trying, and at times Barlow's enthusiasm for continuing service waned. As early as June 1861 he assured his brother, "You will see me in New York the moment our time is up," and by January 1862 he felt that "On the whole" the military made for "a damned stupid life." When disease and combat had depleted the Sixty-first New York Infantry to a fraction of its original strength after Fair Oaks, Barlow expressed his desire to resign as soon as Richmond fell because he was "sick of this damned life + have no idea of beginning to drill + discipline a Regt. over again which will have to be done if this is recruited

[22] Barlow letter, [June 2, 1862] ("cool + obedient," "singing," "dying," "cheered"). Barlow to mother, June 5, 1862 ("pleased"). Barlow to mother and Edward Barlow, June 10, 1862 ("crack Regt.").
[23] Barlow to mother, June 3, 1862 ("accustomed to dead," "shocking wounds"). Barlow to mother and Edward Barlow, June 10, 1862 ("not born," "horrid scenes").

up." Following the Seven Days, Barlow's morale sunk so low that he wanted to resign, though he realized that doing so at that point would hurt his reputation, and when his spirit recovered he emphatically denied even considering such a move. Then again, the high praise and calls for his promotion that started to pour in following his performance in the campaign, as well as his knowledge that friends at home were similarly trying to get him nominated for a brigadier generalship, affected his mood.[24]

Despite his valuable record of combat leadership, Barlow thus revealed to his family the rough and sometimes uncertain road he faced in trying to perform his duty, and though he remained in the armed services until the end of the war, he wavered at times and contemplated leaving the service. Reading Barlow's letters, one truly gets the sense of internal debate, as he sometimes leaned toward the contemplative life of scholarly thought and other times toward the active and vigorous life and engagement with society. Although he remained in the army and learned to accept and even welcome the life experiences it offered, a powerful impulse nearly drew him back to the "delicate life of New York." From this came a long-term transformation, and by the end of the war Barlow eagerly accepted the responsibility of high political office and prosecuted his duty with vigor and self-assured skill. He may have entered the war as an intellectual, albeit one confident he could lead men and take part in affairs. He left it as an active participant and a leader who had not only proven his command abilities but honed his skills and sense of authority; a quiet postwar life was no longer an option after the galvanizing experience of war. In a letter written to urge Barlow's promotion and signed by some of Boston's most prominent intellectuals, Ralph W. Emerson aptly noted with a subtle choice of words, "we have looked on him as one of those valuable officers which the war was creating."[25]

---

[24] William H. French, Headquarters French's Brigade, July 12, 1862. John C. Caldwell, Harrison's Landing, Va., July 14, 1862, both in Barlow Papers NA. Barlow to Edward Barlow, June 19, 1861 ("you will see me"). Barlow to mother, January 18, 1862 ("on the whole"). Barlow to mother, June 12, 1862 ("sick"). Barlow to Edward Barlow, July 8, 1862. Barlow to Richard Barlow, July 24, 1862.

[25] Ralph W. Emerson to Ethan Allen Hitchcock, Concord and Boston, Massachusetts, February 28, 1863, in Rusk and Tilton, *Letters of Ralph Waldo Emerson*, 5:315–16.

Immediately upon arriving in the camp of the Sixty-first New York Infantry as its lieutenant colonel in late 1861, Barlow demonstrated that he was a goal-oriented and vigorous leader. Finding the camp lax in discipline, he immediately took action to set about improving order in the ranks, educating the officers in military tactics, and drilling the men. Although second in command, Barlow relished his position as the de facto commander of the Sixty-first, and while the unit's Colonel Spencer Cone was "not fit to command a drove of hogs," Barlow boasted to his mother that he was "busy the whole time overseeing the whole camp getting things straight. I am supreme here + my position is a most pleasant one." Authority agreed with the young officer, and he seemed to enjoy that he had to "attend to innumerable matters of Camp regulation and answer innumerable calls" in his regiment. He knew that he had the education and the theoretical training for leadership but now found he could put this into practice, especially in the enforcement of military discipline. Despite his young age (compounded by a youthful appearance) Barlow had the self-assurance to make "them step round + some wish they never had been born. It makes me laugh sometimes to have to blow up the Chaplain . . . + Dr. while one old enough to be my Grandfather." He did try to administer justice evenly, however, and when two family friends sought commissions in the Sixty-first New York, Barlow warned that "whoever comes under me will have to submit to severe discipline for I keep them all right in my hand."[26]

Barlow's high premium on a strict brand of military discipline continued throughout his service and became a common theme in letters home. He had abandoned the tomfoolery of his Harvard years, but he further realized that "hard knocks and a tight rein will make them fight," and that was his duty as a commander. Furthermore, he probably joined others of his class in believing that such an attitude would help lead the country out of a sense of national decadence and help reestablish respect for authority. Some who served under Barlow realized that the

---

[26] Barlow to mother, December 3, 1861 ("busy"). Barlow to mother, December 12, 1861. Barlow to mother and Edward Barlow, December 14, 1861 ("attend," "submit"). Barlow to mother, December 24, 1861 ("not fit"). Barlow to mother and Richard Barlow, May 17, 1862 ("step round").

intense drilling and strict military rule he imposed would benefit them on the battlefield, and in this way initial "animosity was turned into confidence and admiration." Augustus C. Hamlin recalled that when Barlow took a brigade in the Eleventh corps in 1863, his disciplinary ways earned him the reputation of a martinet, though his men came to respect him "as intrepid as Decatur, and as fond of a fight as the naval hero of earlier times." Robert Gould Shaw approved of his former tutor's strictness and countered his sister's criticism with the judgment that Barlow's professionalism and compliance with military rules "went to show that he was a better Field-Officer than 9 out of 10[.]" In other cases, Barlow's strictness earned him the resentment of those under his command. A member of the 153rd Pennsylvania Infantry observed that Barlow's tenure as their brigadier was a period never to be forgotten "by those who had the misfortune to serve under him. As a taskmaster he had no equal. The prospect of a speedy deliverance from the odious yoke of Billy Barlow filled every heart with joy."[27]

Officers often found it difficult to balance an emphasis on discipline while keeping in mind that the Federal army was composed of civilian soldiers and not professionals, and Barlow might not always have succeeded in this. Yet, he did often consider how his troops felt about him. As an officer in the Sixty-first New York, he wrote his brother, "I am probably the strictest disciplinarian in the Brigade but am not despotic. My men I think like me." Upon taking command of a brigade in the Eleventh corps in spring 1862, he assured his mother, "There has been some murmuring at my drawing the reins but I am told they are beginning to like me better[.]" When he assumed leadership of a Second corps division and deemed it "rather loose in some matters of discipline," Barlow also informed his mother that he was "making a good impression" and had "not lost my

---

[27] William Simmers, *The Volunteers Manual* (Easton, Pa.: D.H. Neiman, 1863), 26–27. Charles A. Fuller, *Personal Recollections of the War of 1861* (Sherburne, N.Y.: News Job Printing House, 1906), 9–10. Augustus C. Hamlin, quoted in New York Monuments Commission, *In Memoriam: Francis Channing Barlow*, 88. Robert G. Shaw to Josephine Shaw, Near Edenburg, Virginia, April 16, 1862, in Duncan, *Blue-Eyed Child of Fortune*, 191. Barlow to Charles Dalton, June 2, 1863 ("hard knocks"). Frederickson, *Inner Civil War*, 104–6.

temper or spoken or acted hastily to anyone"—that although "thought strict I think I am well liked." Nonetheless, in the same letter, he expressed the view that the pardon of a man convicted for desertion and sentenced to be shot was a "mistaken humanity," since such action detrimentally weakened discipline within the army and therefore prolonged the war.[28]

In addition to Barlow's gravity and personal discipline, other apparent themes throughout his letters are his aggressive streak and the value he placed on energetic action both on a grand scale as well as in individual lives. His early letters are full of references to his vigor in running affairs within the Sixty-first New York, and he seized the opportunity presented by his colonel's weakness in order to imprint his own active view of military life onto the unit. Barlow quickly condemned those he viewed as complacent, such as a regimental surgeon, whom he considered "an old granny of no skill or energy." His anger at apathy shines through in his criticism of division commander Israel Richardson. Barlow condemned him as a "damned miserable" officer because "Other Divisions have had all manner of military instruction this winter + the Division Genls visit their Brigades daily. Nothing of the kind has been done with us," and the young colonel exaggerated in exasperation, "I believe we are the most miserable Division, Brigade + Regt. in the Army."[29]

Throughout the war, Barlow's aggression manifested itself in his desire for more active and vigorous efforts to quash the rebellion. Early on, Barlow believed that the Federal government had delayed mobilizing a sufficient wagon train to enable an advance and he condemned, "They are greatly to be blamed for not having begun the preparations earlier + for having dawdled along in the way they have." His increasingly critical attitude toward Major General George B. McClellan most clearly displays Barlow's frustration with slowness and lack of aggression, though this sentiment might also have been exacerbated by political differences between the two officers. After the disheartening defeat

---

[28] Barlow to Edward Barlow, December 28, 1861 ("strictest"). Barlow to mother, April 24, 1863 ("murmuring"). Barlow to mother, April 9, 1864 ("loose," "well liked," "mistaken").

[29] Barlow to mother, January 18, 1862 ("granny"). Barlow to Edward Barlow, April 23, 1862 ("miserable," "miserable Division").

of the Seven Days, Barlow opined that "McClellan has been completely outwitted + that our present safety is owing more to the severe fighting of some of the Divisions than to any skill of our Generals." While the young colonel praised the army's junior officers and soldiers, he felt that most had lost confidence in McClellan, who rode among them on the withdrawal unnoticed.[30]

In the weeks following this retreat, Barlow's opinion grew even stronger:

> I am thoroughly disgusted with our Generals + think we had better give up the struggle at once unless we can have a radical change. You have no idea of the imbecility of management both in action + out of it. McClellan issues flaming addresses though everyone in the army knows he was outwitted + has lost confidence in him. His statements that he lost no materials of war or ammunition are simply false. I believe that this Army properly handled could march into Richmond even now, but with our present Generals never. We are surprised to learn from the New York papers that we gained a great victory. We thought here that we had made a disastrous retreat leaving all our dead + wounded + prisoners + material + munitions of war in the hands of the enemy, though it is true that the <u>men</u> by hard fighting often temporarily repulsed the enemy.[31]

> You ask my opinion of this retreat + of affairs generally. I think McClellan + many more of our Generals are damned miserable creatures + that unless there is a radical change in the leaders, the enemy will whip us again + again. I think officers + men are disgusted with + have lost all confidence in McClellan + are disgusted with the attempts of the papers to make him out a victorious hero. I have not <u>seen one officer or man</u> (+ I have talked with many) who has any confidence left in him. The stories of his being everywhere among the men in the fights are all untrue. I fought in three Divisions at the most critical times + in the hardest fights + never saw him but once + then not under fire. I have found no one else who saw him. I hope McClellan will be removed.[32]

---

[30] Barlow to mother, May 2, 1861. Barlow to mother, July 5, 1861 ("blamed"). Barlow to mother, July 4, 1862 ("outwitted").

[31] Barlow to Edward Barlow, July 8, 1862.

[32] Barlow to Edward and Richard Barlow, July 12, 1862.

For Barlow, however, this lack of spirit went beyond just individual officers, but infected the entire North. During the *Trent* affair, when war nearly erupted with England, Barlow believed that such a conflict "would bring out a spirit" that even the Civil War could not. While on the Peninsula, he felt that if the Federals suffered a defeat, the North would give up the fight, and by late summer 1862 he held that the Confederacy would ultimately maintain its independence, as the "affairs of the Country look melancholy," with "no prospect or hope of success in this war," hampered by a government "too rascally + corrupt besides being imbecile." A similar low point came with Jubal Early's raid against Washington in summer 1864, a scare which emphasized to Barlow that the Union was filled with "the cowards of the North." Barlow confessed to being "utterly disgusted with the craven spirit of our people" and went so far as to express his wish that "the enemy had burned Baltimore + Washington[.]"[33]

Although Barlow generally avoided discussing politics in his letters home, such issues weighed frequently on his mind. He thoroughly read and analyzed New York newspapers, and in the early days of the war he hoped to attend meetings of Congress often. At least some of his disenchantment with McClellan probably stemmed from political differences with that Democratic general. One of the most telling statements on Barlow's political views, however, comes from a letter written to him by Charles Russell Lowell. Through the missive, it becomes apparent that Barlow had criticisms of Republican Lincoln as well. "Don't mind Lincoln's shortcomings too much," assured Lowell. "We know that he has not the first military spark in his composition, not a sense probably by which he could get the notion of what makes or unmakes an Army, *but* he is certainly much the best candidate for the permanency of our republican institutions, and that is the main thing." What Barlow perceived as a lack of efficiency and vigor in the war effort led to his skepticism about the competence of the administration prosecuting it.[34]

---

[33] Barlow to Edward Barlow, December 28, 1861 ("spirit"). Barlow to mother and Richard Barlow, May 17, 1862. Barlow to mother and Edward Barlow, August 9, 1862. Barlow to mother and brothers, September 6, 1862 ("melancholy"). Barlow to mother, July 15, 1864 ("cowards," "utterly").

[34] Barlow to mother, July 5, 1861. Barlow to mother, December 24, 1861.

Initially, Barlow criticized the Southern lifestyle as slow paced and disordered, a common perception articulated by other Northern soldiers in their letters home. When he visited the town where John Brown was tried and sentenced for his famous raid against Harper's Ferry, Barlow thought it looked "like all Virginia towns, is slovenly + wretched with occasionally some large old pleasant looking places + houses." In his opinion, the South appeared "generally poor with a worn out look + the people seem very ignorant." During winter quarters of 1861–62, he asked his mother to visit but warned of the place she would lodge—"The table is poor + the whole housekeeping disorderly + unpunctual + Virginian"—and another time he went so far as to express, "I hardly think this disgusting country is worth fighting for."[35]

Yet, despite his original assessment of the Southern land, Barlow grew to respect the elan and spirit with which the Confederates fought, displaying bravery, courage, and endurance under hardship. Having fallen into Confederate hands after his severe wounding at Gettysburg, Barlow observed the Rebel officers and men and became convinced that they were "more heroic, more modest + more in earnest than we are. Their whole tone is much finer than ours," and he commented that except for those fighting on antislavery grounds, there was "not much earnestness" or "noble feelings" involved among the Northern ranks.[36]

Barlow's opinions concerning blacks and immigrants provide some of the most interesting commentary contained in his letters, and he displayed disdain for German immigrants despite

---

Barlow to Edward Barlow, December 28, 1861. Barlow to mother, January 9, 1862. Barlow to mother, January 18, 1862. Barlow to mother, February 18, 1862. Barlow to mother, June 5, 1862. Barlow to mother and Edward Barlow, June 10, 1862. Barlow to mother and Edward, June 15, 1862. Barlow to Richard Barlow, June 18, 1862. Barlow to Edward Barlow, July 8, 1862. Barlow to Edward and Richard Barlow, July 12, 1862. Barlow to mother and Edward Barlow, August 9, 1862. Charles R. Lowell to Francis C. Barlow, Ripon, Va., September 10, 1864, in Edward W. Emerson, ed., *Life and Letters of Charles Russell Lowell* (Boston: Houghton, Mifflin, and Company, 1907), 343–44.

[35] Barlow to Edward Barlow, July 18, 1861 ("Virginia towns"). Barlow to mother, January 9, 1862 ("table"). Barlow to mother, January 18, 1862 ("disgusting").

[36] Maria L. Daly diary entry, October 23, 1862, in Hammond, *Diary of a Union Lady,* 190. Barlow to mother, July 7, 1863 ("heroic," "earnestness").

the fact that they were still white. Barlow's service in the Eleventh corps, with its high proportion of foreign-born troops and officers, only reinforced this perspective. Shortly after Chancellorsville, he told his family that he had "always been down on the 'Dutch' + I do not abate my contempt now," though he did admit that some of the Yankee regiments broke and ran when the Confederates attacked. Nonetheless, he was so disappointed in the Eleventh corps' performance that he considered trying to get his brigade transferred to the Second corps, though Howard's "mortification" and "disgust" led Barlow to "pity him" and refrain from abandoning his friend. Barlow looked down upon the intrigues of the Germans, finding their quarreling where "One Dutchman accuses another of misconduct in the last battles + the Dutch accuse the Americans" to be pointless.[37]

Upon assuming command of a division in the Eleventh corps, Barlow trusted the native-born Yankee units under command of Brigadier General Adelbert Ames. He immediately dedicated himself, however, to his "German Brigade" under Colonel Leopold von Gilsa and moved into their camp so as to keep a closer watch on them. Barlow continued to consider switching over to the Second corps, even though it would have meant giving up division command to take over a brigade. He grew exhausted trying to discipline "these miserable creatures under him," and when von Gilsa's brigade was temporarily detached shortly before Gettysburg, Barlow dismissed them with the sentiment "I suppose I shall have it again in case of a battle but I don't care much if I don't." The performance of the corps at that battle bolstered these condemnations, despite the fact that much of the blame for the Eleventh corps' rout came from Barlow's own poor deployment of his brigades. Nonetheless, that defeat confirmed to him that the Germans would not fight and he vowed "never" to "set foot in the 11th Corps again," even if it meant demotion to brigade command. Although acknowledging that "some of the German officers behaved well" at Gettysburg, Barlow heartily believed "we can do nothing with these German

---

[37] Barlow to mother and brothers, May 8, 1863 ("'Dutch'"). Barlow to mother, May 29, 1863 ("One Dutchman").

Regts." who "won't fight" and, worse, "ruin all with whom they come in contact."[38]

Despite having gone to college near Boston during a time when nativist sentiments ran high, Barlow barely mentions Irish Americans in his letters. It is striking that while he scorned the fighting ability of the German Americans, he did not articulate such disdain for that of the Irish Americans. At least some members of the Irish Brigade, fighting under his command during the 1864 campaign, felt that Barlow "rarely omitted any opportunity of showing his dislike" toward the unit "by the exhibition of many petty acts of tyranny and persecution." One such incident giving rise to this sentiment was Barlow's criticism that the Irish Brigade had "behaved disgracefully and failed to execute" his orders at Deep Bottom on August 13, 1864. Barlow made comparable remarks about other units within his command, however, and the scathing report likely came from both Barlow's mental exhaustion at the time of writing as well as genuine disappointment in his division's fighting spirit on that day (Winfield Scott Hancock attributed the command's poor performance to extreme battle attrition among both the officer corps and enlisted troops). Furthermore, Barlow praised the Irish Brigade's "briskly engaging the enemy" at Antietam and in 1865 complimented "Irish soldiers, whom he said he grew much attached to; they would follow any leader who was brave anywhere." His letters rarely mention Irish Americans, other than a few passing references to locations of the Irish Brigade. Additionally, while living in New York he had met and befriended the influential Irish American judge Charles Daly, who gave Barlow a book of tactics in late 1861, and was acquainted with Irish-born Thomas F. Meagher. Paradoxically, Barlow could articulate contempt for one group of white immigrants while having tacit acceptance for, or perhaps at least ambivalence toward, another.[39]

---

[38] Barlow to mother, June 2, 1863 ("'German Brigade'"). Barlow to Charles Dalton, June 2, 1863. Barlow to mother, June 7, 1863 ("miserable creatures"). Barlow to Richard Barlow, June 26, 1863 ("I suppose"). Barlow to unknown, no date [but after Gettysburg] ("German officers"). Barlow to Moses Blake Williams, August 5, 1863 ("set foot," "do nothing,"). Barlow to Robert Treat Paine, August 12, 1863 ("ruin").

[39] Barlow to Edward Barlow, December 28, 1861. Barlow to mother, March 5, 1862. Barlow to mother, March 17, 1862. Barlow to mother, June 2, 1862.

Moreover, in spring 1863, Barlow expressed a willingness to command a brigade of black troops, and he possibly felt that such a posting would be an improvement from dealing with the Germans. Proponents of arming black troops to fight for the Union saw him as the perfect leader to help ensure the success of the experiment. Shortly after taking command of the Fifty-fourth Massachusetts Infantry, Colonel Robert G. Shaw urged his father, as well as Charles Russell Lowell and Massachusetts Governor John Andrew, to attempt to have Barlow assigned to command a brigade of African Americans. Andrew enthusiastically endorsed the idea to Secretary of War Stanton, though Barlow's severe wounding at Gettysburg shortly afterward removed this option for the moment.[40]

By June 1863, Barlow also contemplated taking a position as superintendent general of a program for freedmen and putting his antislavery beliefs in action. Emancipation of the slaves had created a plethora of issues that needed to be considered and addressed. Toward this end, on March 16, 1863, Secretary of War Stanton appointed a commission of three to investigate the condition of the newly freed blacks and "to report what measures will best contribute to their protection and improvement, so that they may defend and support themselves; and also how they can be most usefully employed in the service of the government for the suppression of the Rebellion." Robert Dale Owen, James McKaye, and Boston's Samuel Gridley Howe comprised the

---

Barlow to mother, July 4, 1862. Barlow to Edward Barlow, July 8, 1862. Barlow to mother and Edward Barlow, August 9, 1862. Maria L. Daly diary entry, November 24, 1861; November 25, 1865, both in Hammond, *Diary of a Union Lady*, 80–81, 379. David P. Conyngham, *The Irish Brigade and Its Campaigns* (1867; repr. New York: Fordham University Press, 1994), 474 (page citation is to reprint edition; this portion of Conyngham's book was written by Irish Brigade surgeon William O'Meagher). *The War of the Rebellion: A Compilation of the Official Records of the Union and Confederate Armies,* 128 vols. (Washington, D.C.: Government Printing Office, 1880–1901), vol. 29(1): 289; vol. 42(1): 218, 248. All citations are to series 1 unless noted, and the Official Records are hereafter cited as *OR.*

[40] Barlow to mother, April 24, 1863. Robert G. Shaw to Sarah Shaw, Readville, Mass., March 17, 1863; Robert G. Shaw to Sarah Shaw, Saint Simon's Island, Ga., June 18, 1863; Robert G. Shaw to Charles Russell Lowell, Saint Simon's Island, Ga., June 20, 1863, all in Duncan, *Blue-Eyed Child of Fortune,* 309, 354–55. Governor John A. Andrew to Edwin M. Stanton, Boston, June 29, 1863, in *OR,* ser. 3, 3:423–24.

American Freedmen's Inquiry Commission that examined the conditions and employment of blacks in Union-held territory in Virginia, Kentucky, Tennessee, Missouri, and New Orleans. One of the committee's first propositions was to apply blacks as soldiers and military laborers along the Southern seaboard. Their plan created three departments, each administered by a superintendent of colonel's rank and further partitioned into smaller sectors with roughly five thousand freedmen each. In charge of the entire system would be a superintendent general of brigadier general's rank, and Barlow must have seemed an ideal candidate for the posting, both for his abolitionist views and his active sense of discipline and leadership. After all, the program was not only meant to assist in the Union war effort but, more important, teach displaced former slaves self-sufficiency.[41]

Despite the political advantages of the superintendency, Barlow was initially reluctant to leave the command of men in battle. By June 26, 1863, however, he resolved to accept the "Darkey Superintendent" position and corresponded with Howe and Owen about it. His wound at Gettysburg left him unable to assume the position, though, and after he recuperated he desired to return to field command. By April 1864, Barlow seems to have abandoned the possibility of taking the "Darkey Bureau" position, though the exhausting pace and grim casualties of the Overland campaign led him to a renewed interest toward the end of May and again in July. After the war, Barlow continued with his interest in a position working with the freedmen, writing Oliver O. Howard "You know the interest I have always taken in these Freedmen[']s affairs + I have just written to the Secretary of War asking him to assign me to a command in the Southern States + suggesting that at the same time I might be made Superintendent of Freedmen in my District." Yet, for all Barlow's mention of the position in letters to his family and elsewhere, he never discussed a vision for what he would do if he received the office, and his nonchalant attitude about the post becomes striking. In fact, after mentioning the position several times and

---

[41] Richard William Leopold, *Robert Dale Owen* (Cambridge, Mass.: Harvard University Press, 1940), 360–62. *OR*, ser. 3, 3:73–74. Barlow to mother, June 2, 1863.

asserting his intention to fill it, Barlow offered no rationale, explanation, or justification for the move—just the bald statement to his family that he would become superintendent. Furthermore, though he opposed slavery as an institution and seemed more enthusiastic about commanding black troops than Germans in battle, not one of those references displayed any sympathy for the plight of blacks. Along with many Boston abolitionists, he could condemn the institution of involuntary servitude while maintaining a racist sense that blacks were an other in their midst. Thus, Barlow could call African Americans "Darkeys" with a sense of detachment and refer to the position trying to help them as going "into the nigger business."[42]

In the end, Grant's campaign and Barlow's own personal issues culminated in perhaps the most trying summer he had experienced thus far in his young life. Nearly continuous combat led Barlow to long, by May 20, 1864, "for this damned Campaign to be over." A few weeks later, the officer who cherished spirit saw his own begin to flag, and he identified that the army's recent casualties seriously hampered its ability to carry out attacks. "The men feel just at present a great horror and dread of attacking earthworks again and the unusual loss of officers . . . leaves us in a very unfavorable condition for such enterprises," Barlow warned. "I think the men are so wearied and worn out by the harassing labors of the past week that they are wanting in the spirit and dash necessary for successful assaults." By June 1864, he determined to resign when the campaign was over, but within a few weeks a severe illness coupled with the death of his wife compelled Barlow to seek a lengthy leave from the army. Barlow accompanied friends on a trip to Europe, and though he still

---

[42] Barlow to Richard Barlow, June 26, 1863. Barlow to Charles Dalton, September 26, 1863. Barlow to mother, April 19, 1864. Barlow to Charles Dalton, May 24, 1864. Barlow to mother and brother, July 19, 1864. Francis Barlow to Colonel E. D. Townsend, Boston, December 18, 1863, in Barlow Papers NA. Winfield S. Hancock to Francis C. Barlow, Washington, D.C., December 12, 1863, in Francis C. Barlow papers, Massachusetts Historical Society, Boston, Mass. Francis C. Barlow to Oliver O. Howard, Brookline, Mass., July 24, 1865 ("You know the interest"); Francis C. Barlow to Oliver O. Howard, Brookline, Mass., September 17, 1865, in the Oliver Otis Howard Papers in the Special Collections & Archives, Bowdoin College Library, Brunswick, Maine (hereafter cited as Howard Papers).

xl FEAR WAS NOT IN HIM

wore Arabella's ring on his finger in mourning in late March 1865, Barlow rejoined the Army of the Potomac just in time to see it finally victorious, at Appomattox.[43]

Barlow's return witnessed him energized and willing to accept a prominent position within the community and participation in political events. That is a matter for this book's epilogue, however. First, here are the writings of a civilian at war and an officer in command. They reveal not only the encounters and thoughts of a Northern intellectual but also the internal tensions and struggles of a soldier transformed by the new experiences presented by war.

    [43] Barlow to Edward Barlow, May 20, 1864 ("Campaign"). Barlow to mother and brother, June 23, 1864. Francis C. Barlow to Lieutenant Colonel Francis A. Walker, June 6, 1864 ("men feel"), in *OR*, 36(3): 646–47. Maria L. Daly diary, March 26, 1865, in Hammond, *Diary of a Union Lady*, 345. Special Order No. 87, Army of the Potomac, April 6, 1865; General Order No. 12, Second Corps, both in Francis C. Barlow's Generals Papers, RG 94-9W4/6/10/A, Box 2, National Archives, Washington, D.C. (hereafter cited as Barlow's Generals Papers NA; also cited in this book are Francis C. Barlow papers, M-1064 microfilm roll 241 [Barlow Papers NA] and Francis C. Barlow File, Field and Staff Officers Papers, Sixty-first New York Volunteer Infantry [Barlow Field and Staff Officers Papers NA]).

1

1861: "A surprising change from the delicate life of New York"

Barely over a week after the Confederates fired on Fort Sumter, the volunteers of the Twelfth New York Militia turned out to do their duty in defense of the Union. Assembling at New York City's Union Square at nine in the morning of April 21, most of the regiment wore Austrian army–style uniforms, though a shortage led some to turn out in civilian garb. From there, the Twelfth marched down Broadway, Mercer, and Canal Streets to the North River pier. Undoubtedly, Arabella Barlow packed into the throng that watched the unit and craned her neck for a last look at her husband as he went off to the seat of war. The regiment boarded the steamer Baltic, *and the ship departed from New York to arrive at Fortress Monroe the next day. From there, the unit sailed to Annapolis, where it remained for several days before relocating to Washington, D.C., and assuming initial quarters in the Assembly Room on Louisiana Avenue and a church on Sixth Street.*

On May 2, the Twelfth assembled in front of the Capitol building to muster in for three months' service to date from April 16. The regiment then reported to Colonel Joseph K. F. Mansfield's command charged with protecting the District of Columbia, and on May 8, moved into barracks they had constructed themselves at Camp Anderson in Franklin Square. The neatly laid-out camp had a main street, where officers' cabins stood, and ten smaller company streets running off it, each with six huts capable of housing sixteen men. Barlow had enlisted as a private because he had never before held a gun, but when the regiment mustered in he accepted a first lieutenant's commission. In the coming months, Barlow studied military tactics and learned about soldiering under the Twelfth's Colonel Daniel Butterfield, who established a strict schedule for his troops with reveille at five in the morning followed by various drills and target practice through the day. Barlow and the other officers of the unit were fortunate to receive special additional drilling from Lieutenant Emory Upton, an officer who would achieve high rank and even higher renown as a tactician during the Civil War.[1]

Washington May 2 /61

My dear mother,

Edward will tell you what an exhausting + laborious life I am leading at present. This has prevented my writing to you for a week past. I should have continued to do so had not E. been here + I knew he would let you know what was going on. I expected you here until I got a note from E. on Thursday morning saying you were not coming. You could have had a room here + I was very sorry not to see you. Edward I have seen very little + it has caused me much regret that I could do nothing to make it pleasant for him. I am afraid he had a very dull time + I hope he will go to Maine in June on his fishing excursion.

ASE will tell you I am left in charge of the Camp + have to be officer of the Guard every other day which keeps me up 24 hours.

---

[1] Born in 1831 in Utica, New York, Butterfield graduated from Union College and studied law before entering the business world. He served as colonel of the Twelfth New York Militia and, after its term of enlistment expired, was commissioned brigadier general effective from September 7, 1861. He led a brigade in the Fifth corps and suffered a wound at Gaines's Mill during the Seven Days. Butterfield received command of a division on October 30, 1862, and was appointed major general to date from November 29, 1862. When Major General Joseph Hooker took command of the Army of the Potomac, Butterfield became his chief of staff and served in that capacity until wounded at Gettysburg. In October 1863, Butterfield accompanied Hooker to the Western theater and during the Atlanta campaign, led a division of the Twentieth corps. He is known for having developed the corps badge system adopted by the Army of the Potomac and for composing the bugle call "Taps." George Templeton Strong diary entry, April 22, 1861, in Allan Nevins, ed., *Diary of the Civil War 1860–1865: George Templeton Strong* (New York: Macmillan Company, 1962), 132. Frederick H. Dyer, *A Compendium of the War of the Rebellion*, 3 vols. (Des Moines: Dyer Publishing Company, 1908), 3:1409. New York Monuments Commission, *In Memoriam: Francis Channing Barlow*, 60, 62. Julia Lorrilard Butterfield, *A Biographical Memorial of General Daniel Butterfield* (New York: Grafton Press, 1904), 11, 18–23. Ezra J. Warner, *Generals in Blue* (Baton Rouge: Louisiana State University Press, 1964), 62–63, 519.

I see nothing of Washington or of anyone. I have not been into any house here except my own for a week past. Edward will so fully describe things here that I will say nothing of it.

I wish you would write + tell me fully about Madison + the Gardners + everyone I know of. [George] Bliss wrote me a very kind letter saying that he had sent to Edward the $50 he was to lend me + saying that he would get me credit for some military equipments, which offer I accepted.[2]

I wrote to R. last week discouraging his going into the army at present or until he can get some paying non-combatant position. Bliss says he will make a push with Barney this week.

This sort of life is not pleasant but I did not come for pleasure + can endure anything for 3 months. An active campaign would be much preferable to this sort of life. I expect to stay here for the present.

This morning at 6 A.M. when I was in the Guardhouse who should come in but old Toppen who came on last night to return tonight. I was very glad to see him but could only do it for but 5 minutes. He comes on solely to see the fun. Please send this to R. as I don't know when I can get time to write him. Love to the Gardners + write me a long letter.

Your affectionate son
FCB

The weather is very enervating here but I am very well except being tired.

---

[2] Barlow and George Bliss were partners in the practice of law before the Civil War. Bliss graduated in the Harvard College class of 1851 and studied at that institution's law school before becoming a member of the New York bar in 1857. A staunch Republican, he became a close friend of Governor E. D. Morgan and joined his staff at the start of the Civil War. In 1862, Bliss became a New York State paymaster with the rank of colonel and was later commissioned captain in the Fourth New York Heavy Artillery. He also helped recruit African American soldiers when the North began to organize black regiments. Bliss returned to practicing law when the war concluded, and from December 1872 to January 1877 he served as U.S. attorney for the southern district of New York, where he helped uncover fraud within the customs service. He also wrote treatises on life insurance law and New York civil procedure. Although Bliss avoided elected office, he was an influential and important figure within the Republican Party and New York politics after the Civil War. Dumas Malone, ed., *Dictionary of American Biography* (hereafter cited as *DAB*), 10 vols. (New York: Charles Scribner's Sons, 1927–1936), 1:373–374.

Of course I never have + never should show your letters to any one.

Although Butterfield proved strict with his men, he also allowed them certain enjoyments while in Washington. One night, civilians walked amidst the regimental camp, enjoying music from the unit's band at a time when the war was still defined in terms of pageantry rather than violence. Earlier that day, Butterfield had rewarded the unit's good behavior by giving his New Yorkers leave for the day until four o'clock, at which time every man returned except two who arrived late and drunk from beer.[3]

Mansfield urged Federal occupation of Arlington and the Potomac River's Virginia shore in order to safeguard the capital's security, and the day after Virginia citizens approved secession from the Union, his troops mobilized. For several days preceding this move, the New Yorkers had slept on arms ready for any alarm, but the order to advance into Virginia came suddenly on the evening of May 23 after the results of the Old Dominion's referendum became known. Following several hours' preparation, the regiment assembled on its parade ground shortly after midnight, remaining so silent that the civilians around Camp Anderson did not wake up. After leaving a camp guard, 829 soldiers of the Twelfth marched in column down Fourteenth Street and, following some engineers, crossed Long Bridge as moonlight glistened off their muskets. At one in the morning on May 24, the Twelfth excitedly entered Virginia, the first regiment to do so. Proceeding toward Alexandria, the unit took a position at Roach's Mills, six miles from Washington, and several companies took shelter in the mill building while others bivouacked nearby. The Twelfth remained in this position until relieved by the Second Connecticut Volunteers and ordered to return to Washington on June 2. Being a Sunday, after the regiment had marched five miles out of camp, it formed a hollow square with its officers, band, and flag in the center. After the singing of a hymn and the reading of a psalm, the chaplain delivered a short sermon emphasizing the qualities of a good soldier and need to defend

---

[3] Butterfield, *Biographical Memorial of General Daniel Butterfield*, 33–34.

the Union. Afterward, the regiment formed in column and re-sumed its march in the sweltering heat to reach Washington by the afternoon and make its way up Pennsylvania Avenue and Fourteenth Street to its old camp.[4]

Wednesday 19th [June 1861]

Dear E.

I enclose letter read from mother some days ago. I wrote her the same day + just wrote again. I am glad she seems in such good spirits + hope she will continue so.

My Capt has just got back which relieves me from my arduous duties as Captain. For the last week I have hardly had time to eat.

The collars have not come. Please send them in a letter for I need them. Our pay rolls are made out + they say we shall get the money very soon. You <u>will</u> see me in New York the moment our time is up + shall not enlist again at least for the present. I am sick of this damned Regt.

I have seen no one or been no where since I wrote last. We are still in Washington + shall not leave unless to defend the City if attacked. I have commanded the Co. with credit during the past week + feel quite competent to be Capt.—with the exception of one thing—that is I have not the desire to make the damned scoundrels like me + I do not think they do especially. Has anything been heard from Dalton.[5]

Yours in haste
F.C.B.

---

[4] Ibid., 24, 25, 42.

[5] This probably refers to one of the four Dalton brothers, the sons of Dr. John Call Dalton and Julia Ann Spalding. John Call Dalton Jr. was born in 1825 and studied at the Harvard Medical School before teaching at the University of Buffalo and Vermont College. He then became a professor at the College of Physicians and Surgeons in New York City, where he taught until he entered the army in 1861 and served as a surgeon until 1864. Charles Henry Dalton was born in 1826 and became a partner at J. C. Howe & Company besides being involved in the New England cotton industry. In 1861 he served as an agent of Massachusetts, and he also performed various other functions for Gov-

On July 4, a special session of Congress convened by presidential proclamation to address the growing national emergency. Later that day, the New York units stationed in Washington held a parade, and over twenty thousand men organized in more than twenty regiments made an impressive display. The Twelfth received compliments from general in chief Major General Winfield Scott for their disciplined marching and sharp appearance, after which Butterfield gave his men leave of duty for the day. That evening, Camp Anderson was the scene of speeches and dances to the music of the regimental band and the light of Chinese lanterns, while throngs of civilians, including prominent Washington women, passed through Franklin Square.[6]

Washington
July 5th 1861

My dear mother

Edward sent me this morning a letter from you dated July 2nd from which I am very glad to learn that you are improving under the treatment of Mrs. Pike.

Whether it be imagination or otherwise it makes no difference so long as you flourish under it.

Washington I hope will be a little more pleasant now that Congress has met. I could not go to the opening yesterday as we all

---

ernor Andrew; several of Barlow's letters to him written during the Civil War are reprinted in this volume. Edward Barry Dalton was born in 1834 and also became a doctor, served as a surgeon through the Civil War, and later was sanitary superintendent on the Metropolitan Board of Health for New York City. Henry Rogers Dalton was born in 1839 and worked at J. C. Howe & Company, but when the war broke out he became a lieutenant in the First Massachusetts Heavy Artillery. Later, he performed on staff duty until November 1864. "Charles Henry Dalton Letters, 1861–1865," *Proceedings of the Massachusetts Historical Society, October 1922–June 1923* (Boston: Massachusetts Historical Society, 1923), 56:354–495: 354–55 (letters from Barlow have been reprinted in this volume).

  [6] Butterfield, *Biographical Memorial of General Daniel Butterfield,* 25. Margaret Leech, *Reveille in Washington 1860–1865* (1941; repr. Alexandria, Va.: Time-Life Books, 1980), 109–10 (page citation is to repr. ed.).

paraded but shall attend there often. We have a Congressman from New York in our house + know several who will give us every facility for getting into the house + seeing the proceedings.

When we come home I shall come on to see you and then I think I shall go to Somerville for 3 months until Nov. 1st as I see no cheaper way of being in the country + I do not wish to go to the City so early.[7] Board near New York at any place where we could afford to go + would go I regard as impossible.

You do not tell me whether you have seen the Hedges or Mrs. Clark or the Cathcarts or any of the Massts people, nor whether you mean to make a visit to the Dinemores.

I have not seen one person in Washington who was above the ranks of commonplace + should like to get into the society of intelligent people. I should enjoy making a long visit at Massts when I come home but I have been away so much + at the same time drawing my share of the proceeds of the office that I do not feel at liberty to be gone long when we get back.

Our 4th of July celebration was to parade before the Prest. + [Major] General [Winfield] Scott.[8] There were some 35000 troops from New York alone. Our Regt surpassed them all + Genl. Scott said "They are really magnificent." I was in command of my Company the Capt being on guard.

You allude to not having read a 2nd letter from Mrs. Sheppard. What was the contents of the 1st one?

The delay of this army to move to Richmond is supposed to be caused by the want of means of transportation. The enemy as they retire will destroy everything which they can't consume (if indeed anything is left now) + our troops must depend entirely upon what they can carry with them. You can imagine what immense stores of cattle &c. will have to be carried on for the men grumble at the least hardship or shortness of food. The Govt are waiting for an immense number of waggons to be finished + then it is thought they will move on. They are greatly to be

---

[7] Arabella Griffith Barlow's family lived in Somerville, New Jersey.

[8] A hero of the War of 1812, Major General Winfield Scott went on to lead U.S. forces to victory during the Mexican War. Early in the Civil War he acted as nominal general in chief, though his age and poor health prevented more active service. He soon retired but survived to see the Union victorious. Warner, *Generals in Blue*, 429–30.

blamed for not having begun the preparations earlier + for having dawdled along in the way they have. The impression seems
to be that there will very soon be an advance or a fight. If I had
stayed at home + gone out + slept in a pig pen at night I should
have had about the same experience that we have had here. Now
that I have got familiar with my duties &c.—it is a very easy idle
life—Write soon

Yours affectionately
F.C.B.

On July 7, the Twelfth moved out to reinforce Major General Rob-
ert Patterson's force at Martinsburg, in northwestern Virginia.
After marching to and then through Baltimore, the recent scene
of anti-Federal demonstrations, the New Yorkers went by rail to
Harrisburg, Pennsylvania, and then on to Hagerstown, Mary-
land. After arriving there on the evening of July 8, the Twelfth
bivouacked in nearby woods until breaking camp on the evening
of July 9 to march to Williamsport, where it forded the Potomac
River and pushed on for Martinsburg. The Twelfth arrived at
Camp Meigs there at five in the morning on July 10, after a
twenty-nine-mile march.[9]

N.Y. Friday July 12. Noon
Dear mother, nothing from you today
I wrote a few words yesterday
Hope you are well
    Affecty Edw.

---

[9] A native of Ireland born in 1792, Robert Patterson moved with his family to
Pennsylvania in 1798. He participated in the War of 1812, attaining the rank
of colonel, and afterward remained in the state's militia. He fought in Mexico
as a major general and Winfield Scott's second in command. With the Civil
War, Scott recommissioned Patterson a major general, though he was relieved
shortly after First Manassas and discharged from the army. Butterfield, *Bio-*
graphical Memorial of General Daniel Butterfield, 25. William C. Davis, *Battle*
at Bull Run (Baton Rouge: Louisiana State University Press, 1977), 5–6, 151.

Hagerstown Maryland
Tuesday July 9th 1861

My dear Mother

We left Washington at 3 p.m. on Sunday, reached Baltimore at about 7 marched through the City + left for Harisburg at 12, reached there at 12 the next day + arrived here last night at 10 p.m.

We came this round about way instead of going by the Baltimore + Ohio road direct to Harpers Ferry for the reason that there is no means of crossing the River at Harpers Ferry, the bridges being destroyed + the water deep. Tonight we leave here + march to Williamsport + then wade across the River + march on to Martinsburg to join [Major] Genl. [Robert] Patterson. I think we shall then all march on Richmond simultaneously with an advance on all sides.

The scenery all the way from Baltimore is lovely. It is a wheat growing country with fine wide spread fields of grain + everything looks rich + prosperous. This place is only 6 miles from the Penn. Line + that we passed through in the evening, so that we have not seen much of Maryland. Our journey from Harisburg yesterday afternoon was a perfect triumphal journey. We had 3 engines + 92 cars containing our Regt + the 5th N.Y. all under command of [Major] Genl. [Charles W.] Sanford.[10] The men women + children all turned out to greet us + brought provisions &c. wherever we stopped.

Hagerstown is a very old quaint looking town of about 4100 inhabitants, with a good many secessionists. I have just had a good breakfast at the Hotel + a good bath in a mill stream.

Direct to me here in care of Capt. Cromie 12th Regt N.Y. State Troops. This is our post town at present.

Arabella is in Washington for the present until we see what we are going to do. She may follow us on here if we encamp in a civilized place. We hear nothing of fighting yet but may get some.

Write often and I will write whenever I can.

I send this to Edward who will please forward to mother + Richard.

---

[10] Major General Charles W. Sandford (spelled "Sanford" by Barlow) was a major general in the New York militia. Davis, *Battle at Bull Run*, 9.

I am very well and bear the heat + fatigue as well as "any other man" if not better.

Yours affectionately
F.C.B.

Don't be frightened at any rumors of battles.

While at Camp Meigs, the Twelfth was brigaded with the Fifth, Nineteenth, and Twenty-eighth New York Regiments. Butterfield led the brigade, and Lieutenant Colonel William G. Ward assumed command of the Twelfth. Although the regiment's term of enlistment expired on July 16, Butterfield volunteered its services until August 2, and the War Department accepted the offer. Anticipating upcoming action, the regiment celebrated a religious service conducted by its chaplain on Sunday, July 14. The next day, Patterson's fifteen thousand men marched to Bunker Hill, Virginia, trying to keep eleven thousand Confederates under Brigadier General Joseph Johnston occupied so that they would not join Brigadier General P. G. T. Beauregard's army near Manassas. However, the sixty-nine-year-old veteran of the War of 1812 had waited a few days too long. Shortly after his force moved out, it became apparent that the Confederates had already withdrawn. On July 17, Patterson mobilized his entire corps and advanced to locate the Confederate force, rumored to be at Winchester. During the march, reports of enemy troops caused Patterson to halt his column and form in line of battle, but Johnston had already slipped away, heading off to reinforce Beauregard. After staying in line for several hours, Patterson marched his troops to Charlestown, Virginia, where the Twelfth bivouacked in a field outside town.[11]

---

[11] Butterfield, *Biographical Memorial of General Daniel Butterfield*, 26–27. Davis, *Battle at Bull Run*, 88–89. James M. McPherson, *Battle Cry of Freedom: The Civil War Era* (New York: Oxford University Press, 1988), 335, 339.

Charlestown, Virginia
July 18th 1861

My dear Edward,

Your letter including one from Mother reached me a few days ago and I have not heard from any of you since. I last wrote from Martinsburg. On Monday morning early we left there + after a fatiguing march of 11 miles reached another village called Bunker Hill about 1/2 way between Martinsburg and Winchester. Our Regt. was about the only one that carried their knapsacks, all the others having theirs carried in wagons, + we had to halt continuously because of the baggage trains in front of us + yet we made a most excellent march. My Regt. marches, I think, better than any other. We encamped at Bunker Hill all day on Tuesday. We were surrounded on all sides by troops (our own) + the strict military rule made us understand the realities of war. We threw out heavy pickets but saw no enemy. At 3 a.m. of Wednesday we left for Winchester as we supposed. It was reported at Bunker Hill that there were some 21000 of the enemy at Winchester (12 miles distant) determined to make a stand, + that they had cut down trees to block up the road + had a strong battery thrown up across the road 1 ½ miles from Winchester to stop our march. We had some 35000 troops (having left 40000 at Martinsburg) + it was fully expected that we should fight. I had fully made up my mind that we were to have battle + so did all the other men. But after a march of 7 miles on Wednesday morning we were halted for some 6 hours + then told us we're to go to Charlestown, Va. where we started from our halt at 5 p.m. + marched 7 miles to Charlestown, where we arrived at about 7:30 p.m. Yesterday on the march I was thrown out with part of my Company as skirmishers on the side of the road in the fields, but none of us saw any enemy. We got in after dark last night + after marching about + about we were brought into a wheat field having a stubble of some six inches very sharp. Here we lay down without any supper or tents + slept for the night. This last expedition of ours has given us a thorough taste of camp life for one week is pretty much like another. It is a surprising change from the delicate life of New York but we have all got used to it. At Martinsburg we were formed into a brigade with 3

other N.Y. Regts the 5th, 28th, 4th, 19th of which Butterfield is
Acting Brigadier General which leaves Lt. Col. [William G.] Ward
in command. I like him very much better than Butterfield for I
know him to be a gentleman. Butterfield makes our Regt. his
head quarters but has nothing to do with the details of our Regt.
When along side of other Regts I see the superiority of ours. Our
camp was laid out with regular streets according to military
rules. The others were all straggling + unmilitary. The other
Regts had not heard of dress parades apparently + began them
after our example apparently being shamed into it. We four officers slept together in a tent wrapped up in our blankets sometimes on the ground + sometimes on some hay. We messed
together, some 6 of us, as I wrote you. As soon as we arrive at
any place we officers make a rush to every home for food. At
some small towns like Bunker Hill we have very hard times +
very amusing times in getting anything to eat. The towns have
been thoroughly eaten out by the Seccessionists who have been
at all these places off + on before us. At Bunker Hill I talked
with a very intelligent man who used to live in Phila. who says
that the Seccessionists have plenty of gold + silver which they
spend very lavishly. That the villagers used to pick up purses with
$30 & $40 in them + nice new shirts only worn once + various
new articles thrown away. This man seemed to be a good Union
man and I think gave a true account. In marching we usually
march either four abreast or by sections (some 10 abreast) each
company by itself. First go the flags, the band, then the staff
mounted with the Colonel at the head of the staff + mounted,
then the Companies in their order in line of battle, which depends upon the order of the Captain in seniority. My company is
2nd in line and we march 2nd, the Captain at the head of the
Co. (that is when we march four abreast) on the left side of the
front left hand man, + the 1st Lt. at the rear of the Company in
the left hand side as per diagram

Captain . . . .
. . . . 2nd Lt
. . . . 3rd Lt.
. . . .
. . . . 1st Lt..
. . . .

When marching by sections we are placed as follows
    Captain

_____

2nd Lt.

_____

3rd Lt.

_____

1st Lt.

Each commanding a section. We march without music (except when passing through towns) at what is called a route step, which does not require the men to keep step or to keep strictly in the ranks, + they carry their muskets as they like. My company sings a good deal on the march + there are several very amusing men in the ranks who make a good many amusing jokes &c. + have really a good deal of humor. The style of profanity of the whole regiment is frightful. We hear that [Major General George B.] McClellan is in Winchester + Johnston gone + that we have come here to cut off Johnston's retreat. There is quite a large force here with Patterson in command + [Captain Abner] Doubleday's battery.[12] We are encamped close to the field where they say John Brown was hung + they point out the spot where his gallows was erected.[13] I went into the Court house

_____

[12] The son of a two-term congressman from New York, Abner Doubleday graduated from West Point in 1842 and served in the artillery branch of the army. He served in the Mexican War and as part of the garrison of Fort Sumter when the Confederates fired on it in April 1861. After serving in the Shenandoah Valley, Doubleday was commissioned brigadier general and led a brigade during the Second Manassas campaign. He commanded a First corps division at Antietam and Fredericksburg and led the corps on July 1, 1863, after the death of Major General John Reynolds. After Gettysburg, Doubleday served in Washington through the rest of the war. Doubleday is credited with having refined many of the rules of baseball, and he is often referred to as the originator of that sport in its modern form. Warner, *Generals in Blue*, 129–30.

[13] On the evening of October 16, 1859, abolitionist John Brown led eighteen men to capture the armory at Harpers Ferry and then sent out a patrol to inform local slaves of his action and seize prisoners, including a great-grand-nephew of George Washington's. Virginia and Maryland militia, and U.S. Marines commanded by Colonel Robert E. Lee and Lieutenant J. E. B. Stuart, quickly surrounded Brown, and Brown's goal of starting a slave revolt failed. Less than thirty-six hours after he began his operation, Brown and his men

where he was tried this morning. This town is like all Virginia towns, is slovenly + wretched with occasionally some large old pleasant looking places + houses. Last night we had no supper. I got part of a dinner of coffee + heavy biscuit + butter at about 3 p.m. yesterday at a farm house near where we halted, from which I was hurried by the sound of the bugle giving the signal to march. We all eat like pigs at all irregular hours + the most indigestible food but keep well. When we are quartered in a town large enough to get settled we live better. This morning I got up at 5 a.m. + about six got a biscuit (chip) + a piece of _fat_ salt pork fried from the Company cook which I eat + wiped my hands on my head, the brook which runs by our encampment being so dirtied + riled by the thousands quartered higher up that it dirties one more than it cleans him to wash in it. Yet thousands of naked forms can be at this moment seen washing in it. At about 9 this morning Carlton Richards (one of the engineers) + myself started into the town, all unwashed, to get breakfast. At the town pump in the most frequented part of the town, close to the Courthouse, we took off our coats + shirts + stood entirely naked except trousers, stockings + shoes + washed + cleaned ourselves in the face of the multitude among soldiers of all climes. We then foraged about to 4 or 5 houses for breakfast without success; they saying that they were eaten out + stolen out by those who had proceeded us. The people are rank Secessionists + lie a good deal about food saying they have none. At one place they said they would give us some biscuits which they brought to the door evidently thinking we were beggars of the most degraded kind. At last we found a place where we got a good breakfast for .50 cts. each with some women who talked rank treason. They are openly Seccessionists here almost entirely + the women[14] talk openly + freely, but good humoredly. One girl remarked pleasantly to some of our men that she had 3

---

were captured; following a hasty indictment and trial, Brown's sentence to hang was carried out on December 2. McPherson, *Battle Cry of Freedom,* 205–6.

[14] The remainder of this letter is missing at this point, and I have relied on a typescript copy in the Massachusetts Historical Society for the rest of Barlow's text. Ellipses after one paragraph indicate that perhaps Barlow's family did not want certain information to be recorded for posterity and destroyed the page.

brothers in the Secession Army each of whom could whip any 3 of our men; another said she should like to have the cooking of the Federal Army to do + plenty of arsenic. The people here believe implicitly the stories of their papers + think they have beaten us as every move. The country is generally poor with a worn out look + the people seem very ignorant.

We have given up any hope of seeing any fighting since our disappointment of yesterday. We are only 7 miles from Harper's Ferry from whence there is railroad communication to Washington + we shall probably crawl along to Washington + home very soon.

Last night I lost my pocket book out of my pocket with $10 in it. Bliss will send check for about $76 belonging to me which please retain until I direct its disposition. You ask of my duties in battle. The evolutions, as far as the management of a company is concerned are the same in battle as on parade + we just carry our companies there + make them load + fire + charge just as we are ordered by the Colonel or General. Our duties are comparatively simple. As for fighting we ordinarily stand in the rear of our Companies + of course in the firings are there. In charging a battery or in charging bayonets I suppose the officers or at least the Commandant of a Company leads his men up to the object or the enemy to be attacked but he must fall back, I should think, before bayonets are crossed, as he would stand little chance with his sword agt. a bayonet. I confess I understand but little of the practical duties of an officer in battle + no one else here does. We ought to be instructed in it. In battle I should obey orders when they were given + use my discretion when they were not.

This letter is intended for mother + R. as well as you all. I hope mother will go with Mrs. Hedge. She has a hard summer + needs the cheerful influence of such pleasant company. She has been nowhere which involves any expenditure + I should think could well afford it. . . .

Bliss applied at once for R as soon as he (Bliss heard of it). I have not yet heard yet what his success was. As for R's plans + the plans of all of us, I shall be home so soon that we will talk them all over rather than write of them. At Martinsburg the

Mass'ts 2d was encamped and I went over one evening, saw them all [Wilder] Dwight, Choate (Rufus) Willie Wms (who came into a tent where I was + to whom I was introduced as if we were strangers) (+ we acted accordingly) + [Stephen G.] Perkins, my friend, who is a 2nd Lt. [Henry Lee] Higginson was not about + Bob Shaw was asleep.[15] It is a very fine Reg't, much the finest in the Volunteers service. I just met Choate, Williams

---

[15] Born in 1833, Wilder Dwight attended Phillips Academy in Exeter, New Hampshire, before graduating from Harvard College in 1853. He studied law and was admitted to the Massachusetts bar in 1856, but when war broke out he helped recruit the Second Massachusetts and was appointed its major. He suffered a mortal wound at Antietam and died shortly after that battle. Rufus Choate studied at the Boston Latin School before attending Amherst College and studying law. He entered the Second Massachusetts on May 28, 1861, as a second lieutenant, receiving promotions to first lieutenant on December 13, 1861, and captain in August of the following year. Malarial fever forced his resignation from the service in October 1862 and he died three years later, still affected by the illness. William B. Williams, whose grandfather served in the Revolutionary War, studied engineering and worked on building several railroads before entering the Second Massachusetts as a first lieutenant. He was killed at Cedar Mountain on August 9, 1862. Born in Boston in 1835, Stephen G. Perkins entered the Harvard class of 1855. Illness forced him to graduate in the class of 1856, however, after he received special tutoring from Barlow. Afterward, he obtained a degree in mathematics and joined the Second Massachusetts as a second lieutenant; he was killed at Cedar Mountain on August 9, 1862. Henry Lee Higginson was born in New York in 1834, though he and his family soon thereafter moved to Boston. After attending the Boston Latin School, he graduated from Harvard in 1851 and spent much time in Europe before becoming a second lieutenant in the Second Massachusetts. He was commissioned captain in the First Massachusetts Cavalry on October 31, 1861, and its major the following March, though disease forced him to leave the service in August 1864. After the war, the wealthy Higginson founded the Boston Symphony Orchestra. Born in 1837 into one of the wealthiest families in the United States, Robert Gould Shaw's childhood home was located adjacent to Brook Farm, and the household was a gathering spot for abolitionists and social reformers. In 1847 his immediate family moved to Staten Island, New York. After he spent time touring and living in Europe, he entered Harvard College, though he left in 1858 without having graduated. With the outbreak of the Civil War, Shaw became a second lieutenant in the Second Massachusetts Infantry and fought at Cedar Mountain and Antietam, suffering two wounds in the process. When Massachusetts Governor John Andrew raised the North's first black regiment, the Fifty-fourth Massachusetts, he turned to Shaw to serve as its colonel. Shaw died on July 18, 1863, leading his unit in the charge at Battery Wagner, South Carolina. Alonzo H. Quint, *The Record of the Second Massachusetts Infantry* (Boston: James P. Walker, 1867), 477, 488–89, 493–95, 497. Thomas Wentworth Higginson, *Harvard Memorial Biographies*, 2 vols. (Cambridge, Mass.: Sever and Francis, 1866), 1:373–81. For more on Shaw, see Duncan, *Blue-Eyed Child of Fortune.*

+ Sam Quincy in the town where I was with a patrol to pick up the stragglers + directed them to my breakfast place.[16] This morning I went about a mile from Camp, borrowed a pail at a farm house, washed all my dirty clothes, stripped stark naked behind a shed close to the road + washed all over.

My paper is giving out. Shall be home very soon.

Love to all.

Arabella is in Washington. Direct to that place in future. They will probably be forwarded.

Affectionately yours,
F

On July 21, the Twelfth marched to Harpers Ferry and occupied a position atop nearby Bolivar Heights, and on July 26 four of its companies crossed the Shenandoah River and occupied part of Loudon Heights. On July 28, shortly before being relieved from command, Patterson evacuated Harpers Ferry and concentrated his force at Charlestown. For the men of the Twelfth, their part in the early days of the war was over. On August 1 the New Yorkers began their journey home, travelling by railroad via Baltimore, Philadelphia, Perth Amboy, and then New York. Late in the afternoon of August 2, the regiment reached the wharf, greeted by a throng crowded along Broadway to catch a glimpse of the returning defenders of the Union. The Twelfth New York Militia mustered out at Washington Square, New York City, on August 5, 1861, to conclude its three-month term of service.[17]

---

[16] Samuel M. Quincy, the son of Josiah Quincy Jr., was born in Boston in 1833. He graduated from Harvard in 1852, studied law, and in 1861 represented Boston in the House of Representatives. He was commissioned captain in the Second Massachusetts and was wounded and captured at Cedar Mountain, ending up imprisoned in Richmond's Libby Prison. Quincy was paroled in October 1862 and returned to lead the Second as its colonel at the battle of Chancellorsville before he resigned in June 1863. Quint, *Record of the Second Massachusetts Infantry*, 484–85.

[17] Dyer, *Compendium of the War of the Rebellion,* 3:410. Butterfield, *Biographical Memorial of General Daniel Butterfield,* 26–28.

Office of Bliss & Barlow,
Attorneys & Counsellors. Notaries Public.
No. 50 Wall Street
New York, Oct. 25 1861

Dear Mother

I have not heard from you though perhaps the boys have. I saw
R. a moment day before yesterday but have not seen either of
them besides. R. goes to Phila. today or tomorrow.

They have probably written you how much they liked the 7th
St. rooms. I have not heard what the decision of the woman was.
There is not much news with me. I have been every night to
Soml but may stay in town tonight.[18]

Is not the war news abominable. It seems now pretty clear that
it was a defeat after all as the papers say we have left the Virginia
side of the river + are just where we started; less some 620 men
killed wounded + missing + with the discouragement of a defeat besides.[19]

It seems to have been an outrageous movement to advance
over a deep river into only one or two boats in the face of a large
army + yet it was done apparently by the command of an old
army officer (Col [Charles P.] Stone).[20]

---

[18] This refers to Arabella's town of Somerville, New Jersey.

[19] Barlow refers to the Battle of Ball's Bluff on the banks of the Potomac
River, on October 21, 1861. McClellan ordered Brigadier General Charles P.
Stone to demonstrate against the Confederates across the river while other
Federal forces tried to maneuver the Rebels out of the town of Leesburg, Virginia. Stone assigned the mission to Colonel Edward Baker, a former senator
from Oregon and friend of Lincoln (who named his second son after him), who
sent most of his brigade across the river, where it faced a strong Confederate
force posted atop the hundred-foot embankment at Ball's Bluff. In short order,
Baker was killed, the Federals were driven into the river, and many Yankees
who were fortunate enough to escape Southern lead ended up drowning. In
all, the Federals had a total of 921 casualties out of 1,700 engaged: 49 killed,
158 wounded, and 714 missing. The Confederates suffered but 155 casualties,
and the debacle prompted congressional investigation. McPherson, *Battle Cry
of Freedom*, 362. E. B. Long, *The Civil War Day by Day* (Garden City, N.Y.:
Doubleday & Company, 1971), 129.

[20] Born in Massachusetts on September 30, 1824, Charles P. Stone graduated from West Point in 1845 and served with distinction in the Mexican War.
In 1856, he resigned from the army to survey the state of Sonora for the government of Mexico. In 1861 Stone served as inspector general of the District
of Columbia militia, and as such he protected Lincoln's safety upon the presi-

James Lowell is in Col. [William R.] Lees [Twentieth Massachusetts Volunteer] Regt. but I do not see his name on any of the killed + wounded.[21]

How do you enjoy yourself? Are they all secessionists in Charlestown? I have heard nothing from the Governor about my Majority + shall do nothing about it + do not care much whether I get it or not.

I hear since I wrote the above that Edward has written to ask if you will agree to an arrangement which will include C. Miles in the 7th St house.

Write me.
Your aff. Son
F.C.B.

Love to the Crosbys

As both North and South settled in for a longer war than either side anticipated, new regiments were recruited, and it would not

---

dent's arrival in the capital. On May 14, 1861, Stone was appointed colonel of the Fourteenth U.S. Infantry and he was promoted to brigadier general on August 6, to rank from May 17. After leading a brigade in Robert Patterson's Army of the Shenandoah during the First Manassas campaign, Stone commanded a three-brigade division deployed on the Potomac River. One of Stone's subordinates, Colonel Edward D. Baker, rashly brought about the Federal debacle at Ball's Bluff, but Stone bore most of the blame for the disaster. At the instigation of Radical Republicans in Congress, Stone was arrested in the middle of the night on February 8, 1862, and confined for 189 days in Forts Lafayette and Hamilton without ever being charged. After his release in August, he went unemployed for nine months until Major General Nathaniel P. Banks requested Stone's assignment to the Department of the Gulf, where he served at Port Hudson and on the Red River campaign. On April 4, 1864, he was mustered out of his volunteer commission, and he resigned from the army altogether in September of that year. After the war, he served for thirteen years as chief of staff of the Army of the Khedive of Egypt and then as the engineer for the foundation of the Statue of Liberty. He died in New York City on January 24, 1887, and is buried at West Point. Warner, *Generals in Blue*, 480–81.

[21] One of the finest volunteer regiments in the Federal army, the Twentieth Massachusetts lost heavily at Ball's Bluff, where 148 of its 318 effectives became casualties. Among the wounded, Lieutenant Oliver Wendell Holmes Jr. suffered a serious chest wound and Lieutenant James Lowell a leg wound. *OR*, 5:317–18.

be long before Barlow resumed the soldier's life. Although it ap-
pears from the above letter that Barlow briefly practiced law
again at his old office, he also mentions, albeit with a probably
affected nonchalance, the possibility of a major's commission.

Meanwhile, Colonel Spencer Cone, a contributor to the New
York Mercury *known for his stentorian voice, organized a regi-*
ment designated the Sixty-first New York Volunteers, at Fort
Wadsworth on Staten Island. Almost immediately, trouble
brewed within the unit's officer corps, and Cone suggested a vote
as to whether he would remain the regiment's commander. Cone
refused to step aside after the tally came out against him, how-
ever, and he was physically ejected from the camp. Cone re-
turned to the camp, now at Silver Lake, several days later to
resume his position and, after turning out the regiment, par-
doned those who had joined the cabal against him once they
vowed good behavior in the future. When the Sixty-first's Lieu-
tenant Colonel Manning and Major Lynch refused to do so and
left the unit, Barlow received appointment as the regiment's sec-
ond in command. The Sixty-first returned to Fort Wadsworth,
but during the move several hundred deserted, a further harbin-
ger of future disciplinary problems and difficulties under Cone.[22]

On November 9, the Sixty-first left for the nation's capital,
though numbering only seven hundred strong. After taking a
steamer to Perth Amboy, the New Yorkers boarded a train and
reached Philadelphia in the evening, where they were treated to
a banquet. At 8 a.m. the next morning, the Sixty-first resumed
its journey to the seat of war and reached Washington, D.C., by
nine that evening. After spending the night in the Soldiers' Rest
building near the depot, the New Yorkers set up camp in Kendall
Green, a field not far from the Capitol building, where they spent
the next several weeks.[23]

Barlow remained in New York for a while longer. On November
23, he and Arabella called upon Judge Charles Daly and his wife,
who recounted that Arabella looked large, as if pregnant, though
it seemed that married life suited her well. The New York diarist
did find something odd about the couple, however, considering

---

[22] Fuller, *Personal Recollections*, 6–8.
[23] Ibid., 8–9.

their age difference. When the Barlows arrived, Daly's maid opened the door and announced that a soldier and his mother had called, and Maria Daly found it awkward when the youthful Federal officer referred to his wife simply as "Belle." During the course of the evening, Judge Daly gave Barlow a book of tactics, no doubt a welcome and appreciated gift that the young Lieutenant Colonel reviewed thoroughly.[24]

Barlow went to Washington several days later, where the young officer first met his new comrades. A member of the Sixty-first, Charles Fuller, recalled that Barlow initially made an unimpressive performance, being "of medium height, of slight build, with a pallid countenance, and a weakish drawling voice. In his movements there was an appearance of loose jointedness and an absence of prim stiffness." Barlow immediately set about improving discipline in the unit, however, schooling officers in tactics and drilling the men, efforts that comprise a major topic of his next several letters. Fuller recounted that at first, these "exacting requirements and severity" earned Barlow the enmity of the soldiers under him, but they soon realized that such discipline and order would benefit them in combat and that Barlow would be "at the head leading him." In this way, "animosity was turned into confidence and admiration," and Fuller proclaimed him, in the end, a "great soldier."[25]

---

[24] Born in New York City of Irish parents, Charles P. Daly learned the trades of making quills and cabinets before studying law, passing the New York bar examination in 1839. As a Democrat, Daly served in the state assembly in 1843 and sponsored a bill to create Central Park in New York City. Governor William Bouck appointed him a judge of the Court of Common Pleas, the highest court in New York until its jurisdiction was divided between the state's Supreme, Superior, and General Sessions Courts in 1896. Daly served on the bench from 1844 to 1885, the last twenty-seven as chief justice, until he retired at the mandatory age of seventy. In addition to his activities as a jurist, Daly was active among literary circles and wrote on a variety of topics. Maria L. Daly was the daughter of two wealthy and socially prominent New York families, the Lydigs and Suydams. As a member of the moneyed Dutch and German New York aristocracy, Maria's father objected to her courtship with the Irish judge, despite his career as a jurist. They married on September 27, 1856, and during the Civil War, Maria Daly kept a diary that serves as a valuable resource on New York City and its populace during the conflict. Maria L. Daly diary entry, November 24, 1861, in Hammond, *Diary of a Union Lady*, 80–81. Ibid., xxxii, xxxiv, xxxvi, xl. Harold E. Hammond, *A Commoner's Judge: The Life and Times of Charles Patrick Daly* (Boston: Christopher Publishing House, 1954).

[25] Fuller, *Personal Recollections*, 9–10.

On November 28, the New Yorkers broke camp and marched past the partially constructed Washington Monument to cross the Potomac River over Long Bridge. Upon reaching Alexandria, they boarded a train that brought them to Springfield Station, a little over six miles west. The Sixty-first prepared to bivouac when an alarm threw Cone into a panic. Cone rushed about excitedly as other men in the regiment realized that they had not brought ammunition with them, but luckily, the evening passed without incident. The train returned them to Alexandria for the night, and the following day, the New Yorkers marched three miles west on the Little River Turnpike to reach Camp California, located in rolling farmland near Fort Worth. Here, the men of the Sixty-first soon met the other regiments with which their future history would be intertwined: the Fifth New Hampshire, Fourth Rhode Island (later detached and replaced by the Sixty-fourth New York), and the Eighty-first Pennsylvania. It was also here that Barlow first met Nelson A. Miles, future commander of the U.S. Army and lifelong friend.[26] The four regiments were brigaded under Oliver Otis Howard in Edwin "Bull" Sumner's division.[27]

---

[26] Nelson Miles and Francis Barlow served closely together throughout the war. Born in 1839, Miles studied at a local school before moving to Boston at the age of seventeen, where he attended night classes while working in a store by day. Miles also studied tactics with a former French army colonel, and when the Civil War broke out, he was commissioned lieutenant in the Twenty-second Massachusetts Infantry. Miles served on Brigadier General Oliver O. Howard's staff during the Peninsula campaign and commanded a portion of the Eighty-first Pennsylvania during the battle of Seven Pines, where he was slightly wounded in the foot. Afterward, he became lieutenant colonel of the Sixty-first New York, and when Barlow went down severely wounded at Antietam, Miles took over the regiment. He sustained wounds and received commendations for his conduct at both Fredericksburg and Chancellorsville, and though he missed Gettysburg due to his injuries, he returned to duty in spring 1864 as a brigade commander in Barlow's Second corps division. Miles fought well at the Wilderness, and for his conduct in attacking the Mule Shoe at Spotsylvania on May 12, he received his first star. During Petersburg, he commanded Barlow's division in that officer's absence and suffered his fourth wound, and he ended the war as a major general. Miles decided to continue in the military after the Civil War and fought Indians on the frontier, effecting the surrender of the Apache chief Geronimo. In 1895, Miles became general in chief of the army and commanded the forces that captured Puerto Rico during the Spanish-American War. After retiring in 1903, he concentrated on writing; he died during a circus performance in Washington in 1925. Warner, *Generals in Blue*, 322–23.

[27] A good portion of Barlow's military service was as Oliver O. Howard's subordinate. Born in Maine in 1830, the deeply religious Howard graduated from

In camp near Alexandria
Dec. 3rd /61 7.20 p.m.

My dear Mother
Last night I recd. your letter of Nov. 29th + one from Edward
of Nov. 30th.

You must have had a very pleasant time on Thanksgiving evening—I should have liked to be there.

I am glad to hear that Josephine Newcomes matter promises
to turn out so well.[28] I have not been able to see [George] Whittemore but wrote him saying that J's friends took it for granted
that he was coming on to marry her.[29] I hope by this time he has

---

Bowdoin College in 1850 before he attended West Point as a member of the
class of 1854. Afterward, Howard taught mathematics at the Military Academy
and was elected colonel of the Third Maine Infantry in late May 1861. Howard
led a brigade at First Manassas and received a brigadier general's commission
to date from September 3, 1861. He commanded the brigade that included
Barlow's Sixty-first New York at the Peninsula, until he received a wound at
Seven Pines that necessitated the amputation of his right arm. Howard conva-
lesced and returned for Antietam, where he assumed command of John Sed-
wick's division after that general went down wounded. Howard led the division
at Fredericksburg and received command of the Eleventh corps the following
spring, leading it at Chancellorsville and Gettysburg. In both battles, the corps
was attacked in its flank and driven from the field. Later in 1863, Howard went
west with his corps and eventually commanded the Fourth corps in the Atlanta
campaign. After the death of Major General James B. McPherson, Howard took
over the Army of the Tennessee during the march through the Carolinas. After
the war, Howard became commissioner of the Freedmen's Bureau and fought
for black rights as well as helping to found Howard University. He later became
superintendent of West Point until retiring in 1894, when he turned to writing
and continued promoting religious and educational endeavors. Fuller, *Personal
Recollections*, 10–11. Abbott, "Francis Channing Barlow," 531. New York Monuments Commission, *In Memoriam: Francis Channing Barlow*, 62. Warner,
Generals in Blue, 237–38. Mike Pride and Mark Travis, *My Brave Boys: To War
with Colonel Cross and the Fighting Fifth* (Hanover, N.H.: University Press of
New England, 2001), 52.

[28] Josephine Louise le Monnier Newcomb was born in Baltimore on October
31, 1816, and when her mother died while she was a child, she lived with a
married sister in New Orleans. There, she met her husband, a merchant
named Warren Newcomb, and they moved to New York City. When Warren
died in 1866, Josephine inherited a large fortune and eventually donated much
of it to Tulane University in Louisiana. *DAB*, 7:451–52.

[29] George Whittemore Jr. was born in Boston in 1837 and attended the Boston Latin School before graduating from Harvard College in 1857. He studied
law and was admitted to the Massachusetts bar the same day he left as a private
in the First Company of Massachusetts Sharpshooters. He helped defend
Washington, D.C., participated in the siege of Yorktown, and was killed at An-

arrived. You do not write me what are the expenses of her new lodgings.

I suppose that you are by this time in some new quarters.

We are at the old place + under strict rule which I much like. At 6.30 the whole Brigade's turned out under arms in one line officers + all. After that we breakfast + then have a drill from 9 to 11 in which I superintend 5 Companies. Then dine about 12:30—drill from 2 to 4 p.m. Parade at 4 with all four Regts together + then supper. I am busy the whole time overseeing the whole camp getting things straight. I am supreme here + my position is a most pleasant one. I have got my bed very comfortable fixed up. I sleep in the Straddle bag ever night + find it a most comfortable garment.

I intend to write to George [Bliss] to send the money. It was for business done for Hallet + George was authorized to take it out of some money collected by him on a mortgage + did take it + has kept it. Even if it came out of him he should pay it for he always charged me interest when he lends me money.

I have plenty of straw to sleep on + when I get over my cold in the head which I expected at first, shall be very comfortable.

I should like very much to have you keep a diary of all that goes on + send it to me from time to time. When I get over the hurry of fixing things time will hang rather heavy. I do not think we shall fight until Spring.

Do not forget to send on my gloves by A.W.G.[30] Tell Edward that Read + Taylor is the watch man. I want the watch changed unless it goes perfectly correctly.

I am very glad to get E.'s photograph. It is an excellent one easy + pleasant looking + very different from my savage ones. I depend on E.'s coming to make me a visit in Camp + think I can make him comfortable. I expect my horse every day. I will look for lodgings in Alexandria + think I can find comfortable ones.

Has R. heard any thing from Marshall? I will again urge Bliss. Love to all. I hope for a letter tomorrow.

Your Son
Francis

---

tietam with the rank of sergeant. Higginson, *Harvard Memorial Biographies*, 2:404–14.

30 "A.W.G." might refer to Arabella Wharton Griffith, Barlow's wife.

As the weather turned cold, many of the men became afflicted with sickness. Their coughing seemed especially prevalent at night, and many ended up visiting the hospital at some point. The tedium of camp life and the constant drills that Barlow had imposed was broken by the night false alarm described in the following letter. The entire brigade, under temporary command of Colonel Edward E. Cross of the Fifth New Hampshire, marched to Edsall's Hill to counter a rumored Confederate threat. The next day, while returning to Camp California, the entire force was turned around and marched to the hill once again. The maneuvers accomplished little other than to tire the men, as one member of the Fifth New Hampshire opined, "Our marching back and forth did not amount to anything."[31]

Near Alexandria
December 12th 1861
Thursday

My dear Mother

Your letter of Dec. 7th is recd + is the last I have recd from you.

I am sorry to hear that you are no more comfortably lodged.

On Tuesday night at 11 p.m. our Regt. was turned out + ordered to march at once. All others in the Brigade likewise turned out. We found several batteries of Artillery on the road with us and it looked like business. We marched about 3 miles to Edson-hill where we were halted for the night. We had no blankets + all lay on the ground together. I slept very comfortably on the ground by a large fire. In the morning we were ordered back + on getting nearly to camp were again sent back + remained until 1 p.m. when we came to Camp again. They say it was expected that the enemy would attack our line that night + that we were sent out to repel any advance. But we saw nothing of him. In a

---

[31] Fuller, *Personal Recollections*, 11–12. Miles Peabody to his parents, December 14, 1861, quoted in Pride and Travis, *My Brave Boys*, 56.

few days we shall probably go on picket duty for four days. We are drilling violently from morning to night though I have got things pretty well settled + have more time now. I have not been to Washington or Alexandria but once since I reached here on the day after I arrived.

I enclose a letter I read from Whittemore. Will he be able to support his wife at so great an expense as he is doing now?

I do not suppose I could get to Alexandria every day + I could never stay all night at present but I could come in at least every other day + perhaps a few minutes every day. Genl [Edwin V.] Sumner says he shall not be so strict when we become better drilled.[32] Arabella has not been to town since I left. She will not come here for some weeks. She will come see you as soon as she comes to town. I am very well. Good bye. Love to all. Will send the arrears of my "allowance" to you + R when we are paid, about Jan 1st

F.C.B.

On side: Direct to Alexandria Va.

Tell Richard + E. to write me—when is Edward coming

---

[32] Born in 1797, Edwin Vose Sumner earned the distinction of being the oldest active corps commander to serve in the Civil War. Commissioned directly into the army in 1819, he earned the sobriquet "Bull head" because it was said that a musket ball once bounced off his head. In 1833 Sumner became captain of dragoons; he was promoted to major in 1846, and he served on the frontier until the war against Mexico, where he earned another promotion. In 1855 he became colonel of the First Cavalry and in 1861 was appointed one of three Regular Army brigadiers. When the Army of the Potomac was created outside Washington, D.C., he was assigned to command its Second corps. He led it through the Peninsula campaign and was at the head of its lead division at Antietam. He commanded a grand division at Fredericksburg but asked to be relieved when Major Joseph Hooker became the Army of the Potomac's commander in 1863. Sumner was subsequently assigned to the Department of Missouri, but he died en route on March 21, 1863. Warner, *Generals in Blue,* 489–90.

Near Alexandria Va.
Dec. 14 /61
9 p.m.

Dear Mother & Edward,

Today E's letter of Dec. 10 (enclosing Edison's) + mother's of Dec. 11th arrived.

The Police have not + will not try to exercise the right to stop any noise in a house merely because it disturbs the inmates or one of them. A noise or riot which disturbs the neighborhood + is a breach of the peace they will stop. So you can make any such noise as one you mention with safety. I am glad that E answered the damned old minister as he did. You seem to be having spicy times on the B.Q. I hope to hear that you are well located. I want Edward to come down as soon as he can. It will be a fine opportunity for him to see Army life in the field. I am having a log house built about 16 × 12 ft which I shall have plastered in the crevices with clay + windows made + with a good fire it will be as comfortable as a house. The weather is lovely + the country for miles around is crowded with Camps + I shall have considerable leisure to ride about with him. I hope to arrange for Richard to come before winter is over.

As for mother I think she had not better try to come with Arabella, but wait until A. has found some place to live + then come. Any other course would expose her to much uncertainty + discomfort. Arabella always manages to find some good place + mother could easily come on to Washington by herself + I or A can meet her. To come on at once to Alexandria without knowing where she was to go + in a town filled with troops would be very forlorn.

Arabella has not been to N.Y. except perhaps to pass through to Burlington where the sickness of [Eliza] Wallace has called her suddenly.[33] She will call upon you as soon as she goes to N.Y. + bring on the things you mention. She writes me that she answered your letter. I have enquired in one or two places in the

---

[33] Eliza Wallace was the cousin of Arabella Barlow's mother, and Arabella lived with her in the late 1830s while she attended school at Saint Mary's Hall. She died shortly after this letter was written. Lauter, " 'Once upon a Time in the East,' " 8.

neighborhood to get a place for her to board, but without success, but when she comes I have no doubt that she can find a place for you both near by. A rule was made today that no Officer shall go to Alexandria even with a pass, but they won't keep up such strictness long (Genl Sumner said it would be relaxed) + I can get passes frequently if you are here + you could come out. Still I would rather have you out here if we can find a place in the neighborhood.

I have been remarkably well. I always stand fatigue + exposure better than much stronger people. There is much sickness in the Camp. I do not want anymore or thicker shirts or drawers.

Bliss writes today that he will see Marshall. I shall keep pressing him. When I get my pay (about Jan. 1) I shall send arrears to R + mother, I pd. Mother $7.50 + R $5 before I left.

Say to Edison that I shall like an Officer of his brother's experience but see no chance for him here at present. There are at least two young men who were thrown out by the consolidations by which the Regt was formed + who are here waiting for vacancies. They are most excellent + tried Officers + in justice are entitled to the first vacancies which occur. There are no vacancies now + there are not likely to be any until some of our Lts. + one Capt. are disposed of by an examining board which I trust will be in a few weeks. After these two I will bear in mind Edison's brother + Prentice which ever of them first that E. recommends. But at present I can give no more encouragement than whoever comes under me will have to submit to severe discipline for I keep them all right in my hand. As for other Regts. there will be small chance now for recruiting is stopped + there will be a large number of Officers to be assigned. He had better keep his present place until he gets something better. If he resigns is there not a rule that he shan't reenter the service.

My duties + occupations are as following. Reveille at 6 a.m. when the whole Regt turns out on the Colour line under arms + the rolls of the Cos are called. I have been every morning at Reveille. Then I wash + dress + breakfast + sometimes read a little tactics or write a letter until 9 a.m. I also attend to innumerable matters of Camp regulation and answer innumerable calls + questions until 9 a.m. when we go to drill until 11 when I do the same + also dine until 2. Then drill to 4—then parade. Then supper. Then officers school from 7 to 8.30 (I instructing the 1st

Lts.) + then write or read until between 10 + 11 when I go to bed on an india rubber spread on some straw on the floor with five blankets over me. What takes up my time is the making rules + regulations + following them up throughout the Regt from highest to lowest. Neither the Col. nor Major have any capacity whatever for doing this or for overseeing or commanding a Regt + I do it all. I could not have desired things to go on better than they have done + I am perfectly satisfied. The only thing I want changed is the size of the Regt, there are only some 680 men. I have an excellent servant + we have just got a first rate Cook for our mess who feeds us very well. I am fast getting things in order + shall have more leisure.

Every 6 days I am field Officer of the day + have charge of the Guards of the Brigade + make the grand Rounds at 12 midnight. The first two times I was on I did not get to bed until 2 a.m. I got up at 6 + drilled all day as usual. I have not slept a moment in the daytime since I have been here. About Wednesday next it will be out time to go on Picket duty (the whole Regt.) at Edsons Hill some 2 ½ miles from here, for 4 days, without tents but we shall make huts + be very comfortable. This will probably come every 12 days.

I shall write to Dalton + Perkins as you suggest but I suppose neither are near me + I cannot well get at them. I have not been to W.[ashington] since I was here, but once on the day after I got here, nor to Alexandria until this afternoon when the Major + I rode in. My horse is hard + I don't much like him + shall try to change him. I will ask A.W.G. again about the Captains.

Direct to Alexandria Virginia.

Good night with much love to all.

Francis
Lt. Col.

In Camp
Dec. 17th 1861
Tuesday 7 p.m.

My dear Mother

I recd today your letter of Dec. 15th. I wrote E. a long letter last night.

I am very glad to hear of your good fortune on the B.Q. I am very sorry to hear that E. has neuralgic pains. I hope to see him + you about Jan 1st as you suggest. It will do you both good. The weather is now lovely here.

Our whole Regt goes tomorrow on picket duty for 4 days. 7 Companies stay together as a reserve + 3 Cos are thrown out some 1 or 1 ½ miles further to form a line of small outposts. I shall probably take charge of the first 3 Cos. who go out for 24 hours + then some other officer will do the same for the next 24. Your letters will be brought out as usual + I shall also write as usual. Of course you can get out to our Camp + often I hope if you come. Why does not R. write. Bliss wrote in his last that he would attend to Marshall. I hope he has done so. Miss Wallace is dying + Arabella is at Burlington. It will be sometime before she comes to Washington.

Why don't you begin your diary? I should very much like to see it. Do they know about [illegible word] at home?

> With much love
> Francis

> In Camp Dec. 24 1861
> Tuesday 8.30 p.m.

My dear Mother
I am really delighted to hear that you like your new place so well. It would be strange after so many years of trying you found a really comfortable place.

Your letter with Diary to Friday came yesterday. I had my first day of illness yesterday. I had a diarrhea the night before + lay in bed on my cot all day yesterday + took some powders from the Doctor. Today I am well and about again. The sickness here is dreadful. 150 men out of some 650 are sick in the Hospital + some 12 officers. I continue to be very well.

Tomorrow I am going with one of Genl [Oliver O.] Howards aides to ride down to Mount Vernon which is 8 miles from here. It is a holiday with us, no drills &c.

Today is a very cold day, the first really cold weather we have had. My log house is nearly completed + will be very comfortable. I have a brick fireplace + shall have an open fire. The walls will be plastered in the interstices with clay + shall get one of those cocoanut carpets. The wind last night was terrific + our tents shook like reeds in the wind. Mine however stood it. Miss Wallace is dead + was to be buried on Sat. Arabella will go on Monday (last Monday) to Soml. + will come on here at once. She will call on you in town before she comes. I read Phillips lecture in the Tribune (I see the N.Y. papers the following day). I do not think it equal to some of his speeches. I am afraid that the Govt will back down + give up [James] Mason + [John] Slidell.[34] Did I tell you that Bill Paine had gone home to have a surgical opperation performed on him for some ailment which has troubled him for a long time.[35] Mason told me this but did not know what the matter was. It begins to be rather dull here. I have got used to the routine + learned nearly all that is necessary to enable me to discharge my duties. I shall now peruse the higher branches of the Art of War.

I begin to be disgusted with Cone. He is not fit to command a drove of hogs. All that I say about him must be kept strictly to yourself.

Good night.

I am your loving son

---

[34] Barlow refers to the *Trent* affair. The Confederate government decided to send James Mason of Virginia and John Slidell of Louisiana as envoys to England and France, respectively. In Havana, Cuba, Mason and Slidell boarded the British steamer *Trent*. On November 8, 1861, while the *Trent* was en route to Europe, Captain Charles Wilkes stopped it with his thirteen-gun USS *San Jacinto* and removed and arrested the Confederate envoys and their small entourage, before letting the British ship proceed. While Northern public opinion lauded Wilkes's bold move, Britain was outraged at the act and demanded the Southerners' release from Fort Warren prison in Boston Harbor. Tensions escalated so that for a time, war between the United States and England seemed eminent. Lincoln resolved the foreign policy crisis by releasing Mason and Slidell. McPherson, *Battle Cry of Freedom*, 389–91.

[35] Born in Waltham, Massachusetts, in 1834, William Cushing Paine graduated from West Point in 1858 and served the Union army as a captain until having to resign for disability. Mary Carolina Crawford, *Famous Families of Massachusetts*, 2 vols. (Boston: Little, Brown, and Company, 1930), 2:17.

> Francis + hope for a letter
> tomorrow

Let the boys write me a list of their New Years calls + whom they see + what they hear.

In Camp Dec. 28th /61 5 p.m.

My dear Edward

Your letter of Dec. 27th/61 arrived today. One came from you + one from mother + one from R. on Dec. 25th + I answered them all briefly in a letter to R. Now I will answer them more fully. I have never fired the Revolver but once, when I discharged all the barrels at a tree on my way home from the Picket. I have never had it loaded but twice. The rules forbid firing about the Camp + I have never had time to go away + practice. I do not think that a pistol would do much good in a fight whether I were a good shot or not. I always carry it however whenever I go upon any expedition. It shoots very accurately. Like all newspaper stories the Herald paragraph about [Major William Carey] Massett was a gross exaggeration. He went no where near the Fairfax Courthouse. I went nearer than he did + I did not go within 3 miles of it though it would have been perfectly safe to do so. Cone et al tried to make a great thing out on our Picket duty while the truth is we were not within 8 miles of the enemy. General Howard told me this before we went out. Occasional bodies of Cavalry were reported in the neighborhood but they never amounted to anything + in most cases I believe that even this was the offspring of the frightened brain of some jackass.

I rejoice to hear that the Party of Christmas Eve passed off without hostilities.

I certainly do <u>not</u> approve of giving up Mason + Slidell. I would go to war with the whole of them first. We are lost if we show any cowardice or want of spirit on any point. I also believe that a war with England would bring out a spirit which this war never has.

Mother made a ludicrous mistake on her adoption visit. The

idea of her going to such a place. I should think they would always want to adopt from there instead of the other way.

I have just come back from a 16 mile ride. My horse is terribly hard but I have got so used to him not that I ride 20 miles without feeling it. I have been over to the 22nd Mass. Regt. ([Col. Henry] Wilsons)[36] to see Charles Paine who is a Captain therein.[37] The Regt. is in [Brigadier General John] Martindale's Brigade + [Brigadier General Fitz John] Porter's Division.[38]

---

[36] Born in 1812, Henry Wilson worked as a shoemaker before embarking on a political career, first as a Whig, then a Free-Soiler, a Know-Nothing, and, finally, a Republican. By the beginning of the Civil War, he represented his native Massachusetts in the Senate, but when that body adjourned in August 1861, Wilson became a volunteer aide on Major General George B. McClellan's staff. The Lincoln administration asked Wilson to raise a regiment, and the Senator energetically recruited volunteers, going a thousand dollars into debt in the process. In early October he became colonel of the Twenty-second Massachusetts Volunteer Infantry and led his unit down to Washington, D.C. At the end of the month, he tendered his resignation so that he could return to service as a member of McClellan's staff, and, when Congress resumed on January 9, 1862, he took up his governmental duties once again. Wilson later served as vice president during the Grant administration. Richard H. Abbot, *Cobbler in Congress* (Lexington: University Press of Kentucky, 1972), 117–20.

[37] Born in Boston in 1833, Charles Jackson Paine was the grandson of Robert Treat Paine, a signer of the Declaration of Independence. Paine studied at the Boston Latin School and, after graduating from Harvard College in 1853, studied law. After visiting Europe and Saint Louis, Missouri, he opened a law office in Boston, though he recruited a company for service in defense of the Union when war broke out. Commissioned captain on October 8, 1861, he was made major on January 16, 1862, and colonel of the Second Louisiana Infantry on October 23, 1862. On July 4, 1864, his promotion to brigadier general was confirmed by the Senate, and he later commanded a division under Major General Benjamin Butler in Virginia. After the war, Paine became a powerful businessman and amassed great wealth through railroad building. He was also an avid yachtsman. *DAB,* 7:147–48.

[38] A West Pointer and former district attorney, Brigadier General John Martindale led a brigade through the Peninsula campaign and later served as military governor of the District of Columbia. Brigadier General Fitz John Porter graduated from West Point and distinguished himself in the Mexican War before returning to the Military Academy to instruct cadets in artillery. The outbreak of the Civil War prompted his rapid promotion, and he formed a devoted and loyal friendship with Major General George McClellan. Porter eventually attained command of the Fifth corps and served with the Army of the Potomac until his and McClellan's removal in November 1862. Afterward, Porter faced a politically charged court martial that found him guilty of insubordination and retreat at Second Manassas and dismissed him from the army. Sixteen years later, a board exonerated Porter and vindicated him of guilt. Warner, *Generals in Blue,* 312–13, 378–80.

Their Camp is beautiful with large Sibley (peaked) tents +
streets of hand beaten clay + festooned with evergreens +
planted with fir trees + with grass plots + other floral devices. I
had a very pleasant time with Paine who likes it + is very pleasantly situated. Bill's wife has had a son + that was the "surgical
operation" for which he went home.[39] He is now with [Brigadier]
Gen [Don Carlos] Buel at Louisville.[40] C. Paine is about 4 miles
from here if you know the road but I did not + went a long way
around. Butterfield's Brigade is next to Martindales.

When this war is over this part of Virginia will not have a tree
in it. Every tree + fence has been cut down for miles around.
Where we are there is more wood than nearer the Potomac. We
are the next Division to the left. On the left is [Samuel P.] Heintzelman—Than Sumner to his right—Than [William B.] Franklin's Division—Than Porter—Than [Irvin] McDowell—+ so on
clear up to the right of the line.

On my way back this afternoon I came upon McDowell's Division having a sham fight. There were many thousands of Infantry
Artillery + Cavalry, all firing with blank cartridges + charging
+ maneuvering in every way. It gave one a fine idea of a battle.
They have them often + have no doubt that you can see one.

Col. Cone's story of two men being shot is simply a falsehood.
None of our men, nor any man in our vicinity nor any men of
whom we knew were shot. Some days before a Lt. [Hugh] Janne-

---

[39] William Cushing Paine's son, Robert Treat Paine Jr., was born on December 3, 1861, and later graduated from Harvard and became a member of the
bar, as well as an avid yachtsmen. Crawford, *Famous Families of Massachusetts,* 2:18.

[40] Don Carlos Buell graduated from West Point in the class of 1841 before
fighting Indians in Florida, serving on the frontier, and distinguishing himself
in the Mexican War. For the next thirteen years, Buell performed adjutant
general's duties in a number of departments, and when the Civil War broke
out he was promoted to brigadier general. After arriving in Washington, D.C.,
from the West Coast in September 1861, he assisted in forming the Army of
the Potomac before Major General George B. McClellan appointed Buell commander of an expedition into eastern Tennessee. Ulysses S. Grant's victories at
Forts Henry and Donelson allowed Buell to capture Nashville, and Buell later
reinforced Grant on the second day of Shiloh. Promoted to major general on
March 22, 1862, Buell's caution and slowness over the next couple of months
led to his relief from command that October. He eventually retired to operate
a Kentucky coal mine and ironworks after the war. Warner, *Generals in Blue,*
51–52.

way of the New Jersey Cavalry was shot in our neighborhood +
that is all the shooting I know of.[41] Cone's description of the
"discomforts of scouting duty" are equally wild. We lived in a log
hut + were more comfortable than when at home. No one ever
had occasion to <u>dine</u> or to <u>sleep</u> on horse back for no one was
ever out more than a few hours. Cone is one of the most gassy
men I have ever seen + his letters are not at all to be depended
on.

Only one of the officers on the Board is an Army Officer +
he is Genl Howard. Cone is the junior member + <u>records</u> the
proceedings which he does very well. They certainly did not put
him on because they supposed him to know anything of military
matters for its perfectly well understood at Headquarters that he
does not <u>pretend</u> to any knowledge.

The amount of illness in this Regt. is dreadful. Out of 675 men
we have some 140 sick. 3 died in one day a few days ago + we
shall have I fear one death a day on an average for some time to
come. The diseases are measles + a kind of slow camp fever. I
continue to be perfectly well. The Major [William C. Massett] +
several of the Officers are sick. I think the Major has got the
measles. My log hut is nearly done + will be a most comfortable
lodging place. I have a good brick fire place for an open fire.

Let me know whom you see on New Years day. If you see Miss
Townsend give her my regards. [Colonel Thomas F.] Meaghers
[Irish] brigade is next to ours only a few rods distant.[42] Is Mrs
Meagher with her husband? What an outrage Gordon's treat-

---

[41] This refers to Hugh H. Janeway of the First New Jersey Cavalry, later killed
in the closing days of the war. *OR,* 46(1): 1149.

[42] Thomas Francis Meagher was one of the more flamboyant personalities in
the Army of the Potomac. Born in Ireland, he was an active partisan of Irish
liberty, and the British sentenced him to their penal colony on Tasmania in
1849. After his escape, he went to New York, where he achieved prominence
as a lawyer and outspoken Irish American. In 1861, he organized a company
for the Sixty-ninth New York Militia and fought at First Manassas as that unit's
major. That winter, Meagher organized the Irish Brigade, appointed brigadier
general to rank from February 3, 1862. Meagher and his Irishmen served in
many of the Army of the Potomac's battles and performed especially bravely in
charging Marye's Heights at Fredericksburg. Afterward, Meagher served in the
Western theater under Major General William T. Sherman from 1864 until the
end of the war. In peacetime, he held government posts in the territories and
served as acting governor of the territory of Montana until his accidental death
by drowning on July 1, 1867. Warner, *Generals in Blue,* 317–18.

ment of Henry Dalton is. He ought to be court martialed for such an act. What is Henry going to do + also Charles Dalton? I am probably the strictest disciplinarian in the Brigade but am not despotic. My men I think like me.

Love to all
F.C.B.

2

1862: "I was in the thickest of it at the head of my Regt."

After the Sixty-first settled into its winter quarters and it became clear that further military maneuvers would wait until the spring thaw, Arabella came for an extended visit at Camp California. This no doubt heartened Barlow and broke the monotony of his winter routine.[1]

Jan 9th 1862

My dear Mother

If you can come on at once you can stay at the house where Arabella is.

Mrs. Collet is coming, or expected about the middle of Jan. but I don't regard it as at all certain that she will come then. A. has a large comfortable room with 2 large double beds + a fire in it. You would have to occupy one of the beds. Mrs Collet is to have one when she comes + that is why they say you can come until she comes. But even if she does come there is a room without a fire where you could sleep. So you are pretty sure of being put up somewhere even if Mrs. Collet does come. The house is close to the Camp + the bugles + drums would wake you at 6 a.m. but they don't get up until near 9 a.m.

The table is poor + the whole housekeeping disorderly + unpunctual + Virginian, but I think you could stand it for a few days at any rate. You must make your mind to the hardships + if you cannot possibly stand it you will have to go over to Washington for there is positively no other place in the neighborhood.

---

[1] Oliver O. Howard, "After the Battle," *National Tribune*, December 31, 1885.

If you are in pretty good health + Edward can come with you, you had better come at once. Unless E. can come I do not think it would be wise for you to try it, for if you could not stand it here I could not get away to go to Washington with you.

About a carpet for my house, I do not think I will have one. It is so uncertain about our staying anywhere that I do not like to accumulate too much property. The mud + dirt would both ruin it. That Massts Regt of Cavalry is said to be a splendid Regt.[2] I am both sorry + surprised to hear about Ned Stearns. I don't know yet what board will be where A. is. We have not touched on that point yet + don't want to for some days.

Did you read that pleasant article about Clough in the Tribune? Tell Edward I should think he would go oftener to see Miss Townsend. She is one of the most agreeable girls I know of + always very cordial + pleasant. E. speaks of Miss T's "corresponding with Mrs Whitehead." Does not Mrs Whitehead live in New York still?

Anything from Marshall? His behavior is outrageous + Bliss does not seem to do much in the premises.

Good bye
Write me at once about coming on
Your aff. Son
Francis

Jan. 18 1862

My dear Mother
Your letter beginning with Jan. 9th + ending with Jan. 12th miscarried + did not reach me until day before yesterday. For the last few days I have felt very discontented. The weather for the last week has been either raining, snowing or so muddy that it is impossible to drill or ride. We have consequently had noth-

---

[2] Barlow probably refers to the First Massachusetts Volunteer Cavalry Regiment, four companies of which were stationed in Annapolis, Maryland, at the time, though it is possible he is referring to the Second Battalion Massachusetts Cavalry recruited in late 1861. Dyer, *Compendium*, 3:1237, 1239.

ing to do + Camp life is very dull when the ordinary routine is interrupted.

You ask about our Drs. We have two [Asa] Snow, + [Andrew] Merrill, Asst Surgeon. The former has the reputation here of being an old granny of no skill or energy + a great many attribute the large number of sick + deaths in this Regt. to his want of skill + mismanagement. It is difficult to form an opinion on such a point + I confess I have not enough knowledge of the facts to form an opinion, but he certainly does not seem like a man of much energy + general capacity. I certainly should not call him a first rate physician. He has been summoned before an examining Board + will very likely be shipped. Merrill is a better physician though not a first rate one. He has been sick for sometime + has now gone home + I do not believe he will ever return. As Dr. Buckley says, the army physicians are not of the first distinction. I see by the Herald that your Dr Lighthill is mentioned in the South American papers with Carnachan + also as being very skillful in his particular department.

You seem to have taken a great fancy to Wm. Penn lately. I always thought he was funny. I enjoy being with him or my son "Charles" more than with most persons. I hope C. Miles will not be obliged by poverty to leave New York. It is a singular spectacle for Miles to be borrowing pantaloons of Richard.

Both our Surgeons are from Geneva New York—Swiftsplace. S has not a high opinion of them. Do you hear anything of Dalton (Fred). I wrote him sometime ago but have not heard from him.

I continue to be very well. Indeed there is no reason why I should not be, for my house is as comfortable as any other.

You ask how I pass my evenings. We have tea about six + sit some half hour at it. Then at 6.30 I have a class of 1st Lts. to recite in tactics which occupies me until about 8. Since A. has been here I have then generally gone up to the Richards + sat awhile. Sometimes staying up all night + sometimes not. When I stay all night I get up at 6 a.m. precisely so as to get back to Camp for Reveille roll call. When I do not go to the Richards I lie down + read. On the whole it is a damned stupid life. I hardly think this disgusting country is worth fighting for. I would go over to Washington for a day or two did I not want to save my privileges for your coming. I have written quite largely about your coming in the letters to which I have yet read no answer.

[remainder of letter seems to have been lost]

Jan. 23/ 62
7 am.

Dear mother
We go out on picket this morning for four days. You need not be alarmed we are not within 10 miles of the enemy + I shall live in a house this time + shall be comfortable as at home. As soon as I get back I will see about a furlough + if there seems to be no hope of getting one I will cheerfully accept your proposition as to expenses. We have made a strict rule as you say, but in a week or two they will relax it as they always do. I would not have you come just yet anyway. We have not seen the sun for 10 days but it has been raining and snowing the whole time + the mud is more dreadful than you ever imagined. The ladies have not set a foot out to walk for 2 weeks. Ms Collet + her sister have come. They have the room with two beds + a fire in it + A.W.G.B.[3] has a small one without fire. She would have to give you up hers. We are embarrassed by the fact that Mrs Richards seems to intend to take no pay but to treat us all as guests. Both A. + Mrs. Collet have several times tried to pay her but she put them off.
I enclose a letter recd from Bliss. Let R. go to Bliss + deny emphatically that he is not competent to fill the places spoken of. When [Brigadier General Ambrose E.] Burnside gets in the rear of the enemy + the weather gets either dry or frozen I think we shall go forward.[4] That is the impression here.

---

[3] This refers to Arabella Wharton Griffith Barlow.

[4] Brigadier General Ambrose E. Burnside led a joint army-navy operation in North Carolina and by mid-January had twelve thousand troops aboard a small fleet of gunboats, coal scows, and passenger steamboats ready to make a landing on Roanoke Island. Stormy weather, however, forced the seasick soldiers to wait for weeks until the weather calmed, and on February 7–8 Burnside landed seven and a half thousand Federals on the island, capturing its defenders with light casualties. Over the next several weeks he made several other gains along the North Carolina coast. McPherson, *Battle Cry of Freedom,* 372–73.

I am very sorry indeed to hear of R's losses in his East India shipments. His ill luck seems to pursue him in all the old mercantile transactions. Tell him that I do not think that the fact that Latrobe + G. failed before the rebellion will make no difference in his collecting his money. He also can recover though the notes are in the hands of the Charleston lawyer.

Every thing is confusion + I can't write more now. Will do so tomorrow. Arabella wrote you a day or two ago.

FCB

~

Edsalls Hill
Sunday Jan. 26/ 62

My dear Edward

I wrote mother yesterday touching your visit here. You say you can't come until Feb. 3rd. By that time I hope that the weather will be so settled that we can ride about the country. Today is a fine sunny day + a few such will dry up the roads. When we hear of Burnside's Expedition in the rear of the enemy, which must soon occur I think, I think we shall advance. Possibly by the aid of this diversion in the rear which will draw off the enemy, we may accomplish the capture of Manassas, though I should think it hazardous. A few days fine weather will make the roads passable for the last month artillery could have not got half a mile. You have no idea of the mud. Our horses would sink one foot deep in the mire + you could not go faster than a walk in any place. Arabella has not put her foot out of the house for 2 weeks last Saturday (yesterday) + you had better not set out until you are sure that the weather is in some degree settled, for to be here in such weather as we have had would be forlorn enough. I think we can be sure of some settled weather by Feb. 3rd. I think we can have a very pleasant time. I can get you a horse + we can ride to Mount Vernon + about to the Camps. Tell mother that I will pay $16 towards her coming on here, that is what it would cost me to come on, for the incidental expenses I should save by taking out my board here. If you come I shall defer getting a furlough for the present. I hope you will come. It will do you good + I should exceedingly enjoy going about with you + you will never have an opportunity to see such life again. Mother too will enjoy it much better. R. has not told me whether he cannot get a passage to W. in one of the Govt vessels.

Yesterday the major [William C. Massett],[5] the adjutant [David E. Gregory][6] + I went out riding + went up to within 2 miles of Fairfax Court House where the enemies Pickets are. The inhabitants tell us that it was farther than our men had been for some time. I am afraid the riding will be hard on you. The country is a bad one to ride in + we ride across fields + through roads which would scare one at home.

One day last week I went into Washington on business + saw Charles + Henry Dalton + dined with them at Willards.[7] Henry is trying to get the place of aide on [Brigadier] Genl [Charles D.] Jamisons staff—Don't mention this.[8]

Deposit my money with J. C. Howe + Co. + take a receipt as you propose + send it to me. Do I understand you to say that they will pay me interest? Have you credited me with the $5 collected of George? If so, pay the $1 express charge on the money out of it, pay the rest to R. on a/c. If Bliss don't send the money soon I will write him.

F.C.B.

---

[5] Frederick Phisterer, *New York in the War of the Rebellion 1861 to 1865* (Albany: J. B. Lyon Company, 1912), 3:2556.

[6] Phisterer, *New York in the War of the Rebellion,* 3:2565.

[7] Willard's Hotel, located on Fourteenth Street, was the most famous hotel in Washington. Much business was conducted in its halls, parlor, and bar, and it was renowned for serving large, sumptuous meals including a huge breakfast offering of fried oysters, steak and onions, blancmange, and pâté de foie gras. Leech, *Reveille in Washington,* 10.

[8] Born in Maine in 1827, Charles Davis Jameson ran a successful lumber business and commanded a militia regiment before the war. When the Civil War began, he won election as colonel of the Second Maine, a three-month regiment that ended up mustering into service for two years. Jameson also ran in 1861 and 1862 as a War Democrat for the state's governorship. He commanded his regiment at First Manassas and received promotion to brigadier general to rank from September 3, 1861. During the Peninsula campaign, he led a Third corps brigade and he fought well at Fair Oaks before sickness forced him to take a leave of absence. Returning to Maine, he died on a steamboat between Boston and Bangor on November 6, 1862. Warner, *Generals in Blue,* 250–51.

Jan. 30th /62
Thursday 10 p.m.

My dear mother

Today your Diary from Jan 26th to Jan. 28th reached me. Also E's letter of Jan. 28th. Rs letter came yesterday. If you do not think you can stand a night journey we will arrange in this way. Write me a few days before hand just what day you are coming. Either A. or I will go over in the morning + try to find a place + will certainly find <u>some</u> place for you to stay the night in + will meet you at the Depot. If anything should prevent our attending to this on the day you name I will telegraph. Wait a day or two until the weather gets pleasant. Since I wrote last it has been villainous, but tonight the stars are out. If you came in this weather you could not step out of the house as A. has not for 2 weeks. But it cant last much longer + if the weather in N.Y. has been like ours it will be fair to judge that when it is settled there it is here. Write me what day you think you will come.

We are in the midst of a ferment here. Yesterday a petition which has been for some time in circulation was handed in to the Col. for transmission to higher authority setting forth in 9 charges his utter incompetence "in knowledge character or capacity" to be Colonel of the Regt. It was a tremendously strong production + signed by every officer in the Regt. except the Major [Massett] (who is engaged to the Col's daughter) the Quartermaster [Robert H. Ellis],[9] who was not asked to sign it + agt. [against] whom charges are made, and one [Walter Franklin] Jones a 2nd Lt. of no a/c who did not wish to sign it from motives of private gratitude to the Col. It was accompanied with a request to resign + all the absent Officers strongly concurred in it. It was a thunderbolt on the Col. who asked for a Court of Inquiry. Tonight after asking Genl. Howards advice he stated to him (in accordance with that advice) that he would resign in any event + only wanted the Court to vindicate his character. I had nothing to do with <u>starting</u> or <u>originating</u> this though I could of course

---

[9] Phisterer, *New York in the War of the Rebellion*, 3:2564.

do nothing other than concur in it. I shall not believe however that he is out until he is actually gone. I pity him from the bottom of my heart for he is a generous kindhearted gentleman + my personal relations with him have been most pleasant, but he is utterly unfit for his place + under him the Regt. is going to ruin + private feelings must be sacrificed to public good. I will send a copy of the petition when I next write. This has broken up our mess + I cook in my own house which I like better. The Major of course takes no part agt. the Col though I <u>understand</u> he has advised the Col. to resign + agrees with the substance of the petition. I was thrown quite violently from my horse but not at all hurt + did not feel it the next day. It arose from my riding without stirrups which I shall not do again. I did not tell you I was thrown once before over his head from his falling down when I rode him at full speed down hill on a slippery morning. But I am much more careful now. I do not come in any contact with any of the sick. Apply the balance of George's $5 + the balance of the $37.50 after paying what I wrote, to my contribution to mothers coming on here— + let me know what it is. The Brooks bill was assumed by Bliss in our settlement + is to be paid by him. I will write him. Tell Richard to keep at Marshall <u>himself</u> every few days + see how that works. Keep Clark's receipt carefully. I enclose a letter from Ned Dalton. We will try to go to see him when you come. E. must come prepared to stay two weeks. My relations with the Col. are now <u>none at all</u> but that does not impair the pleasure of my life. Every officer in the Regt. is of the same opinion with me. I will observe mother's wishes about the safekeeping of her diary which I much prize + depend on. Are Miles Boston friends a permanent encumbrance? I should miss the society of that excellent young man. I don't know where W. Williams could have seen me. He must have remembered me from last summer. I do not like to ask a favor of the Smiths—I never used to go near them when we were in Washington. Still if I can't get you in a comfortable place to pass the night I will go there with you. My hut is so warm that I have not slept in the straddle bag since I moved into it (the hut) but I still cherish it.

Yours affectionately
F.C.B.

Sunday Morning
7.30 a.m.
Feb. 16th 1862

My dear Mother

I presume you are in New York, where I should exceedingly like to be for a week or two.

The Col. is back + I could go to Washington for a day or two I have no doubt. You came at an unfortunate time in that respect.

The Col. came back on Friday afternoon in pretty good spirits but I have no idea that the influence of such Scoundrels as [Brigadier General Daniel] Sickles will accomplish anything + I have a firm conviction we shall get rid of him before another week is out.[10] Genl. Howard remarked that the Regt. had improved markedly in appearance the last few days (while I was in command). This is so. Under Cone every one is listless + every one even the men begin to be disgusted with him. He told one of the men that we were going back to Washington, but it is a damned lie like every thing else he says. Tell Charles I will write to him as I will to R. also.

I felt quite homesick the day you went. Yesterday I was Officer

---

[10] Born in New York City on October 20, 1819, Daniel E. Sickles was controversial throughout his entire life. As a young lawyer, he got involved in Tammany politics and became corporation counsel to New York City at the age of twenty-eight. After service as a state senator, he represented New York in Congress from 1857 to 1861. During that time, he achieved fame for shooting down, near the White House, his young wife's lover—the son of Francis Scott Key (author of "The Star-Spangled Banner"). Sickles's defense, headed by future secretary of war Edwin M. Stanton, successfully pleaded that the congressman was temporarily insane at the time of the killing, the first time such a defense was used with success in American jurisprudence. When the Civil War broke out, the War Department accepted Sickles's services, and he commanded New York's Excelsior Brigade through the Peninsula campaign. Sickles led a division at Fredericksburg and then received promotion to corps command, leading the Third corps at Chancellorsville and Gettysburg, where he lost a leg. After the war, President Ulysses S. Grant appointed him ambassador to Spain, where he became intimately involved with that country's former queen, Isabella II. In his later years, he served a term in Congress (1893–95) and was chair of the New York State Monuments Commission. Warner, *Generals in Blue*, 446–47.

of the Day. My voice is very much improved since I have had no shouting for the day last past.

Yesterday I dined with Mrs. Richards + I think I shall do so today.

We hear of victories on all sides + the Rebels are getting Hell from all quarters. I am a little afraid that they will make a sudden descent from Manassas upon Burnside + wipe him out + get back again before we can get to Manassas. We are at such a distance that we could not get at them for several days + although a considerable part of the force at Manassas were sent agt Burnside the remainder could hold those strong entrenchments for a considerable time.

Don't worry yourself about my health. My cold is wholly gone + what hoarseness I have arises from shouting only.

Write me your Diary as before.

There is quite a snow on the ground this morning some 3 inches deep, the deepest we have had + the weather is quite cold again.

> With love to all I am your aff. Son
> Francis

> Feb 18th 1862
> 8 a.m.

My dear Mother

Your letter of Sunday reached me yesterday.

I wrote you a letter which should have reached you on Monday morning.

I have not used my horse since he was hurt. It has been raining + we have had no drills + I have not needed him. The rest has done him good + Braman says I can use him when occasion requires, though it will be a month or two before his hoof is wholly healed.

I think on the whole I had better offer to <u>pay</u> Mrs. Richards at the next pay day. We have no right to assume that you were a visitor, + I shall insist on her taking payment. If she absolutely refuses you can send her some present. I shall pay her in a day or two.

I am sorry to hear of R's increased labours (on Sunday) without extra pay. Has he heard anything of abolishing Marshalls place, or the increase of pay under Sedgewicks bill.[11] I shall not let Bliss rest, though I fear he will not accomplish anything.

I would not send the box on just now. I really cannot think of anything which I want enough to have it sent from New York. Moreover I think we shall be sent on in a few days to Springfield or Barker's Station in the direction of Fairfax Ct. House + Centreville + then I do not want to have any more baggage than I can help for I shall have to leave a good deal of it behind. One of the men in this Regt. applied yesterday for a furlough + General Sumner wrote on the application that as the Division was expected to advance every day it could not be granted.

The impression is that as soon as Genl Sumner gets strong enough to ride with ease (which will be in a few days) this Division will be sent on as I have stated above to form a kind of advanced guard.[12]

The Col. question remains in status quo. Genl Howard went to Washington yesterday + I hope stirred it up. He has also talked with Genl Sumner about it + I think the latter will start Cone sooner or later. I have perfect faith that he will go in a few days. Did you see the paragraph in Saturday's Tribune that the work of weeding out incompetent Commanders had just fairly begun at Washington + would be done thoroughly. Also I am told that the Senate just passed a resolution requesting the Prest. to weed out thoroughly all unfit officers.

---

[11] Barlow likely refers to Charles Baldwin Sedgwick, a Hamilton College graduate admitted to the New York State bar in 1848. Sedgwick practiced law in Syracuse until his election as a Republican representative to Congress. After serving from March 4, 1859, to March 3, 1863, Sedgewick codified naval regulations for the Navy Department in Washington before returning to the practice of law in Syracuse. *Biographical Directory of the United States Congress 1774–1989* (Washington, D.C.: Government Printing Office, 1989), 1787.

[12] Outside Alexandria, Virginia, in late December 1861, Sumner's horse stepped into a posthole and threw the general to the ground. Although his shoulder and lungs were injured, Sumner remounted and returned to camp, but he had to recover in Washington until he returned to his men in March 1862. Jack D. Welsh, *Medical Histories of Union Generals* (Kent, Ohio: Kent State University Press, 1996), 329.

Yesterday we heard the news from Fort Donelson, which I devoutly hope is true. The are said to have captured [General] Albert S. Johnston who is expected to be the most formidable of the Rebel Generals.[13] I can't believe the Govt will ever appoint [Major General John C.] Fremont to command the Army of the Potomac.[14]

Will you have ½ doz (or the least number they will take) of Cartes de Visite taken from my photograph in the <u>fatigue</u> dress. They can reduce the size I suppose. Get good ones + send them on here + let me know the expense.

I should be glad to see [Winslow] Homer here + if we are farther out he must come out there. Tell Charles [Homer] I will write him.[15]

---

[13] On February 16, 1862, Tennessee's Fort Donelson and its twelve or thirteen thousand defenders surrendered to Ulysses S. Grant, though General Albert S. Johnston was not one of them. It was a major victory for the North and earned Grant his second star on February 17, 1862. McPherson, *Battle Cry of Freedom,* 402–3.

[14] John C. Fremont was born in Georgia in 1813. He attended Charleston College in South Carolina for several years until expelled, but with the help of Joel R. Poinsett, he received an appointment to teach mathematics aboard a U.S. naval vessel. In 1838, Fremont was transferred to the army topographical engineers and led several expeditions through the West. He participated in the conquest of California and represented that state for a one-year term in the U.S. Senate in 1851. In 1856 Fremont was the presidential candidate of the new Republican Party, where he lost by a half million votes to Democrat James Buchanan. Lincoln appointed Fremont major general to rank from May 14, 1861, and initially posted him in command of the Department of the West, headquartered in Saint Louis, Missouri. During the spring 1862, Fremont was one of several Federal commanders defeated by Major General "Stonewall" Jackson's Rebel army. After the war, Fremont served as Arizona's territorial governor from 1878 to 1887, and he died in New York City in 1890. Warner, *Generals in Blue,* 160–61.

[15] Born in 1836, Winslow Homer matured into one of the preeminent artists of American history. During the Civil War, he often accompanied the Army of the Potomac in order to make engravings for publication in *Harper's Weekly.* Charles Homer, the artist's brother, graduated from Harvard College in 1855, the same year as Barlow, and through this connection Winslow Homer became friends with the colonel of the Sixty-first and spent much time in his camp in the period of mid-April to early June 1862. In his engraving "Our Army Before Yorktown, Virginia," published in the May 5, 1862, *Harper's Weekly,* Homer particularly honored Barlow and the Sixty-first by portraying the unit during religious services. Sally Mills, "A Chronology of Homer's Early Career, 1859–1866," in *Winslow Homer Paintings of the Civil War,* ed. Marc Simpson (San Francisco: Bedford Arts, Publishers, 1988), 16–24: 17–20. Christopher Kent Wilson, "Marks of Honor and

I am very glad you enjoyed yourself.

> Love to all,
> Your aff. Son
> Francis

My cough is wholly gone + my voice restored as I have not yelled for several days.

> March 5th [1862]
> 6.30 am

My dear Mother

Yours enclosing a letter of E's came yesterday.

We are still in the old place. Yesterday the other 3 Regts of the Brigade went out some miles, near Springfield Station, to protect a party who are repairing a burnt bridge over the Railroad. They may come back, or we may join them there + take up our quarters there, or we may all advance. Everything is uncertain + things do no look so much like an immediate movement as they did a week ago.

Don't place any confidence in the rumors you hear + don't believe in a battle until you see the official report + don't believe at all in the "hard fighting" "bayonet charges" or "terrible slaughter."

Keep cool + don't believe anything until I write it to you. I am going to ride out with Howards Adjt Genl this morning to where the Regts are.

Mrs Richards positively refuses to take a payment for your board so you had better send her some present.

I have given up my cooking arrangements + feed with Capts. [Arthur L.] Brooks + [Knut Oscar] Broady.

I[s] C. Miles still engaged in the photograph business? Be sure

---

Death: Sharpshooter and the Peninsular Campaign of 1862," in Simpson, *Winslow Homer*, 25–45: 27.

that my photographs are good before you pay for them. I would rather pay the $4 + have them good.

What a villainous game of backgammon R. must play to be beaten so by you!!! I have played only one game of chess since I have been in this Camp.

I am very sorry that you feel so uncomfortable of late. Summer will soon be here when you always feel better.

Genl. Meagher wrote me a note on Monday saying that his wife had arrived the night before. I think we shall call on her today.

Tell E. that I will leave my receipt where it is, as he suggests.

You aff Son
Francis

Did I tell you that Henry Dalton is a 2nd Lt. in the 14th Mass. Regt. (Col [William B.] Greene) stationed at the Long Bridge.[16]

After a long winter quarters, Major General George B. McClellan prepared for a spring campaign aimed at capturing Richmond and ending the Rebellion once and for all. McClellan intended to mobilize his Army of the Potomac and confront General Joseph Johnston's Confederate army entrenched at Manassas. Before McClellan could move, however, Johnston's force retreated to cover Richmond, and on March 10 the Army of the Potomac reached the Rebel works to find them abandoned. McClellan thereupon implemented another plan: to move his entire army by boat to Federal-held Fort Monroe on the tip of the Virginia Peninsula, the largest coastal fortress in America at a third of a mile across. From that direction, McClellan could drive toward

---

[16] Originally mustered in as the Fourteenth Massachusetts Volunteer Infantry, in early January 1862, the unit changed its designation to the First Massachusetts Heavy Artillery and performed garrison duty until it joined the Army of the Potomac for Grant's 1864 Campaign. The Long Bridge connected Washington, D.C., to northern Virginia over the Potomac River. Dyer, *Compendium,* 3:1240–41.

the Confederate capital without having to cross through the entire state by land.[17]

> Camp at Union Mills Va
> March 13th /62
> 8 p.m.

My dear Mother

We are still where I wrote from yesterday. We have got on faster than our subsistence + have to wait for it. At this rate we shall not reach Richmond for 3 weeks.

The adjutant [David E. Gregory] + I rode today to Manassas. It is an enormous plain of red New Jersey sand. The batteries are few + of the most rude + contemptible description mere heaps of dirt with hardly any ditches. The guns are all removed. We were told by an inhabitant that he heard from the soldiers that we had started early on Monday morning. We did not begin to move until that time which proves that the rebels were informed of our movements by traitors on our side. This man says that the rebels said they were going to make a stand further down. Also that very few troops have been at Manassas. They have deceived us + kept us at bay by the terror of a name. I am told however that the fortifications at Centreville are magnificent + extend for miles. Nice log camps can be seen in the woods on every side + our men have got every conceivable article from them—flour, aces, chairs, tables &c. We are the foremost division. Kearny entered Manassas with his Brigade a few days since and he is said to have acted without orders + has been ordered back to Fairfax.[18] Today [Brigadier William H.] Frenchs Brigade—one of ours

---

[17] Stephen M. Sears, *To the Gates of Richmond: The Peninsula Campaign* (New York: Ticknor & Fields, 1992), 14, 16, 19, 27.

[18] Philip Kearny, born in New York City on June 2, 1815, came from a wealthy and socially prominent family. Although schooled as a lawyer, Kearny pursued his boyhood dream of a military career after he inherited a million dollars from his grandfather in 1836. Commissioned a second lieutenant in the First Dragoon regiment in 1837, he attended the French Cavalry School at Saumur in 1839 and fought with the Chasseurs d'Afrique in Algiers in 1840. Upon his return to America, he served on the staff of Major General Winfield Scott, and during the Mexican War, Kearny lost his left

occupied Manassas + we shall probably go tomorrow.[19] I shall try to visit Bull Run as we pass it. A man who was there today tells me he saw 3 human skeletons lying on the ground.

Last night one of our men captured two rebel Sutlers wagons with a large stock of tobacco, cigars, gingerbread, peanuts &c. I lay on the ground at night under a shelter of boughs with my feet to a fire. March is a cold month for such exposure but I have been very comfortable so far.

Good night my dear mother. Love to the boys. Write me often + fully.

Your loving son
Francis

---

arm at Charubusco. In 1851, Kearny resigned from the army and traveled around the world before settling on his New Jersey estate. He soon sought military adventure again, however, and in 1859, served in Napoleon III's Imperial Guard, participating in cavalry charges at Magenta and Solferino with his mount's reins clenched in his teeth. With the coming of the Civil War, Kearny rushed back to America and received appointment to brigadier general and command of the New Jersey Brigade. During the Peninsula campaign, Kearny rose to division command and received his second star to date from July 4, 1862. At the end of the Second Manassas campaign, Kearny accidentally rode into Southern lines and was shot and killed as he wheeled his horse and tried to escape. His remains were returned to Union lines by General Robert E. Lee under a flag of truce. Warner, *Generals in Blue,* 258–59.

[19] William Henry French graduated from West Point's class of 1837 along with such figures as John Sedgwick, Joseph Hooker, Braxton Bragg, and Jubal Early, all destined for prominence in the Civil War. He fought Seminoles in Florida and participated in the Mexican War, where he earned several brevets for gallantry. French was made brigadier general effective September 28, 1861, and assigned command of a brigade in the Army of the Potomac's Second corps. He fought through the Peninsula campaign and led a division at Antietam. Promoted to major general from November 29, 1862, French participated in Fredericksburg and Chancellorsville before commanding the District of Harpers Ferry during the Gettysburg campaign. He briefly took command of the Third corps in the absence of its wounded commander, Major General Daniel Sickles, but French lost Major General George Meade's confidence during the Mine Run campaign. When the Third corps was dissolved in the spring of 1864, French was mustered out of service. Warner, *Generals in Blue,* 161–62.

Fairfax Courthouse
March 17th /62

My dear Mother

We have been so busy the last 2 days with march + counter-march that I have not had time to write. Yesterday we left Union Mills to return to Alexandria on our way down the river. The division got as far as this place last night + was immediately ordered back to Union Mills to support Frenches Brigade which had been left behind + was threatened by the enemies rear squad. I turned my ancle day before yesterday + it hurt me to ride + I came down yesterday in a wagon with Arabella + Mrs. Meagher who came to Union Mills on Saturday.

We rode around through Centreville + saw the fortifications. We slept here last night at Genl Sumners Hd.Qrs. + as his guest. This morning Genl Sumner says I had better go to Camp California + stay until my foot gets strong again as the division is coming directly back.

You know our whole plan is changed in consequence of the rebels evacuating Manassas. The whole army is to descend the river in transports + land somewhere + march thence to Richmond. [Major General Nathaniel P.] Banks is to hold Manassas.[20] Sumners Army Corps consists of this division, [Brigadier General

---

[20] Born in Waltham, Massachusetts, in 1816, Nathaniel P. Banks received little formal education and worked in a cotton mill his father managed before becoming a member of the state bar at the age of twenty-three. After seven failed attempts, Banks won election to the Massachusetts legislature, became speaker of the House, and presided over the state Constitutional Convention of 1853. That year, Banks was sent to Congress, where, in 1856, he was elected Speaker of the House after 133 ballots. In 1858 Banks won election to the Bay State's governorship, and he served until Lincoln appointed him a major general in January 1861. McClellan originally intended for Banks's corps to protect Washington from a defensive position at Manassas. This all changed, however, after Major General "Stonewall" Jackson attacked one of his divisions on March 23 at Kernstown in the Shenandoah Valley. Banks was accordingly ordered to remain in the Valley and destroy Jackson's forces, something he proved unable to accomplish. Banks later attacked Port Hudson, which surrendered after Vicksburg fell, and commanded the Red River campaign. After the war, he again represented Massachusetts in the House of Representatives, served a term in the state senate, and for nine years was U.S. marshal in the Bay State. Warner, *Generals in Blue*, 17–18. Sears, *To the Gates of Richmond*, 32.

Louis] Blenker's division + [Brigadier General John] Sedgwicks (late Stone's) division.[21] We have seen nothing of the enemy + I rode over the field of Bull Run on Friday + will write of it in my next. I shall go to Camp today + thence to Washington to have my teeth filled. We shall probably set sail in the course of a week. I have recd. no letters since I left except one from Edward.

> In haste + with much love
> Francis

I enclose the letter I found in the Rebel Camp.

> Mrs Richards
> March 18th /62
> 11.30 p.m.

Dear Edward
   Mothers Diary to Thursday last + your letter of yesterday came today.

---

[21] Lincoln transferred Blenker's division to the Shenandoah Valley on March 31, 1862, to reinforce Federal troops attempting to contain "Stonewall" Jackson's Rebel army there. Louis Blenker was born in Worms, Germany, but after participating in the revolution of 1848, he sought asylum in Switzerland and then the United States. He settled in New York, where he operated a farm as well as conducted business in New York City. When the Civil War erupted, he recruited the Eighth New York Infantry and became its colonel. On August 9, 1861, Blenker was commissioned brigadier general and led a division in the Shenandoah in 1862. He was discharged from the service on March 31, 1863, and died later that year. A Connecticut native, John Sedgwick was graduated from West Point's class of 1837 along with such future notables as Braxton Bragg, Jubal Early, and Joseph Hooker. He fought Seminoles and assisted in the relocation of the Cherokees from Georgia to Oklahoma before fighting in the Mexican War. With the Civil War, Sedgwick became brigadier general effective from August 31, 1861; directed a division in the Second corps during the Peninsula campaign; and received his second star to rank from July 4, 1862. He fought bravely at Antietam, where he suffered three wounds, and he took command of the Sixth corps upon his return, leading it until his death at Spotsylvania on May 9, 1864. Sears, *To the Gates of Richmond,* 32. Warner, *Generals in Blue,* 37, 430–31.

I returned here yesterday being unfit for active service by reason of a sprained ancle, as I wrote you from Fairfax Court House.

My horse slipped on Saturday last + fell on my ancle. It was not his fault as the ground was very slippery + I was spurring him by way of salutary punishment + holding him in at the same time. The sprain was painful for one day but it has gone + there is now only a little stiffness. It is inconvenient as it prevents me from riding or walking but it gives me a chance to have a little leisure which I don't regret as there is no active service at present. The Division is at Manassas. We were told that we were to be one of the Army Corps to go down the river but I hear now (unofficially) that this Corps is to wait for Banks + then go with him forward while the River Expedition turns the right flank of the enemy. Among these conflicting rumors I don't pretend to know what we are to do. Richard must come on if he can get a chance. I shall go out to the Regt. in a few days if it don't come in + he can go out with me. If I am still here he can stay with me. If we go down the River I think I can smuggle him along with me. So in any event let him come. I shall be delighted to see him + I only wish you could come on with him. I hope to see you here again with mother before the war closes. Let R. come as soon as he can.

I am very sorry to hear that mother is so poorly. I wish I could be there to add something to her comfort. She need not worry about me at present for there will be no movement for sometime + we (the Regt.) is some 35 miles from the enemy. It is unfortunate that mother has selected an album for Mrs Richards, she has one already given her by some of the officers. However it is a pretty present. I do not see my cartes de visite yet. Will you send me $20 more to my address Alexandria. Draw it from J.C. Howe + keep an a/c of all you draw. I want to lay in a stock of money in case we advance [remainder of letter missing]

On March 17, the first Federal transports departed from Alexandria for Fort Monroe, and in the next fortnight, almost four hundred vessels transported 121,500 troops, forty-four artillery batteries, 1,150 wagons, and almost 15,600 horses and mules, in *addition to other military equipment. The Sixty-first reached the Peninsula on the steamer* Spaulding *on April 5, accompanied by their brigadier, Howard. Along with the Irish Brigade under Brigadier General Thomas F. Meagher and Brigadier General William H. French's brigade, Howard's regiments completed Brigadier General Israel B. Richardson's division of Sumner's Second corps. Around this time, McClellan's army settled in to besiege the Confederate army at Yorktown, scene of the decisive American victory of the Revolutionary War. Barlow's regiment missed the early days of this operation as it remained near its landing point for some time.*[22]

Friday April 11th /62 9 am

My dear Mother

I wrote a letter yesterday to send by R. who thought of going then but he has decided not to go for a day or two + has carried it off to Yorktown whither he + Homer have gone. We are still at Shipping Point where we landed last Sunday. They have turned us out of our Secesh huts into a pine grove where we are bivouacing. For a day or two it was rainy + damp + R + H were quite uncomfortable especially at night. But today is clear + pleasant + R has decided to stay a few days in the hope of seeing a battle. We are building a road from here to Yorktown to carry up the heavy artillery + nothing will be done until this is accom-

---

[22] Israel B. Richardson was born in Vermont the day after Christmas in 1815, a descendant of Revolutionary War general Israel Putnam. He graduated from the West Point class of 1841 and fought against Seminoles in Florida until earning distinction in the Mexican War, at Contreras, Churubusco, and Chapultepec. He resigned in 1855 to farm in Michigan but recruited and became colonel of the Second Michigan Infantry when the Civil War broke out. After commanding a brigade at First Manassas, Richardson earned his first star on August 9, 1861, and received command of a division in Sumner's Second corps for the Peninsula campaign. He received his second star to date from July 4, 1862, and while directing one of his artillery batteries at Antietam received a mortal wound from spherical case shot. He died on November 3, 1862. New York Monuments Commission, *In Memoriam: Francis Channing Barlow*, 68. Stephen W. Sears, *George B. McClellan: The Young Napoleon* (New York: Ticknor & Fields, 1988), 167–68, 175–76. Warner, *Generals in Blue*, 402–3.

plished. They say Johnston has 80000 men behind the entrenchments + we have not much more than that number. I have not
heard from any of you since the letter that R. brought. R. recd
one yesterday from Ella written on Thursday 8th last. I got on
my boot yesterday for the first time + my ancle is nearly well.
My health is excellent as is R's + H's. We have very pleasant
times together + mess with Capt Brooks or rather he with us. R.
will tell you all that is worthy of mention here. Love to all + Mrs.
Dinsmore.

Your loving son
Francis

My horse has arrived safe.

*A major command shift occurred in the Sixty-first around this
time. After a rocky tenure as the regiment's leader, Cone left the
unit. Barlow assumed the Sixty-first's colonelcy on April 14,
fully prepared to lead it through its coming trial by fire. Not
surprisingly, Barlow continued to place a high premium on discipline, and Robert Gould Shaw, serving as a young officer in
the Second Massachusetts Infantry, fully approved of his former
tutor's strictness. Admonishing his sister's criticism, Shaw wrote
her, "You are very much mistaken in thinking Frank Barlow's
conduct as Officer of the Day was foolish. It is his duty to have
the Guard turned out once a day at least, and certainly oftener,
if he thinks the officer of the guard allows the men to leave the
Guard Tent or neglect their duty in any way. . . . All you said
about Frank, went to show that he was a better Field-Officer than
9 out of 10 in these two divisions[.]"[23]*

---

[23] Robert G. Shaw to Josephine Shaw, Near Edenburg, Virginia, April 16,
1862, in Duncan, *Blue-Eyed Child of Fortune*, 191. New York Monuments
Commission, *In Memoriam: Francis Channing Barlow*, 68.

Before Yorktown
Friday 18th April /62
5 p.m.

My dear Edward

Your letter of April 8th came yesterday. That of April 4th with $10 came a day or two ago. No money is recd since.

R. left for Ship. Point today at 2 p.m. on his way to Fortress Monroe + home. I miss him very much + it seems quite forlorn without him. I have enjoyed his + Homer's visit exceedingly. It seemed quite like home to have them here + I have not laughed so much since I left home. It is very tedious living so many months with men who are so little companions for me as our officers are. There is not one who I am at all intimate with or who is any companion to me. Capt. Brooks who is one of the best of them I have taken for a tent mate for convenience sake. I have made requisition for a tent + when I can get a servant shall try + live more comfortably. It is impossible to get a servant here. There are not more than 10 private servants in the Regt. Mine left me to go to Bull Run to see his wife just as we left Alexandria + R + Homer have done the cooking. Tell R that I got my tent covered with pine limbs this afternoon to make it cool + have had a thick floor of pine branches + it is quite clean. Also I have got a man from one of the Cos. to help Homer with cooking + scullion Dpt. + taking R's place.

Each day they say we are to have a battle + make an assault on Yorktown, but we never do it. They seem to think in [Brigadier General Fitz John] Porter's Division yesterday that the place was to [be] regularly besieged by approaches + trenches. It is impossible to tell what the plan is. I think we are trying to bamboozle the enemy until [Major General Irvin] McDowell gets down in their rear.[24] Our Division is some 2 miles in rear of the front + apparently, are to be used as a reserve.

How outrageously the fight at Pittsburg was managed by our

---

[24] Originally, McClellan thought he would have McDowell's corps at his disposal, but Lincoln opted to withhold and use it to safeguard the Federal capital. Sears, *To the Gates of Richmond,* 40–41.

Generals.[25] I am very sorry to think of mothers prospects this summer. We seem to be unfortunately situated for her comfort. It is evident that neither you nor R. can live out of town + there are very few places where she can go alone. I should think she would try + go somewhere with the Gardners. Why don't they try Wmstown for a few weeks? Where is Ludlow going? I wish I were with her to add something to her comfort. Before the summer passes I hope to have a furlough or perhaps be permanently at home + spend some time with her in the country.

[remainder of letter missing]

Before Yorktown
Wednesday 23rd April
8 p.m.

My dear Edward

We are still in the old place. Occasionally we hear the report of a cannon during the day. Both sides are getting the range of their guns + our side is throwing up entrenchments. If the map in yesterday's Herald be correct, we have a mighty hard place to take. Your letter of 19th inst. [instant] in answer to mine of 16th came yesterday + today we have yesterdays' Herald so that we are now very near you. We drill regularly + nothing reminds us of an impending battle. McDowell must be getting pretty near Richmond if he has marched directly on from Fredericksburg. We were much aroused to read that Harpers of last week had nothing of Homers in it but we regard his occupation as gone. He now does not dare to go to the front having been an object of

---

[25] This refers to the battle of Shiloh or Pittsburg Landing on April 6–7, 1862. After a surprise Confederate attack nearly drove Major General Ulysses S. Grant's army into the Tennessee River, Federal reinforcements enabled a counterattack that defeated the Southern army. McPherson, *Battle Cry of Freedom*, 405–13.

suspicion even before. He says he shall go home after the battle.[26]

Send a box of yeast powder in the box if you have not sent it. No news here from R. I sincerely hope he will have no trouble with Marshall. I have recd all the money you have mentioned. There are absolutely no incidents to relate since I last wrote. I drill + read. We have exhausted wood ticks + have now bites from some mysterious animals or insects which we never see but know only from their bites. Food as before—no meat for several days, only bean soup + rice. I alone bear up agt. the former + continue excellently well. Horrible smells environ our dwelling. Richardson turns out to be a damned miserable Division Genl never knowing or caring for his command. Other Divisions have had all manner of military instruction this winter + the Division Genls visit their Brigades daily. Nothing of the kind has been done with us + I believe we are the most miserable Division, Brigade + Regt. in the Army. I have lost my pistol, but shall borrow one if we have a fight. The weather is clear + beautiful again + all nature is lovely. Homer + I have just been talking of the "Forties" + of my armed occupancy of Mrs Mills &c. He is now going to bed. His head is shaven + he looks like Hell. Does G. Curtis write the "Lounger"?[27] If so, he seems quite a supporter of McClellan.

---

[26] The week before Barlow wrote this letter, Federal officials confiscated the issue of *Harper's Weekly*, as it published several detailed illustrations of Union entrenchments. Apparently, Homer's drawings were viewed with skepticism by the army high command as a possible breach that could allow information to fall into the hands of the enemy. Wilson, "Marks of Honor and Death," 27.

[27] Born in 1824, George William Curtis lived both at Brook Farm and in Concord contemporaneously with Barlow's residence at those places. As a reporter for the *New York Tribune* in the 1850s, Curtis traveled extensively through the Middle East, and he later became associate editor of *Putnam's Monthly Magazine* and a columnist for *Harper's New Monthly*. In 1856, Curtis campaigned for Republican presidential candidate John C. Fremont and married Anna Shaw. From 1857 through 1863, he wrote "The Lounger" columns for *Harper's Weekly,* and he campaigned for Abraham Lincoln in 1860. In 1863 Curtis became political editor of *Harper's Weekly* and continued in that role until 1892, the year of his death. Curtis also played an important role in promoting civil service reform in the early 1870s and served as chancellor of the University of the State of New York in the 1890s. Gordon Milne, *George William Curtis and the Genteel Tradition* (Bloomington: Indiana University Press, 1956).

Good night your loving son[28]

Francis

Johnston stealthily evacuated his fortifications around historic Yorktown on the night of May 3, before McClellan could open on him with his heavy siege artillery. On May 4, Barlow's New Yorkers received orders to prepare for a move in pursuit of the retreating Southerners. The next day, they marched but a short distance before pausing in the evening, hampered by rain and the ensuing mud it created. The march resumed until after midnight, with the Sixty-first passing through the Rebel entrenchments, and by May 7 Richardson's entire division camped at Yorktown. It remained there until May 11, when transport ships conveyed it up the York River to West Point.[29]

On May 15, reveille beat at two in the morning, and by four o'clock the New Yorkers marched once again. Torrential rain soaked the soldiers by noon, and, after a fourteen-mile march, they made camp in a nearby wood. Some of the men, still unused to the privations they would learn to endure during the Civil War, were afflicted with dizziness from the exertions of the day. Barlow's unhappy mood is reflected in the following letter, written after the drenching march.[30]

> In a damned little hut
> made of an India rubber
> blanket, in a woods in a
> pouring rain, 1 mile from
> Cumberland on the Pamunkey
> River + 15 miles above
> West Point. Thursday
> May 15th 1862 3 p.m.

---

[28] Note that Barlow addressed this letter to his brother, Edward.

[29] Fuller, *Personal Recollections*, 13.

[30] Ibid., 14.

Dear Edward

Your letter of May 12th has just been handed me under the circumstances + in the place above mentioned. I have recd. the note describing the contents of the box, but none since from any of you except one I think from mother recd on the 10th inst. As I wrote you in my last I can hear nothing of the box + can't catch the Lottie, but shall keep trying for her. Charlie Lowell was in the Yorktown fight, or rather near it + his Regt. was engaged but not his Squadron.[31] We have not smelt gunpowder yet. This morning we left our Camp from which my last letter was written + marched here + as usual it rained like Hell + after a good wetting we were dumped in this wood for the night. My quarters are contracted but tolerably dry. Our forces are gradually concentrating on Richmond. We stick by the River as long as possible on a/c of getting supplies up easily. McClellan is at Cumberland + the whole army is nearby. We are no longer in the rear but stand a good chance of seeing service. We should have gone to Cumberland today had it not rained so like Hell. We are only some 25 miles from Richmond.

Capt. Brooks is dead. He died some days ago of typhoid fever it is said at Yorktown whither he had been removed. His death was very unexpected. Tell Snout that the Capt. died of the hard living which we had when he (Snout) was here + that he (Snout) would probably have died too had he staid a few days

---

[31] Charles Russell Lowell was born on January 2, 1835, in Boston, the nephew of poet James Russell Lowell. He graduated from Harvard at the head of the class of 1854 and then managed an iron foundry in Maryland. In May 1862, Lowell accepted a captaincy in the Third (later Sixth) U.S. Cavalry and served in the Peninsula campaign until he joined Major General George B. McClellan's staff. Lowell's bravery in carrying orders and rallying troops at Antietam earned him the honor of bringing captured Rebel banners from that battle to Washington. Afterward, Lowell recruited the Second Massachusetts Cavalry and became its colonel, served as commander of Washington's outer defenses, and helped repel Confederate Lieutenant General Jubal Early's July 1864 raid on the capital. During the Shenandoah campaign between Early and Major General Philip Sheridan later that year, Lowell commanded a cavalry brigade. Although he had twelve horses shot from beneath him during the war, he was not wounded until Cedar Creek on October 19, 1864. Refusing to leave the field, Lowell continued to direct his brigade until he received a mortal wound, and he died the following day. Sheridan personally insured that Lowell's commission as brigadier general was dated for the day of that battle. Warner, *Generals in Blue*, 284–85.

longer. Where's Snout + what is he doing. I am well + hearty in every respect + stand everything beautifully. My only trouble has been the tooth ache which for two nights kept me awake nearly all night + which aches several times per diem. The Doctor has made 4 more attempts to extract it (besides 3 attempts made some days ago) + he has not yet extracted it. He has however broken off everything which can be seen or appears above the gum besides cutting into the gum largely + has now given it up in despair + I am to grin + bear it until I return to civilised parts. His instruments are of a rude character + hurt like Hell + I have now got so used to the operations that it is a pleasant

[portion of this letter is missing, though what follows might be its conclusion]

Will you take the [illegible words] to Mr. Kollock Superintendent of the outdoor [illegible word] at No. 1 Bond St. + get his receipt for it to be applied to the support of John H. Power so[n] of Patrick Power of the Regt. The boy is 7 years old + is at the House of Industry of House of Refuge or something of the kind on one of the Islands + Kollock will know.[32] Find out how the money will be applied + how long it will last the boy— + just where he is + what will be done with him if his father don't send money + whether if he's put out to service by the Commissioners, his father can have him when he comes home or whether he will be apprenticed for a number of years. Get receipt + send it + answer all these questions in your next. I will keep this $10 for my own use. Please take $10 from mine in your hands. Much love to mother + R. I hope to hear from them both soon. Is Mrs. Gardner at Fort Monroe or G-town? I should like to see her—

Your loving bro
FCB

---

[32] Barlow refers here to the poorhouses on the East River islands near New York City.

Camp near Cumberland Va
May 17th (Saturday) 1862 1 p.m.

My dear Mother + Richard

Your letter dated May 12th + 13th respectively came together yesterday + I must answer them both together. I am much troubled my dear mother at your uninviting prospect for the summer + yet I see nothing to suggest. I presume you will spend it in diverse places as you did last year, enjoying some + having a pretty hard time in the others. Why don't you try + make some arrangement with Mrs. Clark for spending part of the summer in some pleasant place such as Wmstown or the place Mrs. Clark was last summer? Than you might pass a short time with the Gardners, + a short time at Brookline + at the Dinsmores + then I shall without doubt be at home either on a furlough or out of the service long before the summer closes + then we can go somewhere as we did last summer. You may thus work out the summer. If Richmond be practicable you shall certainly come there. Could you not get Mrs. Dinsmore or Mary Gardner or Mary Brown or some other woman to come with you, for you could hardly come alone. But I don't believe we shall be long in Richmond. Whether the Army evacuates or is beaten we shall soon move on + if we are beaten I think the North will give up. Don't on any account bind yourself to stay at any boarding place near New York all summer. I know you will detest it. I should think it would be much pleasanter to go about from place to place in the way I have suggested. As for Edward I heartily appreciate + sympathize with what you say. Would either he or R. like a position as lieutenant in this Regt. I could without doubt get them one. Were the War likely to last much longer it might be worthwhile to take a commission but unless as a sanitary measure it would be unwise to give up any situation simply to take this one, since there is no knowing when we shall be mustered out. Edward or R. might like it for a while if they could stand it in a sanitary point of view. If they say the word I will write or ask for a commission. Their want of human knowledge need be no obstacle. As for myself I shall try to get out of the service just as soon as we have had a good battle. I think this must be quite soon. The rebels seem to be concentrating in front of Richmond

+ we are gradually approaching it. Today some of the troops moved up the River to White House at a lush point the Railroad from West Point to Richmond crosses. We shall probably [go] to Cumberland tomorrow. I presume we are going up the River (the Pamunkey) so as to approach Richmond on the easiest side + that soon we shall strike off + move directly towards it. We know very little of what is going on. I found that Dalton's Regt. was not far from here + yesterday rode up there but found the whole Brigade had gone out on a reconnaissance + so missed him. We are close to our friends one day + far away the next. Yesterday notice came that Massett was promoted to be Lt. Col. + Capt. Brooks to be Major. The latters death leaves the place vacant. Two other promotions were notified. If I am sick I will certainly telegraph + write at once + until I can get to or hear from you. I will go to Yorktown + get into the care of Mary Gardner. I should like to be wounded slightly, just enough to enable me to come home for a while. My tooth has wholly stopped aching for the last few days + I rather think the nerve was killed in the last struggle. I shall write to Capt. Bell today about the box. If it is brought back to N.Y. send by Adams Express + it will reach me some time or other. It must be quite exciting my dear mum to go among the sick as you do. It brings the honor of war home to one intensely. It is admirable conduct on the part of the women who do it + I only hope their sons + husbands + brothers may fall into as good hands. Frank Howe probably gets paid from the state (Mass.) as Bliss does. Were they the sick or wounded whom you saw? Is Ludlow still in the Custom House. Have you seen old Basbee again? Give my love to him. If E[']s health really gets to the point where he can stand it he must get a good long vacation somewhere this summer + go where he can enjoy it. Can't you persuade Charles to take a house somewhere near N.Y. + take you all for a while to board.

Tell R. that I <u>do</u> make them step round + some wish they never had been <u>born</u>. It makes me laugh sometimes to have to blow up the Chaplain [Henry C. Vogel] + Dr. while one old enough to be my Grandfather.[33] I enclose copy of an endorse-

---

[33] Fifty-five-year-old Henry C. Vogel served as the Sixty-first's chaplain from January 19, 1862, until becoming its assistant surgeon on January 29, 1864. Phisterer, *New York in the War of the Rebellion*, 3:2572.

ment made by Genl Howard on an application to the Gov. for recruits. I told the Gov. that he ought either to recruit up the Regt or disband it. Tell R. not to make any compromise with Clarks assignee or to do anything about it. Simply tell the fellow that he (R.) can't pay at present + then let him do what he pleases. He can only examine R. on supplementary process if he (R.) can make over to me all his assets before judgt. is got agt. him if he is sued which I have no idea will be done. Just put on a bold face + tell him to go to Hell.

The mails come in season + regularly now. So all write often + direct as you have done.

[no signature]

On May 18, the Sixty-first marched five miles before making camp, and the next day marched another five to New Kent Court House. By the twenty-first, a ten-mile march placed the New Yorkers only eighteen miles from Richmond, and on the twenty-fourth they marched to within seven miles of the Confederate capital. The men of the Sixty-first remained under arms and ready for action at any moment throughout this period, with rations in their haversacks and a supply of ammunition at hand. On May 28, part of the Sixty-first guarded an engineer mapping the roads near Fair Oaks, an area they would come to know very well in the following days. Meanwhile, other regiments of Howard's brigade helped as Sumner's corps constructed two bridges across the swampy Chickahominy River, including the Grapevine Bridge.[34]

On May 31, the sound of battle across the Chickahominy split the air. Johnston's Confederates attacked Brigadier General Erasmus Keyes's Fourth corps deployed on the southern side of the river, catching Brigadier General Silas Casey's division by surprise and driving it from its position. At 2:30 that afternoon, Sumner followed McClellan's orders to push Richardson's and

---

[34] Fuller, *Personal Recollections*, 14–15. Pride and Travis, *My Brave Boys*, 75–76. Sears, *To the Gates of Richmond*, 113.

Sedgwick's divisions across the swollen, flooded river. Richardson's division made a difficult crossing on the Lower Bridge, a mile downstream from the Grapevine Bridge, and in some places the men practically had to wade across. One member of the Sixty-first, Charles Fuller, recounted that the log bridge "seemed to be resting on the water," and "some of the logs would roll and dip in a manner to shake confidence in its stability," though the men "crossed on it all right." By the time Richardson's division had fully traversed the river, it was too late to participate in the battle. Sumner's divisions formed a defensive position, with Sedgwick's troops facing west toward the Nine Mile Road and Richardson's men facing south along the railroad tracks, with their right near Fair Oaks Station and French's brigade in the front line. By 9 p.m., the division stacked arms and waited in eerie silence. The next morning would bring the Sixty-first's baptism of fire.[35]

At four in the morning, Barlow's 432 New Yorkers ate a quick breakfast and prepared themselves for the day's action amidst the debris of battle lying on the ground from the day before. The sound of increasing small arms fire swept across the battlefield until 7 a.m., when Howard's brigade advanced to reinforce French's brigade against a Confederate attack. Soon, Richardson's entire division of seven thousand men was engaged. Howard's Eighty-first Pennsylvania attacked first but was quickly repulsed, leaving its colonel dead on the field, and Howard personally led his Sixty-first and Sixty-fourth New York regiments forward. After Barlow's men had passed him, two bullets struck Howard's right arm, shattering the bone and necessitating amputation. The Sixty-first deployed facing south with its right a quarter mile east of the station, along the railroad track running through the woods. On its left was the Sixty-fourth New York, though Barlow lost sight of the rest of the brigade. While his regiment waited under arms, Barlow went into the thicket to reconnoiter. Upon emerging from the trees, Barlow found his men lying flat on their stomachs, trying to avoid stray bullets, which had already wounded several of their number. The colonel bel-

---

[35] Fuller, *Personal Recollections*, 15–16. Pride and Travis, *My Brave Boys*, 77. Sears, *To the Gates of Richmond*, 142. OR, 11(1): 763, 764.

*lowed, "Who ordered you to lie down? Get up at once," and as
the men sprung to their feet, the order came for the New Yorkers
to advance into the woods.*[36]

*The men pressed forward, their line broken up by trees, dense
undergrowth, and swampy soil beneath them, until they reached
and relieved the Fifty-third Pennsylvania of French's brigade.
Barlow's men passed the nearby Fifty-second New York of French's
brigade, observing their comrades from the Excelsior State lay-
ing on the ground, out of ammunition, and awaiting relief. Barlow's men dressed in line of battle and fired one or two volleys to
flush out the Confederates in their front but grew silent when no
Confederates could be seen. The New Yorkers pressed onward
until they reached the crest of a small hill near the former camp
of Casey's division, occupied by the Southerners earlier in the
battle. A Rebel volley shattered the New Yorkers' line, and Charles
Fuller later recalled getting a shot off before throwing himself
behind the bodies of two of his friends to reload his gun. Fuller
watched as a bullet struck Sanford Brooks's head, smashing
through his skull and gouging out both eyes, a painful and mortal wound.*[37]

*The Sixty-first did not waver but kept firing until the Confed-
erates withdrew. Barlow allowed his men a brief rest, and when
he realized that his flanks were unsupported and that he was in
advance of the rest of the Federal line, he sent for Colonel John R.
Brooke's Fifty-third Pennsylvania to reinforce him. Suddenly,
firing from the rear shattered the New Yorkers' brief respite.
Many more would have been casualties had they not been lying
down, and though Barlow had heard that Confederates had
slipped behind his line, he forbade his men to shoot lest the information be faulty. Instead, Barlow sent Adjutant Gregory to get
orders, and upon his return the Sixty-first retired from their advanced position and returned to where they had started.*[38]

*After the battle, the men lay under arms and waited to see if
the enemy would attack. Further action did not come, and by
11:30 combat had ended with the Federals having repulsed the*

[36] Fuller, *Personal Recollections*, 16–17. Pride and Travis, *My Brave Boys*,
82. OR, 11(1): 763, 765–66, 772.
[37] Fuller, *Personal Recollections*, 18–19. OR, 11(1): 772, 785, 790.
[38] OR, 11(1): 772–73.

Confederate attacks. Barlow reported the pride he felt in his unit's performance, that its officers bravely did their duty to a man and that most of the men "stood firm and erect during the firing, and only stooped or went down when ordered to do so." The New Yorkers' valor came at the cost of over one-quarter their number, with thirty killed, seventy-six wounded, and six missing, most of whom were attending to wounded comrades when taken prisoner. Richardson's division lost a total of 838 men in the battle. Among them, Howard's right arm had to be amputated, and the next day he encountered Brigadier General Philip Kearny, who had lost his left arm during the Mexican War. "General, I am sorry for you, but you must not mind it," consoled Kearny, "the ladies will not think the less of you!" With a laugh, Howard retorted that the two generals could now purchase their gloves together and they both shook on it with their remaining hands. Meanwhile, the battle had inadvertently caused one of the most important command shifts of the entire war, as Joseph Johnston's wounding led to General Robert E. Lee's assuming command of the Army of Northern Virginia.[39]

[no date, but June 2, 1862]

At about 4 a.m. on June 1st we were roused and I was ordered by Genl Howard to form my Regt in what is called close column of Division. It was dark and raining. My orders were to take a certain position + be ready to form line when ordered or when the line in front of us should break or retreat or when from any cause I should think it best. After having formed line I was to advance upon the enemy. My Regt in column was on the right of the 2nd line, next on our left was the N.Y. 64th + on the left was [the 81st] Penn Regt. The [5th] NH Regt was in some other part of the field. In our front in the same formation as ourselves was Frenchs Brigade of our Division + directly in our rear was Meaghers Brigade only two of his Regts being present [the 69th and 88th New York regiments]. We stood in this position for

---

[39] Fuller, *Personal Recollections*, 21. OR, 11(1): 757, 773–74. Sears, *To the Gates of Richmond*, 143.

some 2 hours, hearing occasional fire (musketry) on our left.
The rain stopped + the men were allowed to make a fire + cook
some coffee + I took some. We had begun to think there would
be no fight. About 7 am we heard a tremendous volley of musketry burst out on the woods on our left. We were at once faced
in the flank as it is called (in four ranks formation) + marched
into the woods in double quick time following the 64th Regt. On
our way the firing continued + we saw several men of other
Regts crouching under bushes. I spoke to several + asked them
why they did not go in + they said they had lost their guns. I
pointed them out to my men as examples of what a coward is.
The wood was a thick second growth of oak interspersed with
some taller trees. After marching some 200 yards we came out
on the Railroad where we formed line of battle with the 64th on
our left. The firing was going on in the woods on the other side
of the RR towards which we were facing, but most of the shots
struck near us. I then ordered our men to cap their pieces, they
having been previously loaded. In a few moments a volley was
fired in the woods + the balls buzzed close over us. All the 64th
crouched down + started back of this but all my Regt stood firm
+ fast except one Co which crouched a little + Genl Howard
saw this + must have noticed the difference between ourselves
+ the 64th. At this time the 5th N.H. + 81st Penn was at some
other point on the Railroad not in sight. In a moment after the
order was given to move forward and we + the 64th moved in
line of battle into woods. A tremendous firing was going on
therein but we could see no one through the leaves; though the
balls came about as very thick. At length we came upon the 53rd
Penn Regt one of French's Brigade. They were firing briskly
upon the enemy in their front. I was riding before the Regt. +
do not know whether we had lost any one up to that time. I asked
the Col. of the 53rd Penn. [John R. Brooke] to stop firing while I
went on in advance of him to relieve him.[40] His men were firing

---

[40] On April 20, 1861, John R. Brooke mustered into service as a captain in
the Fourth Pennsylvania Infantry, a three-month regiment that went home
on the eve of First Manassas. In November of that year, Brooke became
colonel of the Fifty-third Pennsylvania and served during the Peninsula
campaign, Antietam, and Fredericksburg. During Chancellorsville and Gettysburg, Brooke commanded a brigade in the Second corps and was
wounded when his brigade supported the Third corps in the fighting at the

all crouched down. He stopped + we went over him in good order. We began firing as we went on + could plainly see the enemy in the woods in front of us. We were close to them + they fired vigorously. I ordered my men to cease firing which much to their credit they did + we went steadily on until we got to a kind of clearing on the crest of a hill where there was a Camp. The enemy were firing + falling back before us all this time. When we got to the crest of the Hill I halted the line, got it in order, + a most violent firing began on both sides. The singing of the balls was awful. In about 3 minutes men were dying + groaning + running about with faces shot + arms shot + it was an awful sight. In a few minutes Capt [Theodore] Russell Co. H was shot dead, also Capt [James Joseph] Trenor Co. B, also Lt. [William] McIntyre commanding Co. C. 1st Lt. [Peter C.] Bain command-ing Co. D + Lt. [Cornelius P.] Bergen commanding Co K were soon wounded + had to leave the field leaving their companies without any officer. Lt. [William Henry] Coultis Co C was also wounded + left the field leaving his Co. without any officer; also Lt [Walter H.] Maze Co. A. was wounded + carried off.[41] I rode in advance of the line until we got into our position. The horse went on beautifully + calmly + was not at all frightened + did not once shy. He seemed wholly unconcerned. After we got into our position I found I could not move readily about in the woods on horseback + so dismounted. When we had been firing some minutes Genl Howard came through our Brigade on foot + with his arm tied up. He had led the 64th + now was on his way off the field. His horse had been shot + his arm broken in two places. It was amputated last evening + he goes home today.

Wheatfield on July 2. After recuperating, Brooke returned to the Army of the Potomac as commander of a brigade in Barlow's division of the Second corps, and he received promotion to brigadier general to date from May 12, 1864—the day he participated in a successful attack against the Mule Shoe at Spotsylvania. Wounded again at Cold Harbor, Brooke resumed active duty in spring 1865, leading a division in the Army of the Shenandoah. Brooke participated in the Spanish War and served as military governor of Puerto Rico and then of Cuba before retiring in 1902 at the age of sixty-four. Dying in 1926, he was the next to last Federal general who fought in the Civil War to die; the last was another brigadier who fought under Barlow, Adelbert Ames. Warner, *Generals in Blue*, 46–47.

[41] Coultis's wound proved mortal, and he died on June 23, 1862, in a Phil-adelphia hospital. Phisterer, *New York in the War of the Rebellion*, 3:2563.

Charles Howard, his brother + aide, is severely wounded in the thigh. Miles is unhurt except a slight graze on the heel.[42] After about 10 minutes of firing the enemy fell back + we could see them no longer + I stopped the firing + sent Col Massett back to ask for supports as there were no Regts on either of our flanks. The 53rd Penn came up + passed in front of us + a vigorous firing again began. I don't know whether they saw the enemy or not. They soon fell back behind our men + I stopped firing not seeing the enemy. Very soon word was brought that a Regt. of the enemy had got round between us + the railroad in our rear. I sent back to see if this were so + also to notify our people of our position which was not in advance of any one so far as we could see. While gone Col. Massett was shot dead through the head. We have buried him here + marked his grave. At this time we were in very ticklish position—we + the 53rd Penn—we were far advanced + many had been killed + wounded, there was no one supporting our flanks + it was highly probably that the enemy were in our rear. It was so reported to me by those who I had sent back to investigate. Genl Howard had ordered me not to retreat without orders + I should not have dared at any rate to retreat for the woods were thick + I should not have dared to fire lest we should fire on our own men. I got the men quieted + made them lie down + sent one officer after another to notify Genl Richardson of our situation. Finding it necessary to change our position slightly I was moving the men when we got a tremendous volley from our own men + the enemy I don't know. I had my men lie quietly down + the balls passed over us. If we had been standing we should have suffered terribly. At length my messenger came back with orders to march out by a circuitous route. The other Regt. had been notified of our coming + ceased firing. We came out in beautiful order + were the last Regt. out of the woods. We found the rest of the Division drawn up on the RR + in the open field + have been waiting ever since bringing in our wounded + we have been expecting an attack, but this morning I think the enemy have retreated as

---

[42] Nelson Miles, a lieutenant serving on Howard's staff at this time, was wounded in the foot while directing a part of the Eighty-first Pennsylvania. *OR*, 11(1): 770.

I heard them moving last night. It seems we were opposed to the 3rd Alabama Regt over 800 strong. We drove them completely out of sight. The enemy had designed to flank this part of the army but has been repulsed on all sides. My men behaved really admirably. Some of course would hang back but we drove them all up. Genl Howard has said "that he does not believe there are braver men in the world than this Regt" + "that we stood in line + fought like veterans." I give you his own words for what they are worth. The men were certainly cool + obedient to orders + did not break at all. Several times the line wavered + fell back a few paces but we always brought them up. We were the only Regt. of the Brigade which did not break + run at some time or another. Col. [James] Miller of the 81st Penn was shot in the head at the beginning of the fight. Col [Edward E.] Cross is wounded. When we came in Genl Howards aide came + told me I was in command of the Brigade; that Col. [Thomas J.] Parker of the 64th N.Y. (who ranks me) was passed over because his Regt. had behaved so badly. Col Parker however at my suggestion went to Genl Richardson + told him he was senior Col + R. not knowing the facts told him as a matter of course to take command. We shall have another Brig. Genl assigned us as Genl Howard would not be back for a long time + will, I think, resign. Our loss is 4 commissioned officers killed outright + 4 wounded—of the latter one (Coulter) will probably lose his leg. Another (Bain) has his face completely shot away + will be awfully disfigured even if he lives. Of enlisted men our loss is 22 killed outright, 73 wounded + 8 missing (one or two of whom are no doubt wounded) total 108 enlisted men. We went into action with 417 enlisted men + therefore lost ¼ our number. The staff of our flag is shot away + it has 6 bullet holes through it. The N.H. Regt which went in some 650 strong lost 165 killed wounded + missing. The 81st + 64th lost much less. Our loss is heaviest in proportion + in officers, four exceeds all. The Regt is praised on all sides. The latest news is that the enemy are retreating.

On Saturday afternoon we heard very heavy firing + marched at once without tents + at about 7 p.m. reached this place which is on the R.R. from West Point to Richmond some 7 miles from

Richmond on the West side of the Chickahominy. The place is
called Fair Oaks Station.

I have written all these particulars because I supposed you
would be anxious to hear everything. I telegraphed + wrote to
you at once yesterday (June 1st). I + my horse are wholly unhurt. I was in the thickest of it at the head of my Regt. The men
cheered me violently during the fight + when we came out. The
64th broke to pieces + I took 2 of their Cos. into the end of my
Regt. Col Brook[e] of the 53rd Penn. did well. Some 10 of our
wounded will certainly die, so that our killed will be over 30. I
doubt if we go into action again unless we are absolutely needed
as a reserve. We have only 9 Company officers left one of whom
([Captain Edward Zachary] Lawrence) I have no use as a field
officer + have had to put the Regt. into 8 Cos.

We were short of officers when we started.Will you have two
copies of this made + send one to Arabella + the other to Bliss.[43]
Send Arabellas first + at once—I can't write 3 copies.

> In haste + very well
> Francis

> Battle Field
> June 3rd 1862
> 10 a.m.

My dear mother
I wrote you a long description of the action + sent it yesterday.
Yesterday Genl Howard + his brother [Charles H. Howard], who
is also severely wounded left for the North.[44] They go somewhere
down in Maine. If you see or hear of them being at any of the
Hotels or any other place in New York go + see them. Tell Genl
Howard that you are my mother.

Also quite a number of our wounded go North today. See them

---

[43] According to Maria L. Daly, Arabella Barlow was in New York at this
time. Maria L. Daly diary entry, June 15, 1862, in Hammond, *Diary of a
Union Lady,* 146.

[44] Lieutenant Charles H. Howard, who served on his brother's staff as an
aide.

if you can. You can learn something of our action + it will be a comfort to those who are in the Hospital. Bliss may be able to tell you where they are + when they will arrive.

The enemy have not attacked us since the action + the impression is that they have retreated. All the ground fought over is ours + we have brought in all our wounded + buried our dead. Our loss now is 4 Com. Off. + 26 men = 30 killed, 4 officers + 72 men = 76 wounded (of whom 4 or 5 will certainly die) + 6 missing (taken prisoners) total loss 112. The [5th] N.H. + 64th suffered largely; the [81st] Penn. Regt. not so much, though it lost some 50 prisoners. We took about 12 prisoners. We have got entirely accustomed to dead, wounded, + decayed men. The Hospitals are shocking sights with men lying about out of doors with all manner of shocking wounds. I have just been down to Hospital to see my men who were very glad to see me. Shell is now being vigorously fired by us into the woods with occasional shots of musketry from our extreme advanced Regts. They say the enemy are feeling our lines but I think our Generals are always more frightened than hurt.

The heat is getting perfectly awful here, but we all keep very well. The dead decomposed yesterday, it was dreadful work to bury them. We have buried our dead so that they can be identified. We have dug their graves under large trees which are marked + also put headboards to the graves. The dead were lying everywhere in the woods + our Hospitals are full of the enemy as well as our own. I have made an official report of which I will send you a copy when I can have one made. I report to Gen. Howard he to Division H.Q. I don't know whether Howard will make a report or not. If he does I think he will mention the Regt. with high praise.[45] We are still lying in the open field near where we fought + have a dozen alarms per diem. They all seem as unconcerned as possible about it + ready for another. We have only 9 Company + Field officers left. Lawrence is Major for the Regt.

The 3rd Ala Regt supported by the 12th + 41st Va Regt were

---

[45] Howard noted Barlow in particular for commendation: "I desire especially to notice the coolness and good conduct of Colonel Barlow, Sixty-first New York." OR, 11(1): 769.

opposed + there is no doubt that we drove them back the above named + they did not return while we were there.[46] We were in action 4 hours + our wounded who were left on the field state that as soon as we left a Regt of the enemy came forward + occupied the place where we had stood. They say (the Genls) that 5,000 men commanded by [Major General Benjamin] Huger + [Major General James] Longstreet were opposed to us + we certainly beat them back.

Lovingly,
Francis

Fair Oaks Station
Battle field
June 5th / 62[47]

My dear Mother
Yesterday your letter with Diary up to May 29th came, the first in a long time. We are still on the Field + are turned out + tear down tents + form for battle half a doz times in course of the night. The 69th [New York] has a picket here but got frightened night before last + fired a volley + Genl Richardson drew them in to punish them + sent us out. We are held in a good deal of esteem since the fight. Genl Richardson says we shall be the reserve in the next fight we have suffered so severely. Our Brigade loss is fully 500 about ¼ in the Brigade killed wounded + missing. Napoleon's heaviest loss (Borodino) was only 1/8th. I enclose a dispatch it speaks for itself also a letter from Capt Brooks father. Capt Lawrence has gone to the hospital down sick so that we have no acting field officer. We are lying close to the battlefield in the woods where the trees are riddled with bullets + the smell is awful. I stumbled on two dead rebels this morning

---

[46] This was Brigadier General William Mahone's brigade of Major General Benjamin Huger's division, and it was actively engaged in this sector on June 1. Sears, *To the Gates of Richmond*, 143.

[47] The Massachusetts Historical Society holds a copy of the original letter in different hand from Barlow's.

though most of them are buried + marked. Our experience in the way of exposure is awful compared to any the previous days + nights in pouring rain without shelter. I only have bread to eat. I can sleep comfortably in a pouring rain.

They say the 7th New York Regt is at White House + coming up here. If so, I may see Willie Dinsmore. You had better come to R. if Miss Brown will come with you or Mrs. D. or any travelling companion. If I am wounded I shall be sent home in a few days after, but I don't expect we shall fight again except in an emergency.

We have a slight account of the battle in the Herald of June 2nd [Brigadier General Erasmus D.] Keyes, [Brigadier General Philip] Kearney, + [Brigadier General Samuel P.] Heintzelman had no fight at all compared to ours. I trust you will see our wounded + Genl Howard as I asked in a former letter. The new Brig Genl assigned to this Brigade came today. He is one [John C.] Caldwell late Col of the 11th Maine + a man of no military experience or service besides.[48] My men are much pleased with me since the action. I now have several walking before me for various offences. I am in excellent condition but short of paper. Send some stamps.

Lovingly
F C B
Love to all

---

[48] John C. Caldwell was born in Vermont in 1833 and, after graduating from Amherst College in Massachusetts, became a teacher. At the beginning of the Civil War, Caldwell was principal of Washington Academy at East Machias, Maine, but he became the colonel of the Eleventh Maine Infantry on November 12, 1861. He took command of Howard's brigade after that officer was wounded at Fair Oaks, and he led it through the rest of the Peninsula campaign. Caldwell served at Fredericksburg and Chancellorsville and temporarily commanded the Second corps at Gettysburg when Winfield S. Hancock went down wounded. Caldwell was one of eight generals who formed a guard of honor for Abraham Lincoln's body as it proceeded from Washington to Springfield, Illinois. After the war, Caldwell became a lawyer and served as adjutant general of Maine, chair of the Kansas state board of pardons, and consul to Chile, Uruguay, and Costa Rica. Warner, *Generals in Blue*, 63–64.

The Federals remained on the field of Fair Oaks for several weeks, fortifying their line and placing artillery so as to protect against any possible Confederate attack. The Sixty-first held a position straddling the railroad tracks. The camp proved uncomfortable for the Northerners and the area's swampy water so foul that the men often had to drink it as coffee or sometimes mix it with rations of whiskey in order to make it more bearable.[49]

Fair Oaks
June 10 [1862]

My dear Mother + Edward

Your letters of 5th inst. came last night. I am rejoiced to hear that you have bore your suspense + anxiety so well + calmly waited for authentic intelligence. I am a lucky person you know + was not born to be killed in battle I do not think.

The whole Division is now encamped in a field together about ¼ mile from where the battle was fought. We are at this moment all drawn up for battle, the enemy having been shelling us, but hitting no one. None of their shells have come into this field. This turning out for battle occurs several times per diem. I think we should have made some move this morning had not there been a violent rain all night + all day so far. We slept out in it without any tents.

Mr Massett + Dr Trenor + his two sons + Capt Russell's father arrived here yesterday to disinter + take home the bodies of their sons which they have done. I saw Trevor after he was disinterred + it was an awful sight. The effect on Mr Massett was very much dreaded + Capt Russell's mother has lost her reason I am told + they have not dared to tell his wife of his death. It is singular how soon men become used to such horrid scenes we see, the dead + wounded carried past without any emotion. On Sunday morning our Pickets were driven in + we were under arms all day. No attack was made on us + we made none. I do not think we intend to make any at present for we are at work digging rifle pits + fortifying. I am inclined to think there

---

[49] Fuller, *Personal Recollections,* 21.

will be another battle before we get to Richmond. While I am writing 2 Regts. have just gone out to reconnoitre + may attack the battery which has been shelling us. I saw a very flattering notice of me in the Tribune of 7th inst. + an extract from the Journal of Commerce. Except some nonsense about the "steadiness of a parade" + what is said about a bayonet charge it is really not much exaggerated. We made no bayonet charge, but we did advance some 125 yards under fire without firing + the enemy probably thought we were charging on them though our bayts. were not brought to a charge nor did we advance with that intent but for the purpose of getting a better position to fire where we could see the enemy. We did advance farther + drive the enemy further than any other Regt. in the Division. We are seriously considered here as being the crack Regt. in the fight. The Herald a/cs are ridiculous. When we see the men it especially praises ([Brigadier General Thomas F.] Meagher, [Brigadier General Daniel] Sickles + [Colonel of the Sixty-fifth New York Infantry] John Cochrane) we understand the motives of the praise—it is not to do justice but to curry favor.[50]

I have seen Howards Official Report. It is very brief as the character of the man + the circumstances of being wounded would lead us to expect. Except the aside compliment to the staff (which every General pays regularly + alike) he mentions only Col. Cross + myself + though he says very little of any individual in his report yet he speaks more favourably of me then of any. He says—"I commend Col. Cross, 5th N.H.V. for his excellent

---

[50] All three figures were prominent in New York's public eye. Born on August 27, 1813, John Cochrane attended Hamilton College in New York, became a lawyer, and, in 1844, moved to New York City. Staunchly Democratic, he often supported the Southern perspective while serving in Congress from 1857 to 1861 and as a delegate to the Democratic convention. However, when the Civil War erupted, he recruited the Sixty-fifth New York Infantry and became its colonel. He led the unit at Fair Oaks and was promoted brigadier general on July 17, 1862, but he resigned from the army on account of his health the following February. After leaving the military, he was elected New York's attorney general on the Republican-Union ticket and, though he opposed many of Lincoln's policies, campaigned for the president in the 1864 election. A member of Tammany Hall, Cochrane was its sachem in 1889. For a brief biography of Sickles, see note 10 of this chapter; for one on Meagher, see footnote 42 in chapter 1. Warner, *Generals in Blue*, 86–87.

disposition of his command, which I noticed in the morning. I desire <u>especially</u> (the underscoring is <u>mine</u> not his) to notice the coolness + good conduct of Col. Barlow 61st N.Y.V. He then says says [*sic*] he won't particularise for fear of doing injustice, that all did admirably.[51] His report will be published I suppose. We have changed our position since I began this + are drawn up in order of battle. I should like to see M. Gardner + think I will write her to let me know if I am in her vicinity. Send envelopes + P.O. stamps.

Love to all. I shall answer Mrs Dinsmores letter tomorrow. It came last night. I shall come home just as soon as I can.

Your ever loving
Francis

On front: The Irishmen laugh at the idea of their "bayonet charge." They did not even leave the R.R. + were not engaged at all as severely as we were.[52]

Fair Oaks Va
June 12 /62

My dear Mother

We are still in the place where I last wrote. I am exceedingly incensed that my letter should have been published. I presume Bliss did it. It will do me harm here to have commented on other Regts especially as I find that my statements as to their running were much exaggerated. It is damned outrageous to have published the letter. We are lying still fortifying + I don't know whether we are to be the attacking or the attacked party. We are

---

[51] Howard wrote, "I commend Colonel Cross for the excellent disposition of his command, which I particularly noticed in the morning. I desire especially to notice the coolness and good conduct of Colonel Barlow, Sixty-first New York. I cannot too highly compliment all the officers in the brigade. I might do some injustice should I attempt to particularize." *OR*, 11(1): 769.

[52] The two available units from Meagher's Irish Brigade, the Sixty-ninth and Eighty-eighth New York regiments, served in a support and reserve role near the railroad. *OR*, 11(1): 777.

frequently turned out by alarms but no enemy appears. I shall certainly resign as soon as we get to Richmond + I am sick of this damned life + have no idea of beginning to drill + discipline a Regt. over again which will have to be done if this is recruited up. The weather is hot but I continue very well. No news of any kind + no letters from you since the ones of June 5th. I wrote to Mrs. Dinsmore yesterday. I am so incensed at my letters being published that I don't feel much like writing.

5 p.m.

I have just read your letter of Sunday. Mr. Massett saw all the persons who saw or knew anything of his son + will carry back all that information. I asked him to carry an order to the rear for me + never saw him again. I don't know whether he had got back or not before he was killed. He was <u>not</u> on his horse but had dismounted. He threw up his hands before his face + said not a word. He behaved most bravely + there is no doubt of his perfect contempt of danger. He was a man who learned remarkably quick + had a superior knowledge of tactics + <u>many</u> qualities of a good officer. He was rather changeable + fickle + not very persevering. He was very popular with the officers + men personally + was of a gentle + generous disposition. I was sometimes impatient with him for not being vigorous + energetic enough. Lawrence is commissioned as Major. I recommended him after the battle. Who in Hell had my letter published.

> Your loving Son
> Francis

Why don't you keep your Diary + why don't the boys write oftener.

On side: Did you see a notice in the Express saying that Cone commanded this Regt in the battle? It will be contradicted. Send me $15 in $5s.

Fair Oaks Va
Sunday June 15 /62
12 n

My dear Edward + Mother

E's letter of 12th + Mother's Diary to 11th arrived together today with enclosures + I must answer both together. We are still at the place whence I wrote last (day before yesterday) + to which we moved last Sunday.

As you will see we have moved away from the battlefield + are on a rather high + healthy ground. Now for E's questions. I have my box in my tent + have eaten everything in it except the cheese 3 cans of meat + a bottle of jelly which I am saving for an emergency. For the last few days I have been eating with the Quartermaster [Robert H. Ellis] + Adjutant [David E. Gregory] + we have for a Cook a man whom Massett used to employ who makes the most of a little + is skillful in making up nice (for a Camp) things.[53] Yesterday we had some boiled salt beef which tasted very well + some sort of muffins made of flour. With this exception we have had no soft bread for two weeks + not more than four loaves have we had since 4th of April. All the rest of the time we have eaten hard bread. I have not used nearly all the paper which you sent + shan't want anymore to be sent. I forgot I had the paper. I have got all your letters I think except the one sent by Wren who has not arrived.

You ask what I do? Nothing but lie in bed (which is made of saplings laid on uprights) in my tent to get rid of the heat. The heat is intense + no one goes out who can avoid it. We are sometimes turned out by an alarm, which has just happened. It was caused by the pickets firing a volley whereby a Capt. [Samuel Sherlock] of the 81st Penn Regt. was shot dead through the head + several men wounded.[54] They have just been brought by here. The picketing is dangerous. I do not have to go on it, but we send three Companies daily. We have got our tents + all our Camp equipage up here now. The two great events of the day are the

---

[53] Phisterer, *New York in the War of the Rebellion*, 3:2556.

[54] Samuel P. Bates, *History of Pennsylvania Volunteers, 1861–65*, 5 vols. (Harrisburg, Pa.: D. Singerly, State Printer, 1869), 4:1182.

mail + the newspapers. I lie in bed + read the letters + papers. Is not Cone a miserable cuss. He has an infinite brass to dare to write about "making the Regt." when everyone in it + in the Brigade knows his imbecility + holds him in perfect contempt. I am sure I never gave a thought to what the miserable cuss does or writes about me or the Regt. One of the officers wrote an answer to the communication signed "Justice" + has sent it on to N.Y. The one signed "Honour to whom Honour is due" was written by Capt. [Joseph M.] Carville one of our old Capts who resd about June 1st /62 + who despises Cone. I think the Regt. has been noticed as much as can be expected + desired. It may be commended in McClellans official report but I doubt if anything else further is said of it. This hot weather + want of vegetables is playing the devil with the soldiers. Out of an aggregate of 179 enlisted men 50 are sick today + other Regts are suffering as much in proportion. I continue to be very well.

I have just finished my sumptuous dinner for which I stopped after writing the above. It consisted of lemonade + heavy pancake made of flour + fat with a sauce. You need not fear that I shall suffer from unsuitable food. I have got pretty well used to hard living by this time. They would not listen for a moment in the tremendous press of business to my application to transfer Hoylehurst. It is out of the question. Besides I have not heard from the Col. of the 26th to whom I wrote

[remainder of letter missing]

Fair Oaks Va
June 18 /62
7 a.m.

My dear R.

Your letter of 14th reached me yesterday. I am very glad to hear from you. It is the only letter I have recd. from any of you since those whose I answered day before yesterday (or rather Sunday). On Monday they moved this Brigade forward into the front line to replace the Irish Brigade which had before occupied the entrenchments. We are now encamped behind the earth-works which have been thrown up along the whole line of our front. One would think we were acting on the defensive instead of the offensive. There is a good deal of picket firing on our front. The enemies pickets every now + then make a dash down + fire a volley. They killed Sickles Asst. Adjt. Genl a day or two ago + every now + then two or three of our forces are killed.[55] The enemy are said to be in large force just in our front.

We heard a heavy cannonade yesterday + are told today that Fort Darling is taken + that Burnside has landed up the James River.[56] If this be so we shall probably advance soon.

Bliss wrote me some time ago that he had again attacked Marshall + I hope that this time he will accomplish something. I am very glad that he has spoken so well of you + thinks so well of you. Did you succeed in getting anything out of Angel?

As you say the accounts of the battle by newspaper correspondents are outrageous. The a/c of Massett in Herald of 16th is a striking example of it. I have no doubt Cone is at the bottom of the statement about Massetts "handling his Regt." &c. The fact is that as soon as we got to our position I sent him back with a message + as soon as he got back I sent him to the rear with another message + he was killed while he was gone + never came back. Neither are my officers in the habit of giving commands to my Regt when I am present. These attempts to give Massett a reputation by lies only injures him. He was a brave man + did his duty but he was not killed while "gallantly charging at the head of his Regt." nor did he "handle his Regt." or have anything to do with its dispositions.

I want to know who published my letter about the battle. It was a great outrage + if anything of the kind is ever done again I will cease writing.

---

[55] Lieutenant J. L. Palmer accidentally stumbled upon a Confederate outpost during a routine reconnaissance and was shot dead. His party carried his body back to camp, where Sickles was nearly moved to tears at his loss. W. A. Swanberg, *Sickles the Incredible* (1956; repr. Gettysburg, Pa.: Stan Clark Military Books, 1991). 151 (page citation is to repr. ed.).

[56] Fort Darling stood atop Drewry's Bluff, seven miles from Richmond and rising a 110 feet above the James River. Here, Confederate artillery and obstructions in the river blocked a Federal naval squadron from bombarding the Southern capital. Sears, *To the Gates of Richmond*, 93.

We are constantly turned out. Last night the firing of the pickets turned us out three times + then we are regularly routed out at four in the morning.

> Write often to your aff. bro.
> F.C.B.

Love to all. I asked E. to send me some money which he has not done + I am greatly in want of it. Have it done.

On side: I have only just recd Es letter of 10th inst sent by Wren.

On June 25, Lee and McClellan began what became known as the Seven Days battles, only miles outside Richmond. At Gaines's Mill, on June 27, Lee attacked and smashed Brigadier General Fitz John Porter's Fifth corps, isolated on the north side of the Chickahominy River. Meagher's and French's brigades crossed the river just in time to cover the corps' retreat, and in short order McClellan decided to withdraw to the James River. On the morning of June 28, all soldiers unfit for duty were dispatched to the hospital, and all extraneous baggage was sent away as the Sixty-first struck its tents and readied itself to leave Fair Oaks. The next day, the Sixty-first joined its division in moving away from Richmond and passed the Federal supply center at Orchard Station, with its entire stores afire at McClellan's orders. Some of the men slipped from the ranks to take supplies, which they shared with others in the regiment. Although the prospect of getting a little extra sugar was welcome, no doubt the men were disheartened at lengthening the distance between them and Richmond and seeing millions of dollars of Federal supplies go up in smoke.[57]
Caldwell's brigade formed in a wood and endured some artillery fire before falling back to Savage Station, where it joined the rest of Sumner's corps in helping repulse a Rebel attack. The Sixty-first lost only three men, wounded by a ricochet shot. At 9

---

[57] Fuller, *Personal Recollections*, 22. *OR*, 11(2): 50, 54.

p.m., the Federal retreat through White Oak Swamp recommenced, complicated by darkness and slippery ground that resulted in numerous falls and roads clogged with men, baggage, and cannon. Richardson's division served as the Federal army's rearguard, and upon crossing the creek that general personally supervised the destruction of the bridge early on June 30. Upon being given the order to halt, one member of the Sixty-first recalled immediately dropping to the ground and falling asleep without even removing his gear.[58]

The morning of June 30, the men roused to breakfast, and a few hours later Confederate artillery began shelling their position near Glendale. Federal cannon of Captain George W. Hazzard's and Captain Rufus Pettit's batteries responded in kind while the Sixty-first supported them, and Barlow sat atop his horse and calmly watched the action. After the barrage ceased on both sides, Caldwell's regiments received orders to support Brigadier General Philip Kearny resist a Rebel attack at Nelson's Farm. Dry, dusty soil made for a miserable march, but the report of cannon in the distance alerted the New Yorkers that they might once again be called into battle. Just before entering a dense woods at the double-quick, they came across a large building serving as a hospital and saw the soldiers around it, bearing the bloody costs of their bravery. Marching at the double-quick down a road into the dark woods, the men of the Sixty-first encountered wounded streaming back toward the hospital and warning "You'll catch hell, if you go in there." The New Yorkers knew they were entering a desperate fight.[59]

Proceeding along the wooded road, the Federals unexpectedly came within sight of another column of troops who fired off a volley. They were Northerners, however, and though no one was injured, several men had bullets pass through their clothing and one soldier's canteen was shot from his hip. The New Yorkers identified themselves before the opposing column got off another round, but in the confusion the Sixty-first became separated from the rest of their brigade. Barlow placed himself under command of the nearest brigadier he could find, John C. Robinson.[60]

---

[58] Fuller, *Personal Recollections*, 22–24. OR, 11(2): 54–55, 60.

[59] Fuller, *Personal Recollections*, 24–25. OR, 11(2): 55, 61, 65–66.

[60] Fuller, *Personal Recollections*, 25–26. OR, 11(2): 65, 67.

The Sixty-first pressed onward, reaching an open field and lying down behind a fence at its edge. Other Yankee regiments were firing into the field, but Robinson ordered them to cease fire and then conferred with Barlow, saying "Colonel, you will place your men across that road and hold it at all cost." Barlow warned, "General, you know I have but few men" (a situation exacerbated by the fact that about fifty were on detached picket duty), to which the general replied with confidence, "Yes, but they are good ones." As a result of the smoke and darkness, Barlow did not even know whether the Rebels still occupied the field when his men charged into it. The New Yorkers went in with their bayonets fixed but found no Confederates. In their hasty retreat, the Rebels abandoned one of their banners, which Barlow had sent to corps headquarters as a trophy.[61]

When the New Yorkers reached the road, they were confronted with the question called out from a nearby wood, "What regiment is that?" As one shouted out "Sixty-first New York," the Confederates warned them to lay down their arms and surrender or they would be "dead men." Barlow responded in a different manner and with the command "Up and at them, men," and the New Yorkers poured in a volley. Both sides began firing at will, with neither able to distinguish the other in the fight due to the smoke of battle and the darkness of the thick woods. One soldier recalled, "The flashes of their [the enemy's] muskets were all that our men had to guide their aim," while Charles Fuller later recounted that in no other battle "did the bullets sing about my head as they did here." Although initially told through a staff officer that no reinforcements would be available to assist him, Barlow was heartened when Caldwell sent the Eighty-first Pennsylvania in relief, with the instructions that Barlow command both regiments. Barlow's horse was killed and many of his officers were wounded, but save a shift to their right to prevent a possible Confederate flanking movement, the Sixty-first maintained their position until the Rebels withdrew. Later that evening, Barlow had his wounded brought to the rear and moved his regiment back to the road. Although there was no further

---

[61] Fuller, *Personal Recollections*, 26. OR, vol. 11(2), 61, 65, 67.

action, the Federals could hear Confederates removing their wounded from the position they had earlier abandoned.[62]

When the fighting concluded, Barlow visited one of his officers whose leg had been shattered by a Confederate bullet. The officer later recalled that the Colonel "showed all the tenderness of a brother, letting me see a side of his nature that I had never known anything about before. He deplored the fact that there was no way by which he could have me carried off and kept within our lines. And so, after having me moved to the side of the road, and after my friends had come and talked with me and bade me good-bye, that splendid little regiment marched away about two o'clock in the morning, and left me to reach home, nearly dead, after about twenty-four days, by the way of Libby prison."[63]

After the battle, between forty and fifty men of the Sixty-first remained on the field with Barlow, though that number doubled when fifty men detached earlier for picket duty reunited with their comrades. At two in the morning, the New Yorkers began their withdrawal to Malvern Hill and then stacked arms and had a brief rest. With dawn, the men ate their breakfast of coffee, hard bread, and boiled salt pork or beef. In short order, the beating heat of the glaring sun grew unbearable, and several suffered sunstroke from the exposure and lack of shade. While both sides carried on an artillery duel, Captain Broady supervised the distribution of forty to sixty round of ammunition to each soldier, and the exhausted men of the Sixty-first braced themselves for yet another battle.[64]

At this point, Barlow had an encounter in which he visually made clear his feelings toward those who shirked their duty. According to Charles Fuller, one man, who was often used by the regimental officers to take care of their horses and who had a penchant for finding safe places during battle, claimed to Barlow to be sick and unfit for duty. Tired and with little tolerance for those he felt to be cowards, Barlow's "wrath broke out vehe-

---

[62] Fuller, *Personal Recollections*, 26–28, 34. OR, vol. 11(2), 65–67.

[63] Paper given at the meeting of the Maine Commandery of the Loyal Legion, Riverton, May 3, 1899, reprinted in the *Portland Daily Press*, c. May 3, 1899, quoted in Fuller, *Personal Recollection*, 35.

[64] Fuller, *Personal Recollections*, 38–39.

mently. He cursed and swore at him and called him a variety of unpleasant and detestable things and then he began to punch him with his fist wherever he could hit. Finally he partly turned him around, and gave him a hearty kick in the stern and said: "Damn you, get away from here! You're not fit to be with my brave men." As the soldier fled, Fuller recounted that in the regiment, the men "preferred to meet the rebels rather than the vocal scorn and denunciation of Barlow."[65]

The New Yorkers joined their brigade in supporting a battery on a slight rise of ground near an old house and barn. Shell fragments burst around them and wounded several. As both units had become greatly depleted since their service at Fair Oaks and subsequent engagements, the Sixty-first New York and Eighty-first Pennsylvania were consolidated under Barlow's command. When the men took up a new position nearer the buildings, Confederate shells crashed amidst them, making deafening noises and throwing splinters about in addition to the deadly shrapnel. After the Confederate artillery fire on this sector quieted, Barlow's command marched to reinforce the Federal lines at the crest of Malvern Hill, where rows of Union cannon and lines of blue-coated troops stood poised to repulse a Confederate attack.[66]

The Rebels tried in vain to storm the impregnable position, but Northern artillery fire mowed them down. Barlow had his men pour several volleys into the advancing Southerners before ordering his command to fire at will. The New Yorkers and Pennsylvanians fired so furiously that their guns became hot, and some could hold their rifles only by the sling strap. As their ammunition grew low, Barlow called out, "If the enemy make another attack, we will meet them with the cold steel." It did not come to that, as the Confederates realized the futility of their attacks, and fatigued troops on both sides fell asleep on their arms until daylight.[67]

Despite the victory at Malvern Hill, the Army of the Potomac continued its retreat to Harrison's Landing on July 2. In an oversight, the Sixty-first began marching when one of the soldiers

---

[65] Ibid., 39–40.
[66] Ibid., 40–42. OR, 11(2): 68.
[67] Fuller, *Personal Recollections*, 43–44.

remembered that the furled regimental banner remained at their camp, and he went back to retrieve it. Otherwise, however, the march passed without incident and the men reached Harrison's Landing around noon and went into camp.[68]

During the Seven Days, Barlow added to the laurels he had won at Fair Oaks, as his brigadier wrote, "I cannot fail to award the highest praise to Colonel Barlow, Sixty-first New York Volunteers. It will be remembered that this officer distinguished himself at the battle of Fair Oaks. In every engagement since he has only added to the laurels there acquired. He possesses in an eminent degree all the qualities of a good commander—intelligence, coolness, and readiness."[69]

James River
Tuesday July 2 /62

My dear Mother

We have been in two heavy artillery engagements + in two heavy Infantry fights since I last wrote. The artillery fights were yesterday + day before + the infantry night before last + last night. I am not at all hurt + am perfectly well. Night before last my horse was shot under me + a ball passed through my coat. I have lost horse saddle blanket + all. Night before last I came out of the fight with only one officer besides myself (Lt. [Willard] Keach). Capts [Eugene M.] Deming, [Dennis A.] Moore, [William H.] Spencer + [Manton C.] Angel[70] + the Adjt. [Gregory] + Lt. [Lucien B.] Cadwell were wounded + taken prisoners. The first three were shot in the legs + have had them amputated, Angel in the head (not serious), Cadwell not serious, Adjt. in arm (flesh wound not serious) Capts Broady + [Edward P.] Mount were on picket + not in the fight of night before. Capt [Edward C.] Kittle is not hurt + Lt. Keach, Capts Broady + Mount are well + unhurt. Have a <u>condensed</u> statement made as to these officers + published.

---

[68] Ibid., 45.

[69] *OR*, 11(2): 62.

[70] According to Phisterer, the correct spelling of this name should be Angell. Phisterer, *New York in the War of the Rebellion*, 3:2560.

Do not be worried about me + do not believe the reports of my being shot which you will hear. I hear it reported here that I was shot dead. The 81st Penn + my Regt are consolidated + I am in command of them.[71] Our loss in men has been heavy + we number now not to exceed 175 total officers + men at the outside.

Reinforcements are said to have arrived here + we may be able to beat the enemy back.

Send this by mail at once to Arabella + telegraph her at once that I am safe + unhurt.

Your ever loving
Francis

James River
July 4th /62 9 pm

My dear mother

I sent a letter day before yesterday which I fear has not gone + I am afraid that none got off until the one I sent this morning.

I will give you a brief account of our experience for the last few days. The news came on Saturday morning to our Camp that our right flank was turned. It is regarded here as a much more serious matter than the papers represent + it is considered generally that McClellan has been completely outwitted + that our present safety is owing more to the severe fighting of some of the Divisions than to any skill of our Generals.

On Sunday morning at 3 a.m. our Division left the entrenchments + began its retreat. The baggage + tents had been sent on the afternoon before. After marching some 2 miles + witnessing the destruction of a large quantity of stores by our rear guard the enemy apparently threatened our rear for we halted + formed in line of battle. My Regt was placed just inside of a

---

[71] Lieutenant Colonel Eli T. Connor of the Eighty-first Pennsylvania died leading his men at Malvern Hill, though the Eighty-first Pennsylvania and Sixty-first New York had already been consolidated by that point. *OR*, 11(2): 68.

wood + some quite heavy artillery firing was kept up in our rear
+ also some musketry. Here we had almost our first experience
of artillery. A shell struck in the midst of our ranks + took off
the arm of one man clean, broke the leg of another all to pieces
+ badly wounded a third. The two first we had to leave + they
could not survive. In about 4 hours all the troops in the neighborhood were hurried off together towards Savages Station further
to the rear + it <u>almost</u> amounted to a panic. My Regt. marched
in good order but some quite stampeded + we were all huddled
in together. At Savages Station we were again subjected to quite
a shelling + marched considerably about from one position to
another + finally about 11 o'clock marched by an awful road to
the rear some six miles where we got a little sleep until daybreak
where we were drawn up in line with the Irish Brigade to support
Hazzard's Battery + got one of the most violent canonadings of
the war. I lost quite a number or men + my horse was struck
just over the eye by a piece of shell which however did not much
hurt him. After lying there all day under fire without a mouthful
to eat we were withdrawn + the whole Brigade marched at
about 6 p.m. at a double quick some two miles to where the
enemy were heavily pressing up with infantry. My Regt. got separated from the rest of the Brigade in the confusion occasioned
by some of our troops firing on each other + I put myself under
the command of the first Brig. Genl. I came to—Genl Robinson
of Kearneys Division. Out troops had been firing upon the enemy
from behind some fences + parapets but Genl Robinson stopped
their fire + ordered us to charge over the parapet into the open
field. We did this (my Regt. alone) at a charge bayonets + without firing we went at a rush across the large open field. It was
quite dark + very smoky so that we could not distinctly see the
enemy in the open ground but they heard us coming + broke +
ran leaving a flag on the ground with the inscriptions Williamsburg and "Seven Pines" therein, which I captured + sent up to
Genl Sumner. On arriving at the edge of the woods on the opposite side of the field the enemy shouted from the woods "what
Regt is that" to which my men answered "61st NY." The rebels
then shouted "Throw down your arms or you are all dead men."
I gave the order to fire + we poured in a volley which they returned + a vigorous fire was kept up on both sides for a long

time when I sent for reinforcements + succeeded in getting the 81st Penn. sent down to reinforce us. They formed in front of us + fought gallantly. After firing for a long time + losing many men we were withdrawn + subsequently ordered by Genl Kearney to occupy the parapets + hold them with the bayonet (our ammunition was expended). We did so (with the 5 N.H. + 81st which was under my command as being the senior officer present) until about 12 midnight when we were withdrawn + had a horrible march of several hours, the whole army retreating. We went into this action with only about 240 men (one Company being absent on picket). + 9 officers including myself. We lost 6 officers wounded + at least [this number is smudged and illegible] men killed + wounded. Capts Moore, Deming + Spencer were all wounded in the leg + had them amputated + were later prisoners in the Hospital where they were left. The adjutant had his horse shot under him + was wounded in the arm + was taken prisoner at the Hospital. Capt. Angell + Lt. Cadwell were wounded + also taken prisoners at the Hospital + my horse was shot under me + mortally wounded but I was unhurt.

The next day after having about 2 hours sleep we were aroused + formed in line with the rest of the Division + underwent a shelling + cannon shot engagement for some hours. It was terribly hot + many of the men were sun struck lying in the open field. At about 3 p.m. the cannonading ceased + we had begun to get a little something to eat when a furious engagement of artillery + infantry broke out over on out left + we were marched off in double quick to support Couchs Division which was hotly engaged. After losing several men by shells + cannon shot we marched out in line + engaged the enemy who were lying in the edge of the woods we being in the open field. The men fought better than ever before standing in line with great coolness. Lt. Col. [Eli T.] Connor of the 81st Penn. was shot dead + the 81st lost several officers + many men here. We lost no officers but a considerable number of men. I forgot to say that on the morning of this day (Tuesday) the 81st Penn. + my Regt. were consolidated + I was put in command of both Regts. This continued through all the subsequent fights + still lasts. The enemy were very hard to silence here + continued their fire until by the exertions of Miles a piece of artillery was brought

down + some grape + cannister given them which silenced
them. We fired away all our ammunition + the guns became so
dirty that the balls could not be rammed home. Then we lay
down + prepared to hold the place by the bayonet if the enemy
charged out of the woods. It was now dark + no one remained
on the line but the 3rd Excelsior[72] ourselves (the 61st + 81st
consolidated) + a few of the 7th N.Y. of our Brigade. I heard the
enemy come out of the woods + fix their bayonets + than they
charged on us with a yell. We jumped up to give them the bayonet + the 3rd Excelsior which had a little ammunition left gave
them a volley which broke them + they ran. I went out to the
front to give our wounded some water + found the enemys
wounded mingled with them so near had they got to us in their
charge. Our batteries were stationed behind us firing over our
heads + even struck behind us which did not add to the pleasure of the occasion. At last by the exertions of Miles we were
replaced by the whole Excelsior Brigade + drawn off at 11 p.m.
+ lay down without supper. We had not had time to get asleep
when we were roused + began our retreat. I was awfully worn
out + the roads were terrible + it rained violently. I had no
horse + marched with the rest. The whole army was crowding
along the road. Most Regts wholly broken up + straggling + it
was more like a rout than a "strategic retreat." McClellan rode
along among the crowd with only one attendant + no one noticed him. I think the whole Army feels that it was left to take
care of itself + was saved only by its own brave fighting. I think
all confidence in McClellan is gone with the majority of the
Army. We reached this place about 7 a.m. I had not tasted a
mouthfull since 6 a.m. of the preceding morning + then only
had a cup of coffee + a hard biscuit. When we got here it was
raining hard + the mud was awful + we had no blankets or
tents. Mine were lost on my horse + the men had thrown theirs
away on going into the battle of Monday night in accordance with
orders. It is wonderful how I have escaped without a wound. I
had a ball through my coat which is the only mark upon me. (I

---

[72] Another designation for the Seventy-second New York infantry, serving
in the Excelsior Brigade under command of Brigadier General Daniel
Sickles.

just heard one of the men say outside as I am writing "The Col will be shot in the next fight + then every man will go for himself.") But I do not think they will fight us again. We are now in reserve for the first time since Fair Oaks. This small Regt. has fought 3 fierce infantry fights + driven + held back the enemy every time + has great reason to feel proud. We are really veterans now + the men stand shot + shell + ball with the greatest unconcern. I have here some 175 men of whom some 60 are sick—many old chronic cases. I don't know what they will do with us. The horrid part of this fighting has been that we have had to leave on the field all our wounded who could not walk away except such as we managed to carry to hospital + then left there. The officers + men generally behaved admirably. The Adjutant acted finely. His horse was killed in the shelling of Monday morning. He borrowed another which was shot under him in the fight that night. The horses of myself + Col [Charles F.] Johnson + Major [Henry Boyd] McKeen + Adjt Swain all of them 81st Penn were shot under them. The Penn loss is also heavy. We have quite got into the comforts of camp life + letters come ever more quickly than at our old Camp. I have recd some from you + E. tonight + last night.

I rode down to the River today in some expectation of seeing Arabella who writes me that she is coming on as one of the Sanitary nurses. Adams Express has an office here but they have only goods brought around from White House. I am eager for the boxes which you have sent.

Love to all. I must go to bed. Your very loving Francis.

P.S. We have heard nothing of the enemy since we came here + they have fallen back. Reinforcements are arriving daily + the enemy will never attack us here. We are fortifying.

Our total loss in the last few days is 119 killed wounded + missing—our Surgeon is taken prisoner.

July 8 /62

My dear Edward

Your letter of July 2nd with enclosures reached me day before yesterday + is the last letter I have recd from home. I have already written several letters + in the last one gave quite a long account of the late proceedings.

We are lying here still + the weather is the hottest I have ever known. One can do nothing else but be perfectly still in bed + hardly can survive that. I see considerably of Ezra Ripley.[73] He is very much disgusted with his Regt. + the service in general + last night resigned. I do not believe they will accept his resignation + it will hurt his reputation to resign at this time. Be assured that I am eagerly watching my opportunity to get out of it but it is not just now the time to do it. I have recommended Miles to be Lt. Col. + if he is appointed + there is no immediate prospect of an action I may possibly be able to get a furlough. I have only 149 men in the Regt. who are fit for duty—58 sick + 32 drummers, non combattants &c. I have 11 officers here of whom 4 are sick. If I can't resign I should like to get a position as Inspector General or something of that kind. I am thoroughly disgusted with our Generals + think we had better give up the struggle at once unless we can have a radical change. You have no idea of the imbecility of management both in action + out of it. McClellan issues flaming addresses though everyone in the army knows he was outwitted + has lost confidence in him. His statements that he lost no materials of war or ammunition are simply false. I believe that this Army properly handled could march into Richmond even now, but with our present Generals never. We are surprised to learn from the New York papers that we gained a great victory. We thought here that we had made a

---

[73] Born in 1826, Ezra Ripley graduated from Harvard College in 1846 and studied law for ten years before joining the Twenty-ninth Massachusetts Infantry as a first lieutenant in July 1861. Through much of his service he performed staff duties, acting as an aide to various commanders before rejoining his regiment just prior to the battle of Antietam. Afterward, he returned to Boston on recruiting duty before rejoining his regiment. He died with it during its service near Vicksburg, Mississippi, in July 1863. Higginson, *Harvard Memorial Biographies*, 1:107–15.

disastrous retreat leaving all our dead + wounded + prisoners + material + munitions of war in the hands of the enemy, though it is true that the <u>men</u> by hard fighting often temporarily repulsed the enemy—<u>all this is strictly private</u>.

Did I tell you that in the midst of the hottest shelling I saw Willie Storer who is on [Brigadier] Genl [Innis] Palmer's staff.[74] It was he who afterwards brought me the order to go in to the fight of Tuesday Evening. You do not tell me whether R. has got Tobin's place—has he? I am very sorry you find it so dull, but if you were here you would heartily wish yourself back in New York though I know my dear brother, how hard a life you have. Why don't you go up + see the Townsends + write to Mrs. Meagher asking if she has had any late news from the Army + perhaps they will then repeat their invitation. Ezra Ripley has just been in + is going to get a sick leave instead of resign.

No packages have yet come by Express from the Fort but I expect them up in a day or two. There is a breeze today + it is cooler. I am going down to the River to see if I can find Arabella whom I expect on one of the Sanitary Boats. When it gets a little cooler I shall ride round + see what of my friends were killed + wounded.

Your affectionate brother

By this time, Arabella had become involved in the nursing activities provided through the U.S. Sanitary Commission. On July 10, Arabella and fellow nurse Katharine Prescott Wormeley went

---

[74] First Lieutenant W. B. Storer served as an aide to Brigadier General Charles Devens. After Devens's wounding at Fair Oaks, Brigadier General Innis Palmer was assigned to lead the brigade and Storer served as his aide during the Seven Days. Innis Palmer graduated from West Point in 1846 along with George B. McClellan, Stonewall Jackson, and George Pickett. After fighting with distinction in the Mexican War, he served on the Western frontier before commanding cavalry in the First Manassas campaign and receiving his general's star to date from September 23, 1861. He fought with the Army of the Potomac during the Peninsula campaign before being assigned to various command duties in North Carolina. After the war, Palmer again served in the West before retiring to the Washington area. *OR*, 11(2): 214; 14:220. Warner, *Generals in Blue*, 357–58.

*ashore, despite having neither orders nor permission to do so.
Both women investigated the hospital at Harrison House and
Wormeley reported that although it was a temporary medical
facility and not as well provisioned as an actual city hospital,
the wounded there did have every essential care. The two remained there for three hours and wrote letters for the men, of
which Wormeley observed, "Some few told the horrors of the
march; but as a rule they were all about the families at home."*[75]

Harrison's Bar Va
July 12 /62

My dear Edward or Richard
Your letters of July 8th came together yesterday. I had just
written mother a letter to J.C. Howe to be read by you + forwarded. I wrote some days ago quite a detailed a/c of our fights
+ proceedings. I see by the Herald of the 10th that at least one
of my notes has reached you since the 8th.

Spencer I hear was hit in the side or heart besides being hit in
the leg, though I do not think it was a serious wound as he did
not mention it to me when I saw him on the field after the fight.
During the fight I saw him step back + said to him "What are

---

[75] Born in England on January 14, 1830, Katharine Prescott Wormeley
spent most of her childhood in England, where her father was a rear admiral
in the Royal Navy. She later moved to New England, and when the Civil War
broke out she put much energy into relief work for the soldiers. Wormeley
formed the Women's Union Aid Society and became an associate manager
of the New England Women's Branch of the Sanitary Commission. After
spending the winter of 1861 to 1862 organizing women to make army clothing, she nursed soldiers wounded in the Peninsula campaign. On September
1, 1862, she became superintendent of the Women's Department of a convalescent hospital for soldiers in Portsmouth Grove, Rhode Island, where she
had charge of the female nurses in addition to the laundry department and
the kitchens. Wormeley continued performing charitable works after the
war, as well as translated many eminent French literary works into English.
Katharine Prescott Wormeley to A., "Wilson Small," July 10, 1862, in Katharine Prescott Wormeley, *The Other Side of War with the Army of the Potomac: Letters from the Headquarters of the United States Sanitary
Commission during the Peninsula Campaign in Virginia in 1862* (Boston:
Ticknor & Company, 1889), 194–95. *DAB*, 10:534. Lauter, "'Once Upon a
Time in the East,'" 18.

you doing why don't you go forward with your men. He answered I am wounded (this must have been the heart wound) but he again started into the fight + after that must have recd his leg wound. He was a very noble fellow.

I will try + go to Dalton's Regt. + find out something of him.

You ask my opinion of this retreat + of affairs generally. I think McClellan + many more of our Generals are damned miserable creatures + that unless there is a radical change in the leaders, the enemy will whip us again + again. I think officers + men are disgusted with + have lost all confidence in McClellan + are disgusted with the attempts of the papers to make him out a victorious hero. I have not seen one officer or man (+ I have talked with many) who has any confidence left in him. The stories of his being everywhere among the men in the fights are all untrue. I fought in three Divisions at the most critical times + in the hardest fights + never saw him but once + then not under fire. I have found no one else who saw him. I hope McClellan will be removed. Bliss + Judge Daly have talked some of trying to get me promoted to be a Brig Genl + I think are doing or will do something towards it. When I get some recommendations I have in tow they will do something about it. This is to be mentioned to no one but our own immediate family.

I enclose copy of Caldwell's Official Report. Send it + this letter (+ all my letters) to mother. Tell her to exercise some discretion in showing the Report + the extracts from Kearney's &c. sent in my last letter.

Arabella came here some ten days ago with Mrs. [Eliza] Harris the Prest. of the Phila. Sanitary Committee.[76] She is at the large Harrison House which is used as a Hospital. It is only 5 minutes ride from here + I go down there once or twice per diem. The ladies have a very pleasant + well furnished room to themselves + it is very pleasant. I have heard of your boxes (2 of them)

---

[76] As Secretary of the Ladies' Aid Society of Philadelphia, Eliza Harris proved incredibly energetic in her quest to aid Federal soldiers during the Civil War. Shortly after First Manassas she visited the front and spent the next several months inspecting hospitals and donating goods as she received them from the society. She ministered to the wounded, often close to the front, during the Peninsula campaign, Chancellorsville, Gettysburg, and in the battles of 1864. Frank Moore, *Women of the War* (Hartford, Conn.: S. S. Scranton, 1866), 178, 181, 187, 201, 205, 212.

having got as far as a steamer in the River here though they seem to be very slow about landing them.

I am riding the Quartermasters public horse for the present which I like better than my old one. They will certainly have to draft if they expect to raise any more troops + I will make you both Lieutenants in my Regt. Why doesn't C. Miles enlist? Damn that Marshall why don't he do something else than talk about R.

Affect
FCB

On top: Don't let anyone connected with the Press see Caldwell's Report.
On side: I recd both $5's of which you speak.

Calls for Barlow's promotion began to reach the Federal high command from within the Army of the Potomac as well as from George Bliss and Judge Daly. Brigadier General John C. Caldwell recommended that Barlow receive a general's star, contending that "His gallantry, coolness, + good conduct at the Battle of Fair Oaks were the theme of general praise." Caldwell assured that in the battles of June 29, 30, and July 1, Barlow "displayed the highest qualities of a commander" and that he knew of "no more capable or efficient officer." Brigadier General William H. French similarly concurred in the praise "bestowed upon the conduct of the gallant Colonel Barlow" and believed his promotion to be only "part of the acknowledgement by the government for his devotion to its service."[77]

[77] William H. French, Headquarters French's Brigade, July 12, 1862; John C. Caldwell, Harrison's Landing, Va., July 14, 1862, in Barlow Papers NA.

Harrison's Bar Va
July 24 /62

My dear R.

Your letter has just arrived dated July 21st. I wrote you a day
or two ago + also wrote a long letter to Mother + E. I think I
have recd your various letters.

I do not know how the report got abroad that I had resigned. I
have not attempted it or even thought of it since this retreat.
They would not accept a resignation. Deny emphatically this
statement. Bliss writes under date of July 21st that he is going to
Washington in a few days to try + get me nominated a Brig Genl.
So I shall probably know soon what is to come of it. The objection
as to the number of Genls authorized to law has occurred to me.
I do not know how they get over it but I think they have over-
leaped the number in several instances + they may do it in
mine. I do not know whether it will interfere with a nomination
though it may in a confirmation. If I am nominated by the Prest.
I become a Brig Genl until I am rejected by the Senate or until
the next Session of the Senate adjourns without confirming me.
So if the Senate should not reject me I should be a Genl until
the 4th of March next when the Session will end. Then I suppose
I should not become a Col. again, but be out of the service which
would suit me exactly. I have no doubt that Congress will increase the number of Brig Genls at the next Session. If I am
nominated I think it will give me a chance to go home for a short
time.

Nothing has yet been done towards filling up the Regt.

I put [Captain Edward C.] Kittle under arrest for leaving the
field on the Evening of June 30th (when we had ceased firing it
is true, but were still under the enemies fire lying down) + not
returning again until we got here. He says he left the field after
the firing was over to show some men where Capt. Spencer was
+ that he could not find the Regt again. It may be so, though it
is not a very creditable story to him. I have not pressed the matter
but released him from arrest. Don't mention this matter. [Major
Edward] Lawrence has got a sick leave until Aug. 15th + has
written me a letter trying to explain matters. I have no faith in
him.

I am glad Edward contradicted the article in the Mercury. Who wrote it? We only see the Herald here + don't see the Sunday issue of that even. I wish you would cut out + send me all paragraphs relating to the Regt. or any of its Officers. There have been several which I have heard of but not seen.

I do nothing but write + read + eat + sleep + ride down to the Hospital once or twice per diem. If I either remain Col or am promoted don't you want to either come into the Regt. or onto my staff?

How is money making in the tin pan business

I see that D. Griffith has not yet succeeded in taking Vicksburg + that the "Arkansas" has been down after him.[78] I hope they won't drive him back to the [illegible word]

I have not heard of the circumstances to which you allude in connection with your Grandmother. I suppose a letter is on the way from mother containing them.

Write often to your aff. bro. + forward this to mother.

Love to Elvira
F.C.B.

Harrison's Bar Va
Aug. 9th 1862

My dear Mother + Edward

Your letter of Aug. 3rd reached me yesterday + I must answer them both together. The heat is so terrible that letter writing is an awful labor as is the slightest movement of mind or body. Last night I staid at the Hospital + it was without exception the hottest + vilest night I ever passed, rivaling in agonies the celebrated night at Cambridge preceding the commencement of 1855. As I lay + groaned until morning the heat was most intense + stifling + the flies musketoes + other bugs numerous + vigorous.

Yesterday Mr. Dinsmore called twice to see me. I was away

---

[78] The ironclad CSS *Arkansas* operated below Vicksburg, Mississippi, at this time. David D. Porter, *Naval History of the Civil War* (New York: Sherman Publishing Company, 1886), 260.

both times but in the evening went down to the boat to see him + had a good long talk with him. I was very glad to see him. He goes home this morning. He says yesterday was the hottest day he ever saw.

They are shipping the Reserve Artillery + there are indications that the Army is to evacuate this place. If so they will probably go up the Rhappahannock + join [Major General John] Pope.[79]

[Major] Lawrence arrived here this morning with a fine horse + all tricked out. I put him at once under arrest + shall prefer charges agt him for absence without leave.

I hear nothing from Bliss + am in the dark as to the Brig Genlship. I see that both Gov. [Edwin D.] Morgan + Noyes have lately been to Washington.[80] If Bliss got either of them to take hold of my application, they could accomplish it if anyone could. I don't know whether either of them did anything about it.

---

[79] John Pope graduated from West Point in 1841, and after performing survey duty, he fought bravely in the Mexican War. Afterward, he served in the Topographical Engineers until the Civil War, when political and family connections ensured his brigadier general's star to rank from May 17, 1861. In spring 1862, he won a series of victories that opened the upper Mississippi River almost to Memphis, Tennessee, and he earned promotion to major general. After McClellan's defeat in the Peninsula campaign, Lincoln formed a new Army of Virginia comprised of troops from the Shenandoah Valley and McDowell's corps and placed Pope in charge of it. Robert E. Lee soundly defeated Pope at Second Manassas, however, and Lincoln thereafter placed him in the Department of the Northwest, where he dealt with a Sioux uprising in Minnesota. McPherson, *Battle Cry of Freedom*, 488–89. Warner, *Generals in Blue*, 376–77.

[80] New York Governor Edwin D. Morgan's humble beginnings included working on his father's farm when the local school was not in session, as well as clerking in his uncle's grocery store in Hartford, Connecticut. At twenty he joined his uncle in the business and in 1832 was elected to the Hartford City Council, but he moved to New York in 1836 and became a prosperous grocery merchant in his own right. In 1854, Morgan became involved in banking, and in 1858–60 his E. D. Morgan & Company handled over thirty million dollars of securities issued by New York State and Saint Louis, Missouri. During this time, Morgan remained active in politics and served in the state senate before winning election as New York's Republican governor in 1858 in a four-way race. He won easy reelection in 1860, declined renomination in 1862, and in 1863 began a term representing his state in the U.S. Senate. He was defeated for reelection in 1869, but in the 1870s his name was mentioned as a possible presidential candidate. At the time of his death, Morgan's fortune was between eight and ten million dollars, some of which he donated to Williams College. *DAB*, 7:168–69.

Lawrence is not liable to be tried for desertion, for the reason that he returned to duty of his own accord. It is as E. says about men who have taken off their uniforms + have retd. to private life. I have sent to the Police to arrest those of mine when they can find + send them back here. I agree with all you say about enlisting. I would not enlist if I could help it. We shall have to acknowledge the S. Confederacy in the end.

I will now proceed to answer the questions which E. asks.

My Regt. was <u>by far</u> the smallest one in the Corps. I had only 126 officers + men all told. We were the only one within my sight before whom McClellan stopped to make enquiries. Our extreme smallness must have struck him. The Review was by Sumner not by McClellan + therefore the latter had only a small staff with him. Sumners staff also was very small. Charley Lowell was the only one of McClellans staff whom I knew by sight. You ask who compose McC's staff I know only of his father-in-law [Brigadier] Genl [Randolph] Marcy[81] who is his "Chief of Staff" or (Boss of the whole concern) + Brig. Genl. [Seth] Williams[82] his Asst. Adjt Genl. + [Charles Russell] Lowell. I know of no

---

[81] A Bay State native, Randolph Marcy graduated from West Point in 1832 and served mostly on the Michigan and Wisconsin frontier until the Mexican War. After fighting at Palo Alto and Resaca de la Palma, Marcy performed recruiting duty for the rest of the war. Afterward, he performed in various capacities in the Southwest, including participating in Albert Sidney Johnston's campaign against the Mormons in Utah and serving as paymaster in the Pacific Northwest. In 1860, his daughter married George B. McClellan, and in May 1861 Marcy became his son-in-law's chief of staff. Marcy was appointed brigadier general on September 28, 1861, but the appointment expired on March 4, 1863, because the Senate had failed to confirm his commission. From July 1863 through the end of the war, Marcy performed various duties as an inspector general, and on December 12, 1878, he was promoted to inspector general of the U.S. Army and once again wore a general's star. Warner, *Generals in Blue,* 310–11.

[82] A native of Maine, Seth Williams graduated from West Point in 1847, served as an aide during the Mexican War, and was adjutant at the Military Academy from 1850 to 1853. He received promotion to the rank of major in August 1861 and the following month became a brigadier general. From then until March 1864, Williams served as adjutant general of the Army of the Potomac for its successive commanders, until Ulysses S. Grant appointed him inspector general for the army. Williams served in that capacity through the rest of the war and died in 1866. Warner, *Generals in Blue,* 562–63.

other by name even.[83] All I hear + see more + more convinces me that McClellan has little military genius + that he is not a proper man to command this Army. I think the Division Genls + about everybody else here have lost confidence in him. I think someone might do better though I can't say whom. I do not believe that we have more than 50000 effective men now here present for duty—and how much artillery I haven't the least idea. I have once or twice had a very slight looseness of the bowels, but it has never lasted more than a hew hours + I have never had anything like dysentery. I shall certainly get away from here the first moment I can, whether I am sick or well. We have dug deep wells which give us tolerably good water though when we cannot get ice it is very warm. Generally our Hospital gets a large cake of ice per diem which gives all the Officers a bit but in the usual manner of doing business in this region they usually wait until the supply is exhausted before getting up any more. So all the Hospitals have been for a few days past wholly without ice. Whether an officer gets leave to go home depends on the Commander of the Army Corps. Sumner is resolute in refusing leave except in cases of sickness. It is very sad to see my Regt. so much reduced. Almost every officer who started with us is gone. I miss them sadly—See Capts. Spencer + Moore if you can. Both have lost a leg. I don't think it very strange that McClellan should not remember the losses of individual Regts. in this large Army—Napoleon would have done it but not an ordinary Genl. as ours are. McClellan came down to see the Hospital the other day + came up in A's room. He said to me "Colonel I saw one of your wounded men the other day just released on the boat + he sent word to you that he was feeling better + many kind messages." It shows that McC. has a pretty good memory to remember this. I hear very little of what goes on in the Army. I go about very little + so hear but little news. Have you seen Meagher in New York.

My dear Mother makes certain enquiries which I now proceed

---

[83] Among other members of McClellan's staff were Albert Colburn, Nelson Sweitzer, Edward Hudson, Edward Wright, Paul von Radowitz, Herbert Hammerstein, and George Armstrong Custer. Sears, *George B. McClellan*, 237.

to answer. My course of life is as follows. I get up to Reveille at
4:30 a.m. + generally take a nap before breakfast which is about
6 a.m. We have for breakfast tea or coffee, toasted bread, butter
(melted like oil when we have no ice) steak, chow chow, pickles
+ vegetables when we can get them. About 7 a.m. we get the
mail + then I answer letters. I have a great many from the rela-
tives of the men enquiring about them. I have also various orders
to make + Regimental business to attend to which I do at this
time + which takes me an hour or two. After this I take off everything but my shirt + drawers + socks + lie down + finish reading the papers which came the night before. Sometimes I play a
game of poker at this hour with my friend Miles. Between 10 +
11 I generally ride down to see A. which is about 5 minutes ride.
I come back between 12 + 1 + then we have dinner which is
very much like breakfast except that we some time get a bottle of
ale. I have got a good oven fixed up + bake fresh bread daily for
the Regt. + we also have it for ourselves. After dinner I read
sleep or play poker until 6 p.m. when there is a Company +
Regimental drill which I attend. In the evening I generally go
down to the Hospital + see A. I often go there to tea about 7
p.m. The N.Y. papers of the day before came. We always get the
Herald, sometimes the Times + rarely the Tribune. This is our
life one day after another. <u>Very rarely</u> I take a ride to some other
Camp or out to the front. We are pretty well off on the food question.

> Love to the whole world
> From your Loving Francis

Send stamps to him.

*At noon on August 16, the New Yorkers broke camp and began
marching down the Peninsula en route to transport vessels returning McClellan's army back to northern Virginia. On the first
day of the retreat, the Sixty-first marched only four miles before
the men happily halted near a cornfield. Despite orders not to
forage, the men eagerly harvested some of the corn and roasted*

it for an enjoyable meal. The next day, they made twelve miles, passing Charles City Court House and crossing the Chickahominy River over a long pontoon bridge near the junction of the Chickahominy and James Rivers. Charles Fuller recalled that he grew concerned that the thick dust on this march might cause lasting damage to his lungs and that the soldiers' nostrils became so clogged with the dry soil that they occasionally could "fire [slugs of dust] out of their noses almost as forcibly as a boy snaps a marble from his fingers."[84]

On August 19, the Sixty-first marched through Williamsburg and the next day reached Yorktown and settled onto the same campground that it had used several months earlier. On August 21, the New Yorkers made a march of twenty miles despite an oppressive heat, and that evening they received a ration of rough, raw whiskey, the first to be had since the aftermath of Fair Oaks. The next day, the men marched in a pouring rain before the sun appeared and dried them out, reaching Newport News and their transport ship.[85]

The New Yorkers boarded a steamer that brought them to the Potomac River, and by 2 p.m. on August 27, they went ashore at Aquia Creek. Marching several miles inland, they made camp before their orders were countermanded, and at 10 p.m. the Sixty-first marched back and reboarded the steamer for further transport. The regiment went ashore for the second time at Alexandria, where the men set up camp on their old winter quarter grounds.[86]

Mrs Richards
Aug. 28th 1862
10 a.m.

My very dear Mother + brothers,

We are again encamped on our old ground. We got off from Newport News on Monday night + reached Acquia Creek the

---

[84] Fuller, *Personal Recollections*, 48–49.
[85] Ibid., 49–50.
[86] Ibid., 51.

next night. We disembarked yesterday morning + marched 3 miles on our way to Fredericksburg. Having got pretty well tired we learned that an order had been sent four hours before directing us to reembark + proceed to Alexandria. Through the usual stupidity of the officials it had not reached us. We got aboard the boat + reached here this morning + our Brigade is now encamped on our old parade ground. I am writing from Mrs. Richards where I came at once. I had a pair of new boots on yesterday + the marching which we had to do (as our horses had not landed) made my feet ache terribly. I am sitting here with a pair of Mr. Richards loose slippers. Things look very dark here. Yesterday morning early the New Jersey Brigade started out to join Pope + when they reached Manassas they found the enemy there + were opened upon severely + driven back with loss. The remains of the Brigade came in this morning all broken up. [Brigadier] Genl [George W.] Taylor has his knee shattered + will lose his leg.[87] ["Stonewall"] Jackson with some 20000 men is at Manassas + they have advanced to Fairfax Ct. House some 11 miles from here. Our troops are retreating in from there. I think Jackson has broken through our lines + cut off Pope whose subsistence + communications are endangered. How he will get out I don't know. Col. Collet heard firing yesterday afternoon + the direction of Pope + some part of his forces must have been engaged. I do not think the enemy will attack Washington on this side as it is very strong. They will probably try to

---

[87] Barlow refers to Brigadier General George W. Taylor and his brigade, composed entirely of New Jersey regiments. Taylor entered the navy as a midshipman in 1827, resigned in 1831 to become a New Jersey farmer, and returned to service to fight as an officer in the Mexican War. After spending three years in California, he returned to New Jersey and became involved in iron manufacturing, but with the Civil War, Taylor once again took up the military life. He became colonel of the Third New Jersey Infantry assigned to Philip Kearny's New Jersey Brigade, and when Kearny received command of a division, Taylor assumed that of the brigade. After leading the brigade well during the Seven Days, Taylor and his men were sent by train to Manassas Junction on June 27 in response to reports that "Stonewall" Jackson was operating in the vicinity. The brigade deployed, unsupported and without a single fieldpiece, and was routed by Jackson's Confederates already in position. Taylor was mortally wounded and over two hundred of his men, one-sixth of his force, were taken prisoner. John J. Hennessy, *Return to Bull Run: The Campaign and Battle of Second Manassas* (New York: Simon and Schuster, 1993), 126–27. Warner, *Generals in Blue*, 493–94.

cross into Maryland + take W. on that side. We shall probably remain here for the present to defend the City. What is to be done I don't know. People seem dispirited + I don't wonder at it. I have not heard a word from any of you since R's letter of Aug. 21st. I hope to get a mail soon.

> Your loving son + brother
> Francis C. B.

At 6 in the evening of August 29, the Sixty-first relocated to Arlington and remained there until orders came the next afternoon for the men to march. Major General John Pope's Army of Virginia engaged Lee's army at Manassas, and elements of the Army of the Potomac rushed to his support. The Sixty-first saw no action in this Federal defeat, however.[88]

On September 3, the New Yorkers crossed the Chain Bridge and marched to Tenallytown, Maryland, where they rested until September 5. During this pause, the men were reunited with their tents, knapsacks, and other gear left behind in the rush of the last few days, and pie vendors who came out from Washington ensured that they ate well. On September 5, the regiment marched to Rockville, Maryland, where it remained for several days. Meanwhile, on September 4, Lee had begun his invasion of Maryland with a depleted but battle-hardened force coming off of back-to-back victories in the Peninsula campaign and Second Manassas.[89]

During the pause on September 4, Howard weighed in to offer his recommendation for Barlow's promotion, writing of his friend's "unusual coolness under fire" and skills as a "most excellent disciplinarian + tactician." Howard suggested that if "nine months volunteers are to be brigaded under officers of merit and experience I would particularly call the attention of the War Department to this worthy man."[90]

---

[88] Fuller, *Personal Recollections*, 51.

[89] Ibid., 52–53. McPherson, *Battle Cry of Freedom*, 535.

[90] O. O. Howard to the Secretary of War, Tenallytown, September 4, 1862, in Barlow Papers NA.

In Camp near Rockville Md.
Sept. 6th 1862

My very dear Mother + brothers

We have been so marched + countermarched for the last 10 days that we have had no mails + I have been unable to write to you. The last letter I have recd from home is Edwards of the first of this week.

We reached Tenallytown some 6 miles from Washington on Wednesday + I at once set about finding a place for mother + E. to come on, as it was expected that we would stay there some time to refit, if the enemy let us alone. I found a pleasant place close to our Camp where the food was good + the people + place pleasant + I wrote at once for you to come on. On Thursday I went over to Washington to get a few necessary articles. I saw no one there but the Smiths who told me that A. had arrived the day before in company with another lady + gone to Alexandria in search of me. On reaching Camp that night I found A. who had followed me from Alexandria. Miss Hall, one of the Volunteer Nurses was with her. On Friday much to my regret we were ordered to march + now have got some 12 miles from Tenallytown. I had A. telegraph for mother not to come but for Edward to come on as he can follow us about in the field. I hope to see him in a day or two. My great regret is that Mother cannot come with him. However Winter Quarters must come in a few months + then I shall be stationary + can see you all. Sumner + Sedgwicks Corps are here together. The Enemy are reported to have crossed the River with 30000 men + to be at Poolesville [Maryland] in our front. We are lying here in a strong position in case they advance on us. I don't think they will, but that they will turn our right flank unless indeed this be a mere diversion to draw us off while they attack Washington on the Alexandria side.

The affairs of the Country look melancholy enough. It is not worthwhile to make any predictions but I think there is no prospect or hope of success in this war. The Govt. is too rascally + corrupt besides being imbecile. I am in a state of chronic disgust.

I lost Barker just before our retreat from Centreville + have not heard from him since. I think he escaped. I bought a horse at our last Camp for $150 + drew on E. for his price. She is a mare, rather small but admirably built + full of life. She has very good blood in her + is very fast. She is highly thought of by all who have seen her.

I left A. at Tenallytown. She may try to come out to Rockville to see me but will fail of it if she does as we are 2 miles from town + shall probably march tomorrow. Do not be alarmed at not hearing from me as we have had no mails.

I hope to receive news of you very soon + to see E. here.

I am your very loving Son
Francis

The Sixty-first moved out of Rockville on September 9 and reached Clarksville, Maryland, by the eleventh. On the thirteenth, the regiment joined its corps in passing through Frederick, Maryland, where music played, flags and bunting lined the streets, and women smiled and waved handkerchiefs as the bluecoats marched to their camp outside town. While halted on the crest of nearby hills, the men watched a panoramic view of the battle of South Mountain. The tiny Sixty-first New York, bled dry during the Peninsula campaign, numbered but 105 soldiers, in addition to its officers.[91]

Around this time, another letter arrived in Washington to support Barlow's promotion. Writing directly to President Lincoln, New York's Governor Edwin D. Morgan summarized Barlow's career and military qualities:

> *Colonel Francis C. Barlow of the 61st N.Y. Cols. was, on the breaking out of the rebellion, conducting a prosperous law business in the city of New York. He abandoned it and entered the military service in the 12th Regiment N.Y. Militia, where he remained until the Regiment returned from its three months service. He enlisted as a private soldier and held no higher rank in the twelfth than that of a Lieutenant.*
>
> *When the call for additional volunteers came, he entered for the*

---

[91] Fuller, *Personal Recollections*, 53–56. Pride and Travis, *My Brave Boys,* 122.

*War in the 61st N.Y. Cols., and has nobly discharged every duty
as Lieut. Colonel and Colonel of that Regiment, firmly establishing
himself in the confidence of all who knew him. I have seen the
testimonials of several of the general officers as contained in their
reports of battles and in letters to your Excellency recommending
his appointment as Brig. General. I have no hesitation in saying
that they are conclusive as to Colonel Barlows military capacity
and bravery.*

*That justice may, as far as possible, be done to those in the
service, who <u>really earn</u> promotion, I take the liberty of recommending Colonel Francis C. Barlow as one entitled to receive an
appointment as Brigadier General.*[92]

On the fourteenth, the Sixty-first climbed South Mountain in
a battle line but faced no Rebel opposition, though the sight of
several field hospitals, with piles of amputated legs and arms
lying about, demoralized the men. The New Yorkers later de-
scended the mountain to pass through Boonsboro. The regiment,
along with the rest of Sumner's corps, reached Keedysville on the
evening of September 16.[93]

September 17 dawned with a haze, and few of the Sixty-first
suspected that the day would become the bloodiest one in American history. Shortly after seven in the morning, Sumner received
orders to support Major General Joseph Hooker's First corps near
Sharpsburg, and he quickly had his men on the march with
Sedgwick's division in the lead, followed by French's and finally
Richardson's. Barlow's New Yorkers heard bellowing cannon as
Hooker led an attack on the Confederate left, while Barlow took
command of the Sixty-fourth New York in addition to his own
small unit. Richardson's division held in reserve near McClellan's headquarters while McClellan ordered the other two Second
corps divisions, those of Sedgwick and French, across Antietam
creek to join the fight. At 9:30 Richardson received orders to also
move forward, and shortly afterward the Sixty-first forded the
thigh-deep Antietam creek with the rest of the division. The men
paused momentarily to wring the water from their drenched

---

[92] E. D. Morgan to Abraham Lincoln, Albany, N.Y., September 12, 1862,
in Barlow Papers NA.
[93] Fuller, *Personal Recollections*, 56–57. OR, 19(1): 275.

socks before reaching a field in which bullets flew. The regiment formed in battle line when suddenly, out of a large, leafy tree in the foreground, a sniper put a bullet into the head of Capt. Angell, instantly killing him. Barlow immediately called for several of his better shots to take care of the Confederate marksmen, and in short order two Southerners fell from the tree.[94]

Sumner's Second Corps attacked the Confederate center defended by Major General Daniel H. Hill's division. Hill's 2,500 Southerners deployed in the Sunken Road, where generations of farmers had driven their wagons to a nearby mill and eroded the surface to several feet below ground level, creating a natural entrenchment. The tempestuous William H. French, who earned the sobriquet "Old Blinky" for the way he frenziedly fluttered his eyes when he talked, commanded 5,700 men, though only three of his regiments had prior combat experience. French led his division forward into a maelstrom, and the Rebels blasted away at his brigades. The frontal attack cost French's command 1,750 casualties, the second highest Federal division loss following Sedgwick's, engaged on French's right. The Confederate center remained intact.[95]

By 10:30 in the morning, the Sunken Road had been transformed into Bloody Lane, and when Richardson's division came into the sector they passed crimson wounded and haggard stragglers from French's division making their way in the opposite direction. On the Confederate side, Major General Richard Anderson's division reinforced the Southern center. Richardson's men deployed on French's left, with Caldwell's brigade on the left, Meagher's on the right, and Colonel John R. Brooke's in the rear. Ordered forward, Meagher led the Irish Brigade in a charge against George Anderson's North Carolinian brigade, being commanded by Col. R. J. Bennett after Anderson's mortal wounding. Meagher called, "Boys, raise the colors and follow me!" but as the green banner swept forward, scores of Irish American troops fell dead and wounded, meeting with as little success as French's troops had.[96]

---

[94] Fuller, *Personal Recollections*, 58. Stephen W. Sears, *Landscape Turned Red: The Battle of Antietam* (New York: Ticknor & Fields, 1983), 218. Pride and Travis, *My Brave Boys*, 130. OR, 19(1): 275, 277.

[95] Sears, *Landscape Turned Red*, 236–38, 240.

[96] Ibid., 240, 243. Pride and Travis, *My Brave Boys*, 131.

As it grew close to noon, however, continued Federal pressure
began to fray the Southern lines. Caldwell's brigade, on the Irish
Brigade's left, stood ready to outflank the Sunken Road position.
Barlow's New Yorkers held the right of Caldwell's brigade, and
Meagher called to him, "Colonel! For God's sake come and help
me," but Barlow waited until he received orders to advance. Call-
ing "Where's General Caldwell?" Richardson passed through the
sector on foot with sword drawn. When he could not find his
subordinate, he roared, "God damn the field officers" and or-
dered the brigade in at the double-quick to relieve Meagher's
Irishmen. Barlow stood at the head of his command and led it
into battle with his sword drawn and, having observed the heavy
fire endured by the Irishmen in attacking the Sunken Road head-
on, sidled his joint command to the left and took the Confederate
position in its flank. The New Yorkers poured in a vigorous fire
until several white flags appeared, and Barlow's men advanced
to capture three hundred North Carolinians and two battle flags
as the Confederate center began to disintegrate. They also found
a mass of dead and wounded in the Bloody Lane, and they tried
to make the Confederate wounded as comfortable as possible. The
Southern center had held for hours, but at the right moment, at
the right point, Barlow aggressively pushed his men forward and
shattered the gray line.[97]

Daniel H. Hill rallied a small group of scattered infantry from
various regiments, numbering at most a couple hundred and
personally led a counterattack on the Federal left flank. Colonel
Cross swung his Fifth New Hampshire regiment to parry their
blow, and Barlow swiftly wheeled his New Yorkers at a right
angle to their previous position. They advanced and fired on the
Southerners, and though Hill's attack had no chance to push
back the Federal brigades, it did succeed in halting their advance
and bought a small amount of time. Soon, twenty Rebel artillery
pieces fired canister and shell into the Federal line and in the
midst of this maelstrom, Barlow suffered a painful wound in the
left groin from spherical case shot. He left the regiment in the
hands of his Lieutenant Colonel, Nelson A. Miles.[98]

---

[97] Fuller, *Personal Recollections*, 58–59, 72. Sears, *Landscape Turned Red*, 244–47. OR, 19(1): 277, 285, 289.

[98] Fuller, *Personal Recollections*, 60. Sears, *Landscape Turned Red*, 251–52, 290. Welsh, *Medical Histories of Union Generals*, 15.

By this point, the Confederates had suffered 2,600 casualties defending the Sunken Road, and all semblance of unit cohesion or organization had dissolved. Richardson's attack had stalled, however, and as cannon fire mounted casualties among his men, the division commander pulled his unit back to the shelter of a nearby ridgeline at a little before 1:00 in the afternoon. Richardson intended to regroup before renewing the operation to crack the Southern center. At that moment, Richardson received a shrapnel wound that resulted in his death six weeks later, and the threat of further attack against the Bloody Lane ended. By the barest of margins, Lee's center had held.[99]

The next day, both armies remained in their lines, exhausted from the exertions and carnage of the battle. The Sixty-first lost about a third of its men at Antietam, and Barlow found himself recuperating in a hospital. On September 18, General in Chief Henry W. Halleck recommended Barlow's promotion to Brigadier General; although the recommendation was for Barlow's "distinguished conduct at the battle of Fair Oaks," perhaps word of Barlow's wounding had reached Washington that quickly and helped confirm Halleck's decision.[100]

Meanwhile, Barlow's friend Ezra Ripley feared that the colonel had died and wrote a moving letter:

Right here I must speak of Colonel Barlow. Noble fellow! He is dead now, and his name is in everybody's mouth. When our brigade passed Caldwell's brigade, to which Barlow belonged, just at the ford, he was sitting on his horse at the head of his regiment, waiting to go into the fight. He had on an old linen coat and an old hat. We exchanged pleasant greetings with each other (my last with him); and when he came up leading the way to our relief, it seemed to shine with newness,—pants inside high-topped boots, an army hat, and yellow regulation gloves. It seemed as if a new suit must have dropped on him from the skies. And then he rushed up the hill at the head of his little regiment, looking so handsome, facing his men to cheer them, moving with such grace and elasticity, that it seemed as if he were dancing with delight. I have seen brave men and brave officers; I saw that day colonels coolly and

[99] Sears, *Landscape Turned Red*, 252–54.
[100] H. W. Halleck's recommendation, dated September 18, 1862, in Barlow Papers NA. Fuller, *Personal Recollections*, 63.

bravely lead on their regiments; but I never saw such a sight as Barlow's advance, and never expect to again. It was a picture,—it was poetry. The whole regiment gazed with admiration on him. I wish I could do justice to the brave fellow. His praise is now in every man's mouth. He chased the enemy from the ground, and drove them almost a mile,—he and two other regiments following him,—and then died as a soldier should. His loss affected me more than anything else that has happened here. I admired him, and enjoyed his society.[101]

Barlow's wound was treated with simple water dressings and, though he received no medication, Arabella tended to his needs through his entire recovery. She arrived just in time to see Barlow brought to a hospital where a doctor pronounced his wound to be mortal, though the colonel survived and was moved the following day to Keedysville, Maryland. In the course of surveying the gore of the late combat, New York diarist and Sanitary Commission member George Templeton Strong spotted Arabella among "the crowd of ambulances, army wagons, beef-cattle, staff officers, recruits, kicking mules," looking well despite the chaos about her. Strong recounted that she appeared "serene and self-possessed as if walking down Broadway" and spoke "like a sensible, practical, earnest, warm-hearted woman[.]"[102]

Keeterville Maryland[103]
A few miles from Frederick
Sep 18th 1862[104]

Dearest Mother

A battle took place here yesterday in which I was wounded in the groin by a peice of shell which made an ugly looking wound

[101] Ezra Ripley, September 21, 1862, reprinted in Higginson, *Harvard Memorial Biographies,* 1:110–12.

[102] Strong diary entry, September 24, 1862, in Nevins, *Diary of the Civil War,* 261. Welsh, *Medical Histories of Union Generals,* 15.

[103] Barlow was at the hospital at Keedysville, Maryland, at this time. *OR,* 19(1): 289.

[104] The wounded Barlow dictated this letter, and there are a number of spelling and punctuation errors that he likely would not have made.

but not a serious one. it will be painful and a long time in healing but does not endanger life or limb. I am at Sedgwick division Hospital where am carefully attended to by Rev Mr Sloane and Mrs Lee who were at Harrisons Landing with Arabella. I expect A here to day. they will doubtless send me home very soon if not I shall get a room here and you shall come out. don't try to come now for the difficulties are insurmountable of transportation and you will properly [probably] pass me on the road. the Regiment fought splendidly and lost largely. Seven of us Officers where in the fight of whom one (Capt. Angle) was killed and three wounded. Miles behaved splendidly and is unhurt. fighting will properly be renewed to day or tomorrow. Bramans son is killed. the 64 N.Y. was also under my command and fought bravely. the 61st took two colors and the 64th one. Wren writes this letter as it pains me to sit up. I will write more in a day or two if I dont come home. dont be alarmed about me as I am all right except a little pain.

Your very loving Son
Francis C. B.

We drove the enemy back at every point whipping them thoroughly. there loss is very large.

On September 20, Barlow applied for a forty-day leave of absence on account of his wound, though Richardson's replacement, Brigadier General Winfield S. Hancock, only approved a fortnight's recuperation.[105]

Shortly, news arrived that undoubtedly buoyed Barlow's spirits: his nomination for a general's star. Sergeant Isaac Plumb of the Sixty-first New York hand-delivered the message to Barlow, recuperating at Samuel Deaner's house. Arabella then procured groceries and made a celebratory dinner, and the Barlows in-

---

[105] · Much of Barlow's service was inextricably linked with that of Winfield S. Hancock's. Born in 1824, Hancock graduated from West Point in the class of 1844 and fought in Mexico as well as against Seminoles and against Mormons in Utah. Serving as quartermaster in Los Angeles when the Civil War

vited the bearer of such good news to dine with them, Plumb greatly enjoying this alternative to army rations. On October 4, Barlow wrote to Adjutant General Lorenzo Thomas to accept the appointment and enclosed his signed oath. That same day, however, Barlow had to inform Brigadier General Seth Williams, Adjutant General of the Army of the Potomac, that his wound still troubled him and that he would not be able to report for duty at the end of his twenty-day leave. Although the promotion was subject to Senate confirmation, Barlow no doubt felt a sense of accomplishment. He had proven himself in battle, received a wound in service of his country, and accepted the reward of a general's commission.[106]

Barlow was further pleased when, in early November, the War Department appointed his brother, Captain Edward E. Barlow, to serve as adjutant on his brigade staff. Barlow still wanted to

---

erupted, Hancock came east, where he was appointed brigadier general to date from September 23, 1861. The following spring, Hancock led his brigade admirably in the Peninsula campaign and assumed command of Israel Richardson's division when that officer suffered his mortal wound at Antietam. After receiving his second star, Hancock fought well at Fredericksburg and Chancellorsville, and he took command of the Second corps in time for Gettysburg. There, he performed admirable service on all three days of the battle and received a painful wound while repulsing Pickett's Charge on July 3. After recuperating, Hancock resumed command of the corps and led it through the Wilderness, Spotsylvania, Cold Harbor, and other engagements leading to the siege of Petersburg, though a reopening of his wound led him to relinquish corps command. After the war, Hancock ran for president as a Democrat against James A. Garfield in the 1880 election and narrowly lost. He died in 1886 while commanding the Department of the East, after a long career in which he had earned his sobriquet "Hancock the Superb." Francis C. Barlow to Captain George C. Caldwell, Keetersville, Md., September 20, 1862, in Francis C. Barlow File, Field and Staff Officers Papers, Sixty-first New York Volunteer Infantry, National Archives, Washington, D.C. (hereafter cited as Barlow Field and Staff Officers Papers NA; also cited in this book are Francis C. Barlow papers, M-1064 microfilm roll 241 [Barlow Papers NA] and Francis C. Barlow's Generals Papers, RG 94-9W4/6/10/A, Box 2 [Barlow's Generals Papers NA].). Warner, *Generals in Blue*, 202–4.

[106] Thomas M. Vincent, Assistant Adjutant General to Lieutenant Colonel L. V. D. Reeve, Washington, D.C., October 15, 1862, in Barlow Field and Staff Officers Papers NA. Francis Barlow to Lorenzo Thomas, Keedysville, Md., October 4, 1862; Francis Barlow to Seth Williams, Keedysville, Md., October 4, 1862, both in Barlow Papers NA. Lauter, "'Once upon a Time in the East,'" 19.

know, however, if he had the authority to nominate his commissary and quartermaster.[107]

By early October, Francis and Arabella were in New York City. On October 10, Barlow wrote to Thomas asking if he needed to be mustered out of service as Colonel of the Sixty-first New York and, if so, whom he should report to in order to do so. Thomas quickly responded that Barlow should report to Lieutenant Colonel Reeve in New York City in order to muster out to date to October 3, the day prior to Barlow's acceptance of his general's commission.[108] It appears that Barlow did not do so, however, and he wrote to Thomas again in mid-January, this time from Brookline, Massachusetts, to ask authority for Captain Collins in Boston to muster him out of service as colonel of the Sixty-first. Collins doubted his authority to muster out an officer who served in a New York regiment, and he also wanted to know if he could muster in a brigadier general or if this was even necessary. Thomas's response served as Collins's authority to muster Barlow out of service as commander of the Sixty-first to date from October 3, 1862.[109]

Barlow's wound healed slowly, and on October 10 he obtained a surgeon's certificate extending his leave for another thirty days, with similar extensions on November 11 and December 12. Further complicating his recuperation, Barlow developed an abscess on his back, no doubt a result of having to remain lying on a stretcher. On October 22, Judge Daly and his wife visited the Barlows, with Francis still lying prostrate from his wound. During their conversation, Barlow expressed his lack of confidence in McClellan and lauded the bravery and endurance that the Confederates, emaciated but courageous,

---

[107] Francis Barlow to Brigadier General Lorenzo Thomas, New York, November 28, 1862; Francis Barlow to Brigadier General Lorenzo Thomas, Boston, January 1, 1863, both in Barlow Papers NA.

[108] Francis Barlow to Brigadier General Lorenzo Thomas, New York City, October 10, 1862; Brigadier General Lorenzo Thomas to Lieutenant Colonel Reeve, October 15, 1862; Brigadier General Lorenzo Thomas to Francis Barlow, October 15, 1862, all in Barlow Papers NA.

[109] Francis Barlow to Brigadier General Lorenzo Thomas, Brookline, Mass., January 14, 1863; Lorenzo Thomas to Francis Barlow, A. G. Office, January 20, 1863, both in Barlow Papers NA.

displayed in combat. Meanwhile, when Ralph Waldo Emerson learned of Barlow's wounding, he penned a letter to the general's mother expressing his concern and hopes for a quick recovery. By early December, Barlow continued his recuperation in Boston.[110]

[110] Certificate dated October 10, 1862, in Barlow's Generals Papers NA. Francis Barlow to Lorenzo Thomas, New York, N.Y., November 14, 1862; certificate dated December 12, 1862, Barlow Papers NA. Welsh, *Medical Histories of Union Generals,* 15. Maria L. Daly diary entry, October 23, 1862, in Hammond, *Diary of a Union Lady,* 190. Ralph W. Emerson to Almira P. Barlow, Concord, Mass., December 3, 1862, in Rusk and Tilton, *Letters of Ralph Waldo Emerson,* 5:298–99.

Major General Oliver Otis Howard, Barlow's friend and often his superior during the first half of the war. (Library of Congress)

Confederate dead in Bloody Lane at Antietam, near where Barlow's regiment charged. View is looking northeast. (Library of Congress)

Isaac Plumb of the Sixty-first New York, who told the wounded Barlow of his promotion to general after the battle of Antietam. (United States Military History Institute, Carlisle, Pennsylvania)

Confederate dead in Bloody Lane at Antietam on September 19, 1862. (Military Order of the Loyal Legion of the United States, Massachusetts)

Charles A. Fuller, regimental historian of the Sixty-first New York. (United States Military History Institute, Carlisle, Pennsylvania)

Carl Schurz, temporary commander of the Eleventh corps on the first day of Gettysburg. (Library of Congress)

Adelbert Ames, an
excellent young officer
who commanded a
brigade under Barlow
at Gettysburg.
(Library of Congress)

Colonel Leopold von
Gilsa, Barlow's fiery
Prussian brigade
commander at Gettys-
burg. (Archive of the
Military Order of the
Loyal Legion of the
United States at the
United States Military
History Institute,
Carlisle, Pennsylvania)

John B. Gordon, whose brigade shattered Barlow's division on the first day of Gettysburg. (From John B. Gordon, *Reminiscences of the Civil War*)

Major General Winfield S. Hancock, commander of the Second corps on the road to Richmond in 1864. (Library of Congress)

Major General Winfield Scott Hancock (seated) and his division commanders; from left to right, Francis C. Barlow, David B. Birney, and John Gibbon. (National Archives)

Major General Winfield Scott Hancock surrounded by his staff. Barlow is leaning on the tree near the middle. (National Archives)

Nelson A. Miles, Barlow's friend and subordinate, as a major general. (Library of Congress)

Barlow's monument at Gettysburg. (From *In Memoriam: Francis Channing Barlow, 1834–1896*)

3

1863: "I did not expect to get out alive"

Barlow spent the entire winter of 1862–63 recuperating, and on January 12, February 13, and March 13, 1863, he submitted additional doctor's certificates extending his leave of absence so that his Antietam wound and an abscess on his right pectoral could heal. During Barlow's absence from active service, the Army of the Potomac underwent several changes in leadership: Lincoln first replaced McClellan with Major General Ambrose E. Burnside, and, following that officer's debacles at Fredericksburg and the subsequent Mud March, Major General Joseph Hooker received command.[1]

Meanwhile, when it seemed that the Senate had declined to confirm Barlow's nomination to brigadier general, several of Boston's elite immediately rallied into action. On February 14, Charles Russell Lowell Jr. wrote John M. Forbes to recount Barlow's bravery and wounding at Antietam. Several days later, Charles H. Dalton wrote Forbes with the suggestion that the powerful senator from Massachusetts, Charles Sumner, be informed of the situation and ensure that justice be done to Barlow. Forbes immediately wrote Sumner to praise Barlow's gallantry and talent thus far in his military career and asked his intervention. Furthermore, Forbes depicted Barlow as "a man who saw the need" of "carrying on the war <u>without</u> gloves" and whose desire for vigorous action in prosecuting the war indicated that he was a "<u>right thinking</u> military man." Several days later, Sumner forwarded these "excellent letters in favor of Col. Barlow" for consideration with his endorsement.[2]

---

[1] Medical certificates dated January 12, February 13, March 13, 1863, in Barlow Papers NA.

[2] Charles Russell Lowell Jr. to J. M. Forbes, February 14, 1863; Charles H. Dalton to J. M. Forbes, Boston, February 18, 1863; J. M. Forbes to Charles

Ralph Waldo Emerson also took it upon himself to urge Barlow's promotion to Major General Ethan Allen Hitchcock, who provided special services directly for the secretary of war. In a letter signed by some of Boston's most prominent members of the Saturday Club—author Nathaniel Hawthorne, Oliver Wendell Holmes, Charles Eliot Norton, John Russell Lowell, John Murray Forbes, future Attorney General Ebenezer Rockwood Hoar, Samuel G. Ward (Julia Ward Howe's brother), Horace Gray Jr., literary critic Edwin Percy Whipple, Estes Howe, Charles R. Lowell Jr., and Dr. Samuel Gridley Howe—Emerson wrote:

> *I learn with great regret that the name of Brigadier General Barlow of New York originally nominated by the President, after the battle of Antietam, is not returned in the list newly sent to the Senate for confirmation. This omission is deeply lamented by many good persons here to whom General Barlow is known. A man of great natural ability,—from a boy, first among his mates; at Harvard College, first in his class; and in the army, which he entered as a private, so strong was the impression of personal power he made, that he rapidly became Brigadier General,—we have looked on him as one of those valuable officers which the war was creating. I earnestly hope, & I am sure I speak the thought of many informed persons, that his name may yet be brought so prominently before the President, that his service & genius may be secured to the country. His wounds at Antietam, which are slowly healing, & in spite of which the surgeons promise early return to duty, ought to plead strongly in the same interest.*

Hitchcock returned the letter to Barlow with the comment that he should save it due to the signatures of its eminent endorsers.[3]

Sumner, Boston, February 19, 1863; endorsement of Charles Sumner, February 21, 1863, all in Barlow Papers NA.

[3] Formed in the mid-1850s, the Saturday Club was an exclusive Boston Brahmin group. It numbered sixteen members by 1857, fourteen of these Harvard graduates or professors, and in the next seven years, eleven of fifteen additional members were from Harvard; one, Nathaniel Hawthorne, was an alumnus of Bowdoin. This literary club met each month, with select guests, for a Saturday dinner at the Parker House from three until nine, and quickly became respected throughout cultured American society. Gilman M. Ostrander, *Republic of Letters*, 38–39, 185, 188–89, 289. Ralph W. Emerson to Ethan Allen Hitchcock, Concord and Boston, February 28, 1863; Ralph W. Emerson to Francis C. Barlow, Concord, Mass., c. March 10, 1863, in Rusk and Tilton, *Letters of Ralph Waldo Emerson*, 5:315–16, 318–19.

Meanwhile, Charles R. Lowell Jr. also wrote to William Whiting, solicitor of the War Department.

> *I know that you are always ready to aid in anything you believe to be for the good of the service—and it has occurred to me that, if not too late, you might be glad to say a word at the right place for Col. Francis C. Barlow, late of 61st N.Y. Vols., more recently a Brig. General of Vols. Among those returned to the President by the Senate.*
>
> *Col. Barlow is a native of Massachusetts, a graduate of Harvard College in 1855 with the highest honors of his Class—he had just commenced practice at the Bar in New York when the war broke out. He went <u>at once</u> as a private in the N.Y. 12th Regt—was made a Lieutenant by Col. Butterfield within a few weeks—+ on the return of the three months men was appointed by Gov. Morgan Lieut. Col. of the 61st N.Y. Regt. At Yorktown Barlow's Colonel resigned—+ Barlow was immediately promoted; he was in command through nearly all the several battles of the Peninsula + returned to Fort Monroe in Augt. With only 195 men + 3 officers! He was highly complimented + recommended for promotion by all his superior officers among others, Caldwell, Howard, Kearney + Sedgewick. At Antietam he was present in command of his own Regt. + another small regiment which was temporarily attached to it; he greatly distinguished himself by his coolness + judgment at a critical moment, checking a flank movement of the rebels + capturing several hundred prisoners; his horse was killed early in the action; + Col. Barlow badly bruised + later in the day he was very severely wounded in the hip by a canister shot—he is still unable to return to duty in the field.*
>
> *Barlow was among the <u>first</u> Colonels recommended for Brigadierships—+ I believe among the most <u>deserving</u>. I knew him in college—have watched his career since—+ believe he will do honor (he has done honor) to the Service + to the State—it is on this account I write to you. Excuse the length of this letter. I am anxious to get it off by the first mail + have not time to shorten it.*[4]

As evidenced by Barlow's letter to his mother, however, the whole issue of Barlow's nonconfirmation was no more than a mistake.

---

[4] Charles R. Lowell Jr. to William Whiting, Boston, March 2, 1863, in Barlow Papers NA.

Boston
March 8th /63

My dear Mother
I wrote you a letter nearly a week ago at which I have recd no answer. Why don't you write.

We are still at the Howes but go to Concord tomorrow having finished our Boston visits. We have nothing left now but Milton. The Russells are expected home tomorrow + when they get settled will, I presume ask us out there.

We met Mrs Upton (Rivers) at the artists reception + she has called on us + yesterday we dined there. I am glad to go to Concord for I do not much enjoy the going out + about which we have done lately. It gets tiresome. I enjoy it however at the Howes + like Mrs [Julia Ward] H. very much. She is not only very bright + clever but most amiable + kindhearted + an earnest + good woman. The Dr [Samuel G. Howe][5] is rather a taciturn man but is very cordial. They have six children, the two oldest being very pretty daughters of some 18 + 19 years old.[6] I have enjoyed it much more at home here than in going out. You saw my nomination in the papers yesterday. Bliss telegraphed me of the fact + says that Morgan is on the Military Committee + that there is no danger of my not being confirmed.

Genl Hitchcock wrote Mr Emerson a letter saying that he enquired at the War Dept. on March 2nd + found that I had al-

---

[5] Samuel Gridley Howe was a prominent Bostonian abolitionist who watched and promoted Barlow's career whenever he could. Born in 1801, he graduated from Brown University in 1821 and Harvard Medical School in 1824 before fighting in the Greek war for independence. In 1831, Howe returned to Boston and helped found a school for the blind. He married Julia Ward, later author of "The Battle Hymn of the Republic," and by 1851 the couple became involved with the abolitionist paper *Boston Commonwealth*. Later, he was one of the "Secret Six" who helped fund the efforts of radical abolitionist John Brown. During the war, Howe served on a three-member advisory committee formed to analyze issues relating to the freedmen, and afterward he continued his social work and efforts to educate the blind. Deborah Pickman Clifford, *Mine Eyes Have Seen the Glory: Julia Ward Howe* (Boston: Little, Brown, and Company, 1978).

[6] This refers to Julia Romana Howe, born on March 12, 1844, and Florence Howe, born in late summer, 1845. Clifford, *Mine Eyes Have Seen the Glory*, 80, 86.

ready been renominated + that the first list of names sent in was imperfectly given in the papers + my name should have been upon it. So I must have been in the first list of names. I wonder at R's not having a girl. I thought it was very easy to get one in N.Y.

I recd yesterday E's letter of March 6th. He could not get his pay, I think, by coming here. He is on sick leave + it would not do to keep the knowledge of that fact from the Paymaster + I could not certify that he is on any duty with me. When this certificate expires he must send another as otherwise he will be bound to report to Genl Tyler. He <u>would</u> go with me in case my Brigade were changed. Let him get another extension which will do for the present. If I am confirmed he will be—I am sorry to hear that he is not so well. I still think that the country is the best place for his health. Direct to Concord—

Lovingly
Francis

On side: Will Edward call + pay Bliss for two telegrams which he has sent me—let me know the amt.

On April 8, Maria Daly reported that Barlow continued to appear "very frail" and felt that he had not yet fully recovered despite his decision to return to service. By April 17, Barlow reported for duty to the Army of the Potomac and assumed command of a brigade in Brigadier General Adolph von Steinwehr's division of the Eleventh corps, now led by his friend and former brigade commander, Major General Oliver O. Howard. Barlow's new command consisted of the 33rd Massachusetts, 134th New York, 136th New York, and 73rd Ohio. Barlow met a mixed reception from his brigade, as Augustus C. Hamlin recalled that he was "a new comer in the corps and was but little known to its members. His ways were too abrupt and his views too much of those of the martinet to please his brigade, but they soon discovered that he was as intrepid as Decatur, and as fond of a fight as the naval hero of earlier times." Barlow had his own misgivings

about being in the Eleventh corps, as it contained a heavy pro-
portion of German American troops. Barlow's letters over the
next several months articulate that he doubted they would fight
well.[7]

> Hd. Qrs. 2nd Brigade
> 2nd Division 11th Corps
> Army of Potomac
> April 24 1863

My dear Mother

I was very glad to receive last night your letter of April 21st enclosing one from Edward. One from R also came.

I am glad you felt so well in Phila. + wonder you did not get a place to board there + try it for a while. E. writes that you have written to Aunt Mary about coming there + I shall be very glad if it can be arranged. I have written to ask Mr. Williams to let young Moses come out + make me a visit to see how he likes it preparatory to coming on my staff.

Speaking of Dr Hammond, Gen. Howard told me that he was "crazy on the subject of love" which agrees very well with our estimate of him. Gen Howard gave as a reason that when Ham-

---

[7] Adolph Wilhelm August Friedrich, Baron von Steinwehr, was born in 1822 in the Duchy of Brunswick. After attending military school, he became an officer in the duke's service, and in 1847 he took a leave of absence to visit the United States. Although he did not fulfill his hope of participating in the Mexican War, he did meet and marry an Alabaman woman and returned to Brunswick with her in 1849. Five years later, the couple settled on a Connecticut farm, and when the Civil War broke out he became colonel of the Twenty-ninth New York. Von Steinwehr fought in the Shenandoah Valley against "Stonewall" Jackson during the spring of 1862, and he commanded a division in Pope's Army of Virginia at Second Manassas. After serving as a division commander in the Eleventh corps at both Chancellorsville and Gettysburg, von Steinwehr accompanied his corps on its transfer to the Western theater. With the consolidation of the Eleventh and Twelfth corps, however, von Steinwehr was demoted to command a brigade, and he declined the position. After the war, von Steinwehr taught at Yale and became an esteemed geographer and cartographer before his death in Buffalo, New York, in 1877. Maria L. Daly diary entry, April 9, 1863, in Hammond, *Diary of a Union Lady*, 228. New York Monuments Commission, *In Memoriam: Francis Channing Barlow*, 88. Warner, *Generals in Blue*, 530–31.

mond was in Mexico he became violently in love with a beautiful
+ rich Mexican girl + they were engaged + finally married, but
immediately after the marriage + before they had lived together
her family, who were opposed to the match removed her + he
has never seen her since. They have been divorced since. I hope
you told him that I was here + couldn't call on Mrs Hammond.

I am sorry my dear mother you find my absence so hard to
bear. I trust time will make it easier. I shall never be away so long
as I was before without coming home on leave + you will perhaps get a chance to visit me. I would have you down here now
were not our stay so very uncertain. I have sent for Arabella to
stay a day or two + expect her today but before you could get
ready + get to Washington + down here we shall probably have
marched. I still mess with my Staff—our food is fresh bread
baked in one of the Regts, roast beef + potatoes, beef steak +
onions, ox tail soup + nice pudding, tea + coffee. I have not
much appetite but otherwise am well, except that I require a
good deal of sleep. I don't get up until 7.30 or 8 a.m.

Tell Edward I have written to the Paymaster Genl asking him
to send to E at J. C. Howe an order for his payment. If it don't
come he can probably get paid in Washington when he arrives
there. I have heard nothing from the application to transfer him
to me. Tell E. he can bring Edelson down with him as well as
not.

I have written to Lowell that I am still ready to take command
of the Negro brigade if it is desired.

I have for duty in the Brigade about 2100 men <u>present for duty</u>
in the ranks + about 2500 men in all, well, sick, present +
absent. I wrote you a long letter a day or two ago giving an account of my Brigade &c. There has been some murmuring at my
drawing the reins but I am told they are beginning to like me
better + have been very mild. Col. [Orland] Smith[8] is very much

---

[8] A native of Maine, Orland Smith was a railroader working as an official of
the Marietta and Ohio Railroad before the war. In late 1861, he obtained a
colonel's commission in the Seventy-third Ohio and led it at McDowell, Cross
Keys, and Second Manassas, and he served as a brigade commander at Gettysburg. Smith continued in this capacity when the Eleventh corps was transferred west, but in the army reorganization of 1864, he reverted to command
of the Seventy-third Ohio. He resigned in February 1864 and became general
superintendent of the Columbus, Hocking Valley, and Toledo Railroad in 1877

of a gentleman + I have got on excellently with him + Lt. Col. [Adin B.] Underwood.[9] Col. [Charles R.] Coster I have seen but once I think he is all right.[10] Col. [James] Wood is disposed to be a little touchy + I shall have to take him down I fear.[11]

I have not got Braman with me. He brought my horse over + I thought I would apply for him, but it would be difficult to get him + as I have got a good man to take care of my horse I do not think I shall try for Braman.

I do not now sleep cold.

Thank you for the $20 which came safely. I shall be able to repay it the first of the month. I shall not want any more + you had better not send the other $20 if you have not done so.

Thank you my dear Mother for the loan. Tell R. I shall write to him very soon and also Edward.

I wish you would keep a kind of Diary as you did before. Have you got my picture from Fredericks. If it is good please have some cartes de visites taken.

---

and took over as its president in 1882. Harry W. Pfanz, *Gettysburg: Culp's Hill & Cemetery Hill* (Chapel Hill: University of North Carolina Press, 1993), 145, 432 n. 38.

[9] Adin B. Underwood graduated from Brown University before studying law at the Harvard Law School. Admitted to the bar in 1853, he settled in Boston two years later and on May 23, 1861, became a captain in the Second Massachusetts Infantry. On August 13, 1862, he accepted the lieutenant colonelcy of the Thirty-third Massachusetts and became its colonel the following April. Although he saw little action at Chancellorsville, he and the Thirty-third were heavily engaged on the first day of Gettysburg. He accompanied the Eleventh corps when it was transferred west and on October 29, 1863, was crippled for life by a bullet that severely damaged his upper leg. Although appointed brigadier general that November, Underwood saw no further service in the war. He returned to Boston and was surveyor of its port for nearly two decades. Warner, *Generals in Blue,* 518–19.

[10] A New York City native, Charles R. Coster was a private in the Seventh New York Militia when the Civil War erupted. Commissioned in the Twelfth U.S. Infantry in May 1861, he served in the Peninsula campaign, received a wound at Gaines's Mill, and later became colonel of the 134th New York Infantry. He led this regiment through Chancellorsville and commanded a brigade at Gettysburg. When the Eleventh corps was transferred west, Coster resigned and in May 1864 became provost marshal of New York's Sixth District, where he administered the draft. Pfanz, *Gettysburg: Culp's Hill & Cemetery Hill,* 430 n. 11.

[11] James Wood was appointed colonel of the 136th New York and mustered into service on September 18, 1862. He served through the war and mustered out with his unit on June 13, 1865. John Michael Priest, ed., *John T. McMa-*

I will answer all the questions which E. asks when I write him.

Most lovingly
Francis

Direct as at the head of this letter.

In late April, Hooker began a series of maneuvers in an effort to destroy Lee's army in the vicinity of Fredericksburg, culminating in the battle of Chancellorsville on May 1–4, 1863. During the battle, the Eleventh corps bore the brunt of Confederate Lieutenant General "Stonewall" Jackson's now famous flank attack on May 2, but Barlow's brigade was fortunate enough not to have been present for the disaster. On the night of May 1, Jackson and Lee conferred and designed a bold plan to strike at Hooker's larger army when they agreed to send Jackson's corps on a wide movement to strike the exposed Federal right flank. On the afternoon of May 2, while Jackson's "foot cavalry" marched into position, Major General Daniel Sickles observed the Confederate column on the move not far from his line and obtained Hooker's approval to attack it. In the ensuing fight near Catharine Furnace, Sickles called for reinforcements to support his advanced position, and Howard reluctantly sent Barlow's brigade, which he had posted as his corps reserve.

Howard joined Barlow and von Steinwehr in riding to the Furnace area to see what all anticipated would be the main sector of action for the day. Once in position, however, Barlow's brigade saw little action on Sickles's right flank. The same could not be said for the rest of the Eleventh corps. Jackson sent forward three divisions to crush the Eleventh corps' flank and rout it from the field. Howard had barely returned from Sickles's front when he heard rifle and cannon fire to the west and then saw his men running from that direction. He mounted his horse, placed the staff of a U.S. flag under the stump of his amputated arm, and waved a pistol in his hand, vainly trying to rally his men. Meanwhile, Barlow's brigade remained in a forward position on Sickles's right flank, and its commander did not learn of a call for units to pull back and assist the Eleventh corps until a messenger from the Third corps' Brigadier General David B. Birney informed him of the situation. Barlow's brigade lost but nine wounded and fourteen missing in the battle.[12]

> Hd Qrs 2nd Brigade
> 2nd Div. 11th Corps
> Friday May 8th 1863
> 8.30 p.m.

My dearest Mother + brothers

Edward's letter of May 1st, R's of May 6th enclosing mothers of same date have just reached me. Before this you will have recd my letters + telegram announcing my safety + the return of the Army to our old quarters. You can imagine my indignation + disgust at the miserable behavior of the 11th Corps. It does not appear as plainly as I should desire in the Tribune letter of May 4th that my Brigade was not with the rest of the Corps. I trust it will be stated more clearly in the Tribune + other papers. Please send me any papers which have touched or may touch on the subject. You know how I have always been down on the "Dutch" + I do not abate my contempt now, but it is not fair to charge it all on them. Some of the Yankee Regts behaved just as badly + I think that Hookers failure thus far has been solely from the bad fighting of the men.

Howard is full of mortification + disgust + I really pity him.[13] The general impression is that if my Brigade had been there we could have done a good deal towards checking the rout.

---

[12] Ernest B. Ferguson, *Chancellorsville 1863: The Souls of the Brave* (New York: Alfred A. Knopf, 1992), 154, 158, 159, 180–81, 187, 357.

[13] After the war, Howard admitted, "I felt . . . that I wanted to die. It was the only time I ever weakened that way in my life, before or since, but that night I did all in my power to remedy the mistake, and I sought death everywhere I could find an excuse to go on the field." Howard, quoted in *San Francisco Chronicle,* May 23, 1872, quoted in Ferguson, *Chancellorsville 1863,* 181.

There will be some changes in Brigade commanders here. Col. Smith of the 73rd Ohio is assigned to the command of one of the Brigades in the 1st Division which I much regret as he is an excellent officer. I have not heard from Bliss lately but believe he has gone home or at least as far as Washington. Were it not for my dislike to leave Howard just now I should try to get out of the Corps with my Brigade. [Major] Genl [Winfield S.] Hancock who commands Richardson's old Division told me he should be delighted to have me + paid me a high compliment when I met him last Sunday. We are still ignorant of the plans of Hooker or the movements of the enemy.

I telegraphed Edward today to wait if he could until he got transferred. By that I meant for him to get another Certificate if possible. If not to report to Tyler who would probably hurry up the transfer. I telegraphed [Brigadier] Gen [Seth] Williams this morning to ask if the transfer had been made + he answered that he did not know but would ask at Washington. It will doubtless be made but in the present confusion things at Washington are delayed. Edward had better report to Tyler + ask him to see about it at the Adjt. Genls. Office. I write by this mail to Tyler that they have said the transfer should be made + asking him to see about it. If E. can't get another Certificate conscientiously he will <u>have</u> to report to Tyler. I also write by this mail to the Adjt. Genl. on the subject asking him to send order to Edward care J. C. Howe + Co. If E. leaves New York before the order comes (which he must do if he can't get another Certificate) Tyler can find out if the order has

[remainder of letter missing]

Barlow replaced Brigadier General Charles Devens, wounded at Chancellorsville, as commander of the First division of the Eleventh corps. Brigadier General Adelbert Ames and Colonel Leopold von Gilsa headed its two brigades. An impressive man of twenty-seven years, having a military bearing and standing six feet tall, Ames was calm but efficient in battle, and an aide later described him as "the beau-ideal of a division commander." Ames gradua-

ted fifth in his West Point class of 1861, and as a lieutenant of artillery, he suffered a painful thigh wound at First Manassas. Despite his injury, he remained in command of his section and issued orders from atop a caisson until physically unable to continue, for which he later received a Congressional Medal. Afterward, Ames commanded the Twentieth Maine Infantry and helped mold it into the unit that would win glory at Little Round Top a few weeks after he departed it. He received his promotion to brigadier on May 20, 1863, supported by such officers as Major Generals Joseph Hooker and Oliver Howard and Brigadier General Charles Griffin. Barlow valued his assistance as second in command of the division and judged him an excellent officer. Von Gilsa, a former Prussian officer, served as a major in the Schleswig-Holstein war before immigrating to New York, where he lectured, sang, and played piano in music halls of New York City's Bowery district. In June 1861, he helped recruit the Forty-first New York Volunteer Infantry and became its first colonel, leading it in the Shenandoah Valley where he was wounded at Cross Keys. Von Gilsa displayed a talent for enforcing discipline through his liberal use of expletives shouted in his native German. When Howard met von Gilsa during the retreat from Chancellorsville, the corps commander sought to calm his subordinate's anger by speaking on the importance of relying on God. In response, von Gilsa issued forth such a barrage of expletives that Howard thought he had lost his mind. Von Gilsa's New York and Pennsylvania regiments contained many German immigrants in their ranks, including veterans of the Schleswig-Holstein war.[14]

---

[14] After Gettysburg, Ames commanded a division in the Army of the James during the siege of Petersburg. Following the war, Ames served as the Radical Republican governor of Mississippi and as U.S. senator from that state, though in 1875, Ames resigned rather than face impeachment by that state's Democratic legislature. He briefly served in the Spanish-American war and died in 1933, the last survivor of general's rank from either side of the Civil War. Henry King Benson, *The Public Career of Adelbert Ames, 1861–1976* (Ph.D. diss., University of Virginia, Charlottesville, 1975), 18–19. Joseph Hooker to Hannibal Hamlin, Camp near Warrenton, Va., November 16, 1862; Charles Griffin to Joseph Hooker, Head Quarters First Division Fifth Army Corps, April 5, 1863; Oliver O. Howard to Joseph Hooker, Head Quarters Eleventh Corps, April 19, 1863, all in Blanche Butler Ames, ed., *Chronicles from the Nineteenth Century: Family Letters of Blanche Butler and Adelbert Ames*, 2 vols. (Privately pub-

*Barlow had already earned a reputation as a strict discipli-
narian, but the sentiments he expressed in his letter of May 8
may have encouraged him to be even more exacting on his new
command. One member of the 153rd Pennsylvania observed that
Barlow's leadership was "an epoch in our history, which will
never be forgotten by those who had the misfortune to serve
under him. As a taskmaster he had no equal. The prospect of a
speedy deliverance from the odious yoke of Billy Barlow filled
every heart with joy."*[15]

Head Qrs 1st Div. 11th Corps
Friday May 29th 1863
6.30 p.m.

My dear Mother

Your letter written in the cars on Tuesday 26th to Edward has
just reached us. You speak therein of having written me "the day
before" + I have never recd this letter, the last to me being that
of 23rd last.

I have been exceedingly busy ever since I took command here
as Edward will tell you. I am actually employed from morning
until night. There is no end of work to be done.

Edward finds it very dull I think—more so even than in the
Brigade where he liked the adjutant + Aides better than he does
these. He has not yet begun to do anything here as the other
Adjt. Gen. is still here. E. has ridden about daily + a good deal
+ has felt better for it I think. Today however he says he feels
worse than for some time. I am afraid he finds it rather dull
inasmuch as he has not the interest in the life that I have. The
Corps is in a state of continual excitement + quarreling. One
Dutchman accuses another of misconduct in the last battles +
the Dutch accuse the Americans + vice versa. I think that
[Major General Carl] Schurz is intriguing to get command of the

lished, 1957), 1:15–19. Richard N. Current, *Three Carpetbag Governors*
(Baton Rouge: Louisiana State University Press, 1967). Pfanz, *Gettysburg:
Culp's Hill & Cemetery Hill*, 244–47. Ferguson, *Chancellorsville 1863*, 160.
Warner, *Generals in Blue*, 5–6.

[15] Simmers, *Volunteers Manual*, 26–27.

Corps + is trying insidiously to injure Gen. Howard.[16] I do not feel that he will succeed.

An order has come forbidding leaves of absence for more than five days. I shall try to get a longer leave for the purpose of seeing Gov. [Horatio] Seymour about the promotions in some of the New York Regts of this Division.[17] I have written to ask Miles if he will come here if he is made a Brig. Genl. I want to get him to command the German Division now commanded by Col. Von Gilsa.[18] If he says he will come I will get recommendations from all the people I can + see the Prest. in person about him if no better person can be found to do it. If you do not find it tolerable in Charlestown we will try + have you come down here if we

---

[16] Carl Schurz was born near Cologne, Prussia, and attended the University of Bonn. His participation in the revolution of 1848 forced him to flee to Switzerland. When he was later expelled from France, he made his way to England and then the United States. A noted orator, he moved to Wisconsin in 1856 and became an eloquent campaigner for abolition and the Republican Party. Lincoln appointed him ambassador to Spain, and when Schurz returned from that post in 1862, Lincoln commissioned him brigadier general. Despite his lack of military training, Schurz proved a good commander during the war. He led a division at Second Manassas and in the Eleventh corps at Chancellorsville. Having received his second star on March 17, 1863, he assumed temporary command of the Eleventh corps when its regular commander, Major General Oliver O. Howard, became senior officer on the field upon the death of Major General John F. Reynolds. Schurz accompanied the Eleventh corps when it transferred to the Western theater, and during the presidential election, he traveled throughout the North campaigning for Lincoln. After the election, he resumed military duties as chief of staff to Major General Henry Slocum as he marched through the Carolinas. After the war, Schurz was an energetic proponent of black rights, represented Missouri for one term in the Senate, and became an eminent and influential figure in public affairs until his death in 1906. Warner, *Generals in Blue,* 426–27.

[17] Born in upstate New York in 1810, Horatio Seymour attended several local academies before studying law, gaining admission to the bar in 1832. The following year, he became military secretary to Governor William L. Marcy and learned about Regency politics, and after William H. Seward defeated Marcy in 1838 Seymour became a prominent local politician in his own right. In 1845 he became speaker of New York's assembly and was elected governor in 1852, though defeated for reelection in 1856. A staunch Democrat, he opposed nativism, abolitionism, and temperance but helped Governor Edwin Morgan raise troops in the early days of the Civil War. Seymour won the governorship in 1862, then was defeated again in 1864. He briefly retired until accepting the Democratic nomination for president in 1868, and after his defeat by Ulysses S. Grant, Seymour became an elder statesman of great influence within New York and the Democratic Party. *DAB,* 9:6–9.

[18] Von Gilsa commanded a brigade.

can get you a pass. They do not grant passes here for people to come down from Washington as they did formerly, but leave it to the authorities at Washington who have heretofore uniformly refused to do so. Col. [Adin B.] Underwood has sent to Washington to try + get a pass for his wife who is there. His application is endorsed by Gen. Howard + if he succeeds I can get a pass for you. You would have to bring a female servant + to stand considerable heat, but otherwise I think you would be comfortable. But the discomforts are so great as is also the uncertainty, that if you can be tolerably comfortable in Charlestown, I should recommend you not to come down.

Paine wrote me a letter on April 9th saying that the Russells had given him notice that they should move as the land is sold at the May term. Paine offered to try it alone if we would trust him. The letter reached me only a day or two ago, too late of course to do anything. Today I had another letter from Paine saying that receiving no answer to his letter he had to discontinue the case. This ends the case; though we can begin it anew. I don't know whether they got costs agt. us or not. I think Paine was very much to blame for not writing me a second letter when he recd no answer to the first + I shall tell him so. C. Heath will probably be much pleased at the result. We can begin another suit if we please.

With much love
Francis

Love to all the Crosbys

On June 1, Generals Hancock, Howard, Barlow, and other dignitaries reviewed the regiments of Howard's old brigade on the anniversary of their sacrifice at Fair Oaks. Afterward, Howard delivered a brief oration, noting that few of the men he commanded that day remained in the service but that the Federal army would fight until attaining final victory.[19]

[19] Fuller, *Personal Recollections*, 89.

Hd Qrs 1st Division
11th Corps
June 2nd 1863

My dear Mother

Your letter of May (I forget the date + E. has the letter) reached me this morning + I am very glad to hear that you reached Charlestown safely—though I regret that you do not feel better.

It is as you say about Charlestown. It gets more + more dull + sorrowful every year. If you do not come down here I hope you will go somewhere with the Gardners. As to your coming E. will learn tonight how passes are obtained. We have heard that Miss Underwood[20] has come + if she has come down I see no obstacle to your coming if you bring a servant + think you can stand the heat.

I have just recd the enclosed letter from Dr [Samuel G.] Howe which is <u>confidential + is to be kept secret</u>. I have telegraphed to him to write particulars. Politically it would be of great advantage to me, but I doubt my ability to fill the place + I dislike the idea of leaving the active service for which I am well fitted. I will write you more about this when I hear from Dr. Howe.[21] Edward would like me to take the place I think. The old Adjt. General is still on duty here + E has nothing to do yet. He rides a good deal each day. Livingston has been over this afternoon + to tea + Arabella + E. + L. have gone up to Steinwehrs this evening. I am too much occupied to go much of anywhere. There is a terrible amount of work to do here. Gen. Ames will bring his Brigade out all right in time + I shall confine myself particularly to the German Brigade. I am going to move their Camp tomorrow so as to bring them all under my immediate eye. I continue to like Ames very much.

Yesterday Gen. Howard + his brother + Edward + I + Arabella rode over to the 2nd Corps to see a Brigade celebration of the anniversary of Fair Oaks. It was simple but quite impressive

---

[20] The wife of Colonel Adin B. Underwood.

[21] This refers to a superintendent general position in a proposed program for freedmen, discussed in the introduction to this book.

+ touching. The four old Regts (61st + 64th N.Y. 81st Penn + 5th N.H.) that were in the fight were all reviewed together by Gen Howard + myself. The 61st, 81st + 5th are still in the same Brigade + the 64th came over from another Brigade for the occasion. The Regts. are terribly small but brave looking. The 61st had hardly 75 men. Genl Howard made quite a feeling speech to the Brigade after the Review + I went down into the Camp + saw my old men who were very glad to see me. Edward will write you more fully about this. I shall not always be so hurried my dear mother. Now every moment of my time is taken up + Edward will tell you how much I am occupied. In a week I shall have more time for my friends. I may come to New York in a week for a day or two to see Dr Howe about the new matter + Gov. Seymour about appointments in New York Regts + then I can see you there + bring you on.

> Lovingly
> Francis

> Headquarters, 1st Division, 11th Corps,
> Army of Potomac, June 2nd, 1863

My very dear Charles [Dalton],[22]

I hope you have not inferred from my silence that I do not love you, for I assure you that when I look upon the miserable beasts that I have about me I rejoice to think that there is such a place as Massachusetts and such excellent young men as Mr. C. Dalton.

I presume you have heard something of my fortunes since I left Massachusetts. First I commanded a Brigade in this Corps and was fortunate enough not to be among the runaways on May 2nd.

Now I have command of the Division lately commanded Gen-

---

[22] This and several other letters from Barlow to Charles Dalton are in the Charles Dalton Collection at the Massachusetts Historical Society, Boston, Massachusetts, and were published in "Charles Henry Dalton Papers." As a hard copy of this letter was unavailable for my review, I have relied on this published version.

eral Devens.[23] It was the first to break on May 2nd and is in a most disgusting condition as to discipline and morale. But if hard knocks and a tight rein will make them fight they will have to do it. One of the Brigades is wholly German and is commanded by Colonel Von Gilsa (or rather it is now commanded by a Major as Colonel Gilsa is away and I have the next Colonel in rank in arrest). I expect to have to arrest them all the way down until I find some private soldier who will make them do things properly. The other Brigade has three Ohio and one Connecticut Regiment. It is all American. Over this last named Brigade I have General Ames, the last appointed of the Brigadier Generals, a most admirable officer who graduated at West Point in 1861 and who has a very high reputation. I have just come in command and am working hard.

I wish you would write me and tell me of all my friends in Massachusetts. I hear that Ned has gone to Fort Monroe. Is it so? I have seen no one of my friends here except [Henry Lee] Higginson,[24] C. F. Adams[25] and Channing [Clapp]. The latter is

---

[23] Born in Charlestown, Massachusetts, in 1820, Charles Devens Jr. was educated at the Boston Latin School, Harvard College, and the Harvard Law School. Before the war, Devens served as a state senator, militia officer, and U.S. marshal; while in that capacity, Devens was compelled by the law to participate in the return of a captured slave to his owner, though he first attempted to purchase the fugitive's freedom with his own funds. Devens immediately volunteered for service when war came in 1861, and he became colonel of the Fifteenth Massachusetts Infantry. He led that regiment at the disaster of Ball's Bluff, where a uniform button deflected a bullet and saved him from death. On April 15, 1862, he became brigadier general and led a brigade in the Fourth corps at Seven Pines, where he was wounded. At Fredericksburg he led a brigade in the Sixth corps and at Chancellorsville commanded the first division of the Eleventh corps, where he was wounded as "Stonewall" Jackson crashed into his brigades on the Federal right flank. After recuperating, Devens led a division in the Army of the James during 1864–65. Following the war, he became a Massachusetts superior court judge and later a justice on that state's Supreme Judicial Court before President Rutherford B. Hayes appointed him attorney general of the United States. He died in Boston in early 1891 as a celebrated hero. Warner, *Generals in Blue,* 122–23.

[24] Henry Lee Higginson was a major in the Second Massachusetts at this point. Quint, *Record of the Second Massachusetts Infantry,* 493.

[25] Born in 1835, Charles Francis Adams attended the Boston Latin School before graduating in the Harvard College class of 1856. Afterward, Adams studied law and met prominent Republicans in the company of his father. When the Civil War erupted, he obtained a commission in the First Massachusetts Cavalry. He served with the Army of the Potomac and saw action at Antietam

an Adjutant General in the Department and is on the staff of [Brigadier] General [Henry W.] Benham so that I cannot have him unless I have a vacancy in that Department.[26] My brother is now with me and does very well. . . .

Francis C. Barlow

Head Qrs 1st Div.
Sunday June 7th

My dear Mother

Your letter of June reached me yesterday + yours of 4th Inst. to E. came today.

The extreme difficulties of your position + the want of a cheerful home for the summer cause both E. + myself very much uneasiness + pain. But I do not see how the evil can be remedied at present without Edwards coming home at once which I think would be a great injury to him. I think the life agrees with him + that his nerves + digestion are improving. I think that if he stays here a while longer it will materially benefit him.

Charlestown seems to have been very unfortunate as a residence for you. The politics of the place are a great objection to it.

---

and Gettysburg before becoming colonel of the black Fifth Massachusetts Cavalry. He served through the end of the war, though the damage this did to his health prompted him to take an extended vacation in Europe. Afterward, he became a prolific writer, penning essays and books on topics ranging from railroad financing to history, and for twenty-four years he was a member of the Board of Overseers of Harvard University. *DAB,* 1:48–52.

[26] Captain Channing Clapp served as assistant adjutant general to Brigadier General Henry W. Benham, commander of the Army of the Potomac's engineers. Henry W. Benham was born in Connecticut in 1813 and graduated first in the class of 1837 from West Point. Serving in the Corps of Engineers, Benham helped construct coastal defenses and participated in the Mexican War but declined a promotion in the infantry branch so that he could continue as an engineer. In the early days of the Civil War, he served as chief engineer of the Department of the Ohio before a brief tenure as a field commander. He was unsuited for line duty, however, and from the spring of 1863 through the end of the war, Benham commanded the engineer brigade of the Army of the Potomac. After the war, Benham constructed defenses for Boston and New York harbors. *OR,* 27(3): 99. Warner, *Generals in Blue,* 30.

I trust that when we next hear from you you will have made some arrangement with the Gardners—or cannot you go somewhere to the Sea shore with Mrs Clark? I forgot to send you a copy of Dr Howe's letter in my last. I will get Edward to make a copy + send it in this. Dr Howe has not written me the particulars of the scheme in answer to my telegram + I have telegraphed + written him again. I have not made up my mind on that point yet.

I am in a state of uncertainty as to whether I will not go + take a Brigade in the 2nd Corps (Sumners old one) under [Brigadier General John] Gibbon.[27] I have been over there today to see them on the subject. Gen Ames has been sent away on detached service for a few days + I begin to be afraid he won't stay long in his Brigade. I should not care about staying with the Division unless I can have a good General Officer.

I have not had time to write to R. yet. Edward had a letter from him tonight. Willy Penn seems to have been frightened out of his New Orleans trip.

I am busily occupied with these miserable creatures + get very little time to do anything. I am heartily tired of this lying in camp + wish for a fight or to go home. For a day or two past I have had a bad headache + been out of order in my bowels.

I sincerely hope our next letter will bring us more cheerful news from you.

Very lovingly
Francis

---

[27] Although born in Philadelphia, John Gibbon grew up in North Carolina before attending West Point. After graduating from the Military Academy in 1847, Gibbon fought in the Mexican War and against Seminoles in Florida, and then returned to his alma mater to serve as an artillery instructor, quartermaster, and author of *The Artillerist's Manual*. With the coming of the Civil War, Gibbon maintained his allegiance to the Union and was made brigadier general on May 2, 1862. He led the elite Iron Brigade through the Second Manassas and Antietam campaigns before taking a division in the First corps. Badly wounded at Fredericksburg, Gibbon returned to duty to lead a division in the Second corps, fighting well at Gettysburg, where he was wounded on July 3. The following spring, he resumed command of the division and led it through the siege of Petersburg until he was assigned to command the Twenty-fourth corps in the Army of the James. At Appomattox, Gibbon was one of three commissioners who received the Army of Northern Virginia's surrender, and after

In the following letter, Barlow maintained that he still wanted to pursue the "Darkey Superintendent" position. Others wished him to remain in combat service, though in command of the Union's new and untried black regiments. Robert Gould Shaw wrote, shortly after taking charge of the Fifty-fourth Massachusetts Infantry, that Massachusetts Governor John Andrew contemplated raising several more units to comprise a black brigade. Shaw immediately expressed his eagerness to serve under his old tutor, "I hope Frank Barlow can get the command. He is just the man for it, and I should like to be under him." Furthermore, Shaw urged both his father and Charles Russell Lowell to intervene with Andrew to promote Barlow's cause. On June 18, Shaw informed his mother, "Frank Barlow still wishes to get command of a coloured Brigade, and I think it would be a great piece of good fortune for us if we could get him—& for the cause, as well. If Father can do anything towards it, I wish he would," and he expressed similar sentiments to Lowell a couple of days later.[28]

On the eve of the battle of Gettysburg, Governor Andrew followed Shaw's suggestion and urged Secretary of War Stanton to place Barlow over the black regiments in the Department of the South. Besides, Andrew felt uneasy about the other available options: Thomas W. Higginson, a personally brave and cultured man with little military experience, and Colonel James Montgomery, "a good bushwacker," but "hardly a competent brigadier." The governor argued that "for the sake of the reputation of the Fifty-fourth Massachusetts . . . I beg for a brigade commander over it who shall not by his own deficiency peril the reputation of the troops who are under his orders." Andrew then offered a "personal knowledge of General Barlow" and assessment of him as the best person for the job, as well as assuring

---

the war he fought against Indians in the West. When he died in 1896, he was serving as commander in chief of the Military Order of the Loyal Legion and was buried in Arlington National Cemetery. Warner, *Generals in Blue,* 171–72.

[28] Robert G. Shaw to Sarah Shaw, Readville, Mass., March 17, 1863; Robert G. Shaw to Sarah Shaw, Saint Simon's Island, Ga., June 18, 1863; Robert G. Shaw to Charles Russell Lowell, Saint Simon's Island, Ga., June 20, 1863, in Duncan, *Blue-Eyed Child of Fortune,* 309, 354–55.

that Barlow would "cheerfully obey an order placing him over black troops[.]"[29]

Meanwhile, Barlow and the other soldiers of the Army of the Potomac had more pressing issues with which to contend: Lee invaded Pennsylvania with an army that had won victory after victory in the past year. To add to the uncertainty, on June 28, Lincoln replaced Hooker with Major General George G. Meade. This proved a good choice, and Meade served as the Army of the Potomac's commander until the end of the war, though his abilities as an army commander were unknown at the time.

Hd Qrs 1st Division
June 26 1863
9.30 a.m.
near Jefferson Md + 9 miles from Frederick

My dear Richard

I hope you understand why I have not written to you all this time. I have been so busy that I have written only when actually obliged to.

---

[29] Born in Cambridge, Massachusetts, in 1823, Thomas Wentworth Higginson enrolled at Harvard in the class of 1841, at the age of thirteen. Following graduation, he taught for two years before returning to Harvard as a "resident graduate" student, and he eventually graduated from its Divinity School. Higginson became a Unitarian minister and campaigned for abolition of slavery. While Anthony Burns was in Boston in May 1854, Higginson helped lead a mob in an attempt to storm the courthouse where the fugitive slave was held, receiving a severe facial cut in the process. He also helped support John Brown and that abolitionist's violent actions. In November 1862, Higginson held a captaincy in a Massachusetts regiment not yet dispatched to the front when he was offered, and accepted, command of the black First South Carolina Volunteers. Although the regiment participated in no major battles, Higginson wrote an eloquent account of his experiences in a volume entitled *Army Life in a Black Regiment*. He resigned in May 1864 and spent the rest of his years writing articles and books. Colonel James Montgomery was born in 1814 and joined John Brown to participate in the abolitionist's activities in Kansas before the Civil War. On January 13, 1863, he obtained permission to raise a black regiment of troops, and by late February he began recruiting the Second South Carolina in the vicinity of Port Royal. During his military service, Montgomery continued to utilize the tactics he learned in "Bleeding" Kansas, including retaliatory burnings, such as when he ordered the destruction of Georgia's second leading port, Darien. *DAB*, 5:16–18. Duncan, *Blue-Eyed Child of Fortune*, 42–43, 337 n. 5. Governor John A. Andrew to Secretary of War Edwin M. Stanton, Boston, June 29, 1863, in *OR*, ser. 3, 3:423–24.

We arrived here last night in a rain storm + are staying at a very comfortable house. We start again in a few minutes. We are pursuing the enemy I suppose though I don't know where they are. We hear that [Lieutenant General James] Longstreet crossed with 15000 men one mile below Sheppardstown day before yesterday. There seems to be quite a force of them in Maryland + I hope we shall have a battle which will settle the matter one way or the other. You know I presume that when this immediate Campaign is over I am going to accept the "Darkey Superintendent" place if it is then open to me. I am expecting to have a letter from Robt Dale Owen on the subject every day.[30]

I am glad to hear that Ella is better + that the symptoms are not so alarming as supposed.

Mothers ill luck this summer I regret exceedingly. We shall soon be at home + then she will be more comfortable.

I should be very glad to have you pay us a visit if you can do so. Can't you come down for a few days now that we are in Maryland? You will find it pleasanter than your Yorktown experience.

Edward is not so well for a day or two past as he had been. Yesterday we had a march of some 25 miles which used him up. We marched 15 hours. His horse has proved an unfortunate failure. He is lame in his right fore leg + I am afraid it is permanent. He gave $175 for him + I am afraid it is a swindle.

My Dutch Brigade has just been detached for a few days with [Brigadier] Genl [Julius] Stahl + his Cavalry.[31] I suppose I shall

[30] Born in Glasgow, Scotland, in 1801, Robert Dale Owen had a strong interest in the cause of social reform. In 1825 he left his homeland for New Harmony, Indiana, a socialist utopian commune his father had founded, and he grew interested in rights for women and blacks. He won several terms in the Indiana legislature before representing that state in Congress, and he later served as a diplomat to the Kingdom of the Two Sicilies. In 1861 he served the Union as an ordnance commissioner and in 1863 was a member of the American Freedman's Inquiry Commission that proposed the program for newly freed slaves to which Barlow refers. Richard Leopold, *Robert Dale Owen* (Cambridge, Mass.: Harvard University Press, 1940).

[31] Julius Stahel was born in Hungary and served as an officer in the Austrian army before his participation in the 1848 revolution forced him to flee to Berlin and London. In 1859 he arrived in New York City, where he worked for a German-language newspaper, and in 1861 he and Louis Blenker recruited the Eighth New York Infantry. The regiment helped cover retreating Federal troops at First Manassas, and Stahel succeeded Blenker in command of the unit in August 1861. On November 12, Stahel received a general's commission and

have it again in case of a battle but I don't care much if I don't. I am glad to hear you are making so much money. I wish you would give me some idea of how you make it + how much you are worth.

What is W. Penn. doing?

Have you seen Mr. C. R. Miles + how have these two gents. arranged their differences?

<u>Don't speak of my darkey plan</u>.

Very affectionately
F.C.B.

Love to Ella. Send this to Mother.

On June 29, the Eleventh corps marched nearly twenty miles from Frederick before camping around Saint Joseph's College near Emmitsburg, Maryland, not far from the Pennsylvania border. On the night of June 30, Howard reviewed Meade's movement orders to wing commander Major General John Reynolds for the following day and issued appropriate instructions to the Eleventh corps in anticipation of Reynolds's directions. Barlow's division would follow the First corps to Gettysburg via the Emmitsburg Road, while Howard's other two divisions and the corps artillery were to turn east off the Emmitsburg Road and take the Taneytown Road to Gettysburg, a march route three miles longer than Barlow's but on a road with no other military traffic.[32]

served in the Shenandoah Valley against "Stonewall" Jackson the following spring. He led a division at Second Manassas and was assigned the command of the cavalry in Washington's defense in the spring of 1863. The following year, he led a cavalry division in the Shenandoah, and after the war he served as a U.S. diplomat in China and Japan. Warner, *Generals in Blue*, 469–70.

[32] A. Wilson Greene, "From Chancellorsville to Cemetery Hill: O. O. Howard and Eleventh Corps Leadership," in *The First Day at Gettysburg: Essays on Confederate and Union Leadership*, ed. Gary W. Gallagher (Kent, Ohio: Kent State University Press, 1992), 57–91: 67. Harry W. Pfanz, *Gettysburg—The First Day* (Chapel Hill: University of North Carolina Press, 2001), 134–36. *OR*, 27(1): 701.

On July 1, the Eleventh corps' men woke at dawn and prepared for the day's march, getting under way by 8:00, while Howard and his staff rushed to reach Gettysburg ahead of them. Arriving there several hours before his troops would, Howard began reconnoitering the town when he learned that Reynolds had been wounded. At 10:30, Howard received the information that Reynolds had died and that he was now commander of the field. Howard immediately dispatched an aide to inform Schurz of the situation and order him to take command of the Eleventh corps (Brigadier General Alexander Schimmelfennig assumed command of Schurz's division). He then sent Captain Edward P. Pearson down the Emmitsburg Road to urge Barlow and, behind him, Major General Daniel Sickles and the Third corps, to hurry to Gettysburg as soon as possible. Shortly before 11:00, Barlow was about four miles from Gettysburg when he heard the rumbling of battle in the distance and dispatched his aide, E. C. Culp, to ride ahead and ascertain the situation. On the way, Culp met Pearson and learned that the First corps was being heavily pressed, that Reynolds was dead, and that Howard had command of the field. Pearson told Culp to urge "General [Barlow], for God's sake, to push on with the utmost speed." Meanwhile, Barlow grew impatient and sent another aide, Captain Wickham, ahead. Pearson met him as well and they rode toward Barlow, finding him well in advance of his division while his men marched at the double-quick. Barlow immediately ordered Wickham to hurry the marching blue column forward.[33]

Barlow's men endured an uncomfortable march. A rainstorm drenched them as they began their movement, and the First corps troops, cannon, and wagons that preceded their march had rutted the already muddy road on which they traveled. Heat and humidity soon compounded their discomfort as they tramped along at a pace of about two and a half miles per hour. At least

---

[33] From Pearson's account, it seems that he conferred with Barlow in person before going on to find Sickles and the Third corps. E. C. Culp, "Gettysburg: Reminiscences of the Great Fight by a Participant," in *National Tribune,* March 19, 1885. Captain Pearson to O. O. Howard, January 22, 1886, quoted in Charles H. Howard, "The First Day at Gettysburg," in *The Gettysburg Papers,* ed. Ken Bandy and Florence Freeland, 2 vols. (Dayton, Ohio: Morningside, 1986), 1:310–36: 321. Pfanz, *Gettysburg—The First Day,* 136–37.

*the 153rd Pennsylvania found a brief moment that boosted their
morale: upon crossing the Mason-Dixon line, they threw their
caps in the air and gave three cheers for their old Keystone State.
The misery of the march intensified, however, as they hurried to
Gettysburg, and some discarded extra clothing and equipment.*[34]

In light of the impending action, staff officer and German no-
bleman Baron Frederick Otto von Fritsch found Barlow and pled
for the release of brigade commander von Gilsa's from arrest for
allowing more than one soldier at a time to leave the ranks to
obtain water. Von Fritsch conferred with Barlow and asked if he
could return von Gilsa's sword, and Barlow acquiesced with a
warning to enforce strict discipline on the march. "You can do
so, under the circumstances, but keep your men well together,"
warned Barlow, "Staff officers may even shoot down stragglers,
and I demand the strictest discipline."[35] While on the march to
Gettysburg, another officer got in trouble for a similar issue. A
staff officer observed a member of the Seventeenth Connecticut
break ranks to dip a cup of water from a stream. When Barlow
(or perhaps Ames, who knew what had happened to von Gilsa
and who was a strict disciplinarian in his own right) learned of
this, the Seventeenth's commander Lieutenant Colonel Douglas
Fowler was placed under arrest and sent to the rear of his unit.
The regiment refused to enter battle without their colonel, however, and Schurz released Fowler from arrest, not wanting the
regiment to fight with distraction or without its commander over
a "mere unimportant peccadillo."[36]

*At 12:30, Schimmelfennig's division reached Cemetery Hill.
Schurz quickly sent its men forward, "streaming with perspira-
tion and panting for breath" from the sultry weather and fast*

---

[34] Pfanz, *Gettysburg—The First Day*, 138–39. Greene, "From Chancellors-
ville to Cemetery Hill," 68–69. Justus M. Silliman to mother, Gettysburg, Pa.,
July 3, 1863, in Edward Marcus, ed., *A New Canaan Private in the Civil War:
Letters of Justus M. Silliman, 17th Connecticut Volunteers* (New Canaan,
Conn.: New Canaan Historical Society, 1984), 39. W. R. Kiefer, *History of
the One Hundred and Fifty-third Regiment Pennsylvania Volunteers Infantry*
(Easton, Pa.: Chemical Publishing, 1909), 139, 208–9.

[35] Joseph Tyler Butts, ed., *A Gallant Captain of the Civil War: Being the Record of the Extraordinary Adventures of Frederick Otto Baron von Fritsch*
(New York: F. Tennyson Neely, 1902), 74.

[36] Pfanz, *Gettysburg—The First Day*, 226. Carl Schurz, *Reminiscences* (New
York: McClure and Company, 1907–7), 3:8.

march, to deploy to the right of the First corps. Barlow's division marched through Gettysburg a half hour behind Schimmelfennig and likewise rushed to bolster the Federal right. Schurz commanded Barlow to position one of his brigades to connect with Schimmelfennig's right and to the west of Mummasburg Road, with the other in its right rear and protecting Carlisle and Harrisburg Roads. Brigadier General Adolph von Steinwehr's division, meanwhile, received orders to hold Cemetery Hill in reserve. The men of the First corps cheered their comrades' arrival on the field, as hostility toward the largely immigrant Eleventh corps melted in the face of six thousand troops preparing to bolster the Federal right.[37]

As the soldiers of the Eleventh corps marched through Gettysburg, they saw some scared civilians rushing for cover while others doled out food and water to the sweating, blue-clad soldiers. There was no time to accept refreshments, however, as Schimmelfennig's men double-quicked through town, followed by a battery, its cannoneers barely able to cling onto its swift-moving limbers. As Barlow's men tramped through town, the passing of a mounted party resulted in cheering which echoed like a "high surge sweeping across the surface of a flowing sea." It was von Gilsa's brigade welcoming his return to command after Barlow released him from arrest.[38]

Howard rode with Barlow and his division as it marched through Gettysburg, up Washington Street, and east along the northern edge of town, then proceeded left down Harrisburg Road. Both generals saw one young woman who remained on her porch and fluttered her handkerchief to the passing men in blue. Shortly afterward, Howard conferred with the First corps' acting commander, Major General Abner Doubleday. Realizing that the Federal line was thinly stretched and would soon become hard pressed, coupled with Schurz's and Doubleday's requests for re-

---

[37] Pfanz, *Gettysburg—The First Day*, 140. Greene, "From Chancellorsville to Cemetery Hill," 72, 74. OR, 27(1): 727–28. Carl Schurz, "The Battle of Gettysburg," *McClure's Magazine* (July 1907): 272–282: 275, 276. Justus M. Silliman to mother, Gettysburg, Pa., July 3, 1863, in Marcus, *New Canaan Private in the Civil War*, 39–40.

[38] Pfanz, *Gettysburg—The First Day*, 141. Kiefer, *History of the One Hundred and Fifty-third Regiment*, 208–9. Charles P. Hamblen, *Connecticut Yankees at Gettysburg* (Kent, Ohio: Kent State University Press, 1993), 18.

*inforcements, Howard urged Major General Henry Slocum to
hurry forward the Twelfth corps—help that would come too
late.*[39]

*By 2:00 p.m., Schimmelfennig's division deployed on the right
of the First corps, and Barlow's small division swung into position on Schimmelfennig's right, but neither was exactly where
Schurz had initially anticipated. Major General Robert Rodes's
Confederate division had occupied Oak Hill, forcing Schimmelfennig to shift his deployment to the east of the Mummasburg
Road and Barlow to form accordingly. Upon reaching the vicinity of the Crawford farm, Ames's brigade deployed in a meadow
on the east side of Harrisburg road, while von Gilsa's soldiers fell
out to the west of it. Some observed Confederate sharpshooters
skirmishing with Federal cavalry, while the Seventeenth Connecticut's Lieutenant Colonel Fowler ordered his men to load
their pieces and for officers to make sure their pistols worked
after the morning's wet march, knowing that the fight would
soon come to the Eleventh corps. Soon thereafter, Ames ordered
four companies of the Seventeenth to seize the bridge over Rock
Creek, a half mile north of their present position, and to hold
Josiah Benner's brick house just beyond the bridge. Major Allen
G. Brady volunteered to lead the party of four companies, though
others in the regiment felt this advance was futile. Observing as
Confederate pressure pushed Federal cavalry back, they knew
they would engage the Rebels soon enough.*[40]

*Brady's four companies moved forward just as Major General
Jubal Early's division occupied higher ground four hundred
yards north of Benner's farm. Brady sent two companies to advance as skirmishers, while his remaining men supported in battle line, crossing Rock Creek and then swinging toward Benner's
buildings, firing as quickly as possible at Confederate skirmishers. Rebel artillery fired shot, shell, and canister as the Federals*

---

[39] Pfanz, *Gettysburg—The First Day,* 141–43. Captain M. Browne to J. B.
Bachelder, Jacksonville, Fla., April 8, 1864, in David L. and Audrey J. Ladd,
eds., *The Bachelder Papers,* 3 vols. (Dayton, Ohio: Morningside, 1994–95),
1:148. OR, 27(1): 702.

[40] Pfanz, *Gettysburg—The First Day,* 217, 223, 226. Hamblen, *Connecticut
Yankees,* 18. OR, 27(1) 717, 727–28. Captain M. Browne to J. B. Bachelder,
Jacksonville, Fla., April 8, 1864, in Ladd, *Bachelder Papers,* 1:148.

neared the house, prompting Brady to dismount and personally lead his men in capturing the building, set ablaze by the Confederate cannon. Only Benner's personal efforts prevented his entire house from burning down.[41]

Soon, Barlow decided to move the rest of his division forward in order to capture the high ground at Blocher's Knoll (now known as Barlow's Knoll) in his front, rising fifty feet above Rock Creek on its northern base. A postwar memoriam deemed this maneuver one that revealed Barlow's "characteristic vision" and "characteristic daring," though analysis of his decision reveals it was a poor one. Historian Harry Pfanz compared this ground at Blocher's Knoll with the Peach Orchard: both positions were high and could serve as a good artillery position, and both attracted Federal commanders to overexpose their line in taking them. In Barlow's case, Pfanz accurately judged that by advancing his men into a salient and further stretching an already thin line in the process, the young division commander "had blundered, and in doing so he had ensured the defeat of the corps[.]" A. Wilson Greene similarly recognized that Barlow had, acting on his own accord, "committed the tactical error" that sealed the Eleventh corps' fate on July 1. Greene aptly recognized that perhaps Barlow had been tempted to advance so as to flank Brigadier General George Doles's Georgian brigade operating against Schimmelfennig's division. This echoed an opinion offered after the war by Confederate Major General Jubal A. Early, whose division smashed Barlow's line on July 1.[42] Decades after the fight, a member of the Eighty-second Ohio recounted the entire event and accurately assessed that Barlow had mistakenly placed his division that first of July:

> The truth is the whole line, Division, was "flanked and gave way," and the position was one which no troops in the world, of equal numbers, could have held. The entire advance of our line by the right flank was an act of unspeakable folly. Instead of advancing,

---

[41] *OR*, 27(1): 717. Hamblen, *Connecticut Yankees*, n. 25, 136.

[42] Doles's brigade was in Major General Robert E. Rodes's division. *In Memoriam: Francis Channing Barlow*, 29. Pfanz, *Gettysburg—The First Day*, 230–31. Greene, "From Chancellorsville to Cemetery Hill," 57–91: 77–78. Jubal A. Early to J. B. Bachelder, Lynchburg, Va., March 23, 1876, in Ladd, *Bachelder Papers*, 1:459.

*we should have fallen back, as soon as the approach of the enemy
from the right was developed, and should have reformed and bar-
ricaded the line with our right well refused upon the town, and
our left connecting, as well as might be, with the right of the First
Corps. We could then have punished the enemy much more severely, and perhaps, have held the town until dark. I do not know
who is responsible for the advance, but whoever ordered it deserves
the severest censure.*[43]

Nonetheless, after the battle, Barlow never admitted his deployment to be a poor one. In a July 7, 1863 letter, Barlow informed his mother that he formed as directed, though it is nearly
inconceivable that he could have misunderstood Schurz's initial
order to place one brigade in the right rear of the other to mean
advancing his entire line. Barlow either denied to himself or
failed to appreciate the consequences of his decision. Even years
after the war, Barlow wrongfully persisted in arguing that the
attack on him was "square in front" of his lines and that he was
not flanked in the initial assault on his line. All in all, he seems
to have been in a combative mood that day. When Barlow observed the four companies of the Seventeenth Connecticut fall
back in the face of an entire Confederate division later that afternoon, he exclaimed, "What is that skirmish line stopping for?"
In an article about Gettysburg, Schurz noted Barlow's aggressive
attitude as well. Although he covered for his subordinate by offering that Barlow might have misunderstood his orders, Schurz
also felt that Barlow might have been "carried away by the ardor
of the conflict" in advancing his line forward.[44]

Following Barlow's orders, von Gilsa intended to take Blocher's Knoll and then move forward to Rock Creek with his small
brigade, which had been further depleted with the absence of a
regiment detached to guard wagons near Emmitsburg. His men
advanced and slung off their knapsacks in the vicinity of the
Adams County Almshouse buildings, the 153rd Pennsylvania
stacking theirs in a nearby field. Then, the 54th and 68th New

[43] Arthur T. Lee to J. B. Bachelder, Columbus, Ohio, February 16, 1888, in
Ladd, *Bachelder Papers*, 3:1526.
[44] Culp, "Gettysburg." Schurz, "Battle of Gettysburg," 276. Barlow to
Mother, July 7, 1863. Barlow to J. B. Bachelder, New York, N.Y., March 31,
1883, in Ladd, *Bachelder Papers*, 2:938.

York regiments, numbering about two hundred men each, and two companies of the 153rd Pennsylvania moved forward as skirmishers, with the main body of the Pennsylvanians support- ing them in line formation fifty yards to the rear. Von Gilsa rode between the two lines, warning his men to conserve costly am- munition by firing only at visible targets, while Confederate skirmishers and cannon fired on the bluecoats. Men crouched for cover from minie balls, while von Gilsa called out that they had nothing to fear, that as long as they heard the bullet they were safe from it. The brigade double-quicked over the knoll, sending Confederate skirmishers tumbling back and then rushed down the hill to the banks of Rock Creek. Von Gilsa formed a skirmish line on the creek's banks, with the 54th New York holding the right near Harrisburg Road, two companies of the 153rd Penn- sylvania in the center, and the 68th New York covering the left. The remaining four hundred men of the 153rd were held in re- serve.[45]

Barlow's men had some artillery support to bolster their posi- tion. Eleventh corps artillery chief Major Thomas Osborn had earlier dispatched Lieutenant Bayard Wilkeson's Battery G, Fourth U.S. Artillery to report to Barlow. The son of New York Times war correspondent Samuel Wilkeson, the lieutenant was reputed to be the youngest battery commander in the Army of the Potomac. Barlow ordered him to deploy a section of his napo- leons (a type of cannon) east of Harrisburg Road near the Alms- house buildings to cover his division's right flank, while the remaining cannon were to take a position on the knoll itself. Although the knoll provided an excellent position for artillery, Wilkeson's four cannon were not only within range of Confeder- ate infantry, but were outgunned by several batteries of Lieuten- ant Colonel H. P. Jones' battalion but twelve hundred yards away. Wilkeson's napoleons dueled with two Confederate batter- ies for about a half hour while the section near the Almshouse, under Lieutenant Christopher F. Merkle, fired several rounds at

---

[45] Pfanz, *Gettysburg—The First Day*, 231–32. J. Clyde Miller to John Bachel- der, Freemansburg, Pa., March 2, 1884; March 2, 1886, in Ladd, *Bachelder Papers*, 2:1025, 1211–12. Kiefer, *History of the One Hundred and Fifty-Third Regiment*, 210–11.

Major General Jubal Early's Confederate division sweeps Barlow from field, first day of Gettysburg, July 1, 1863

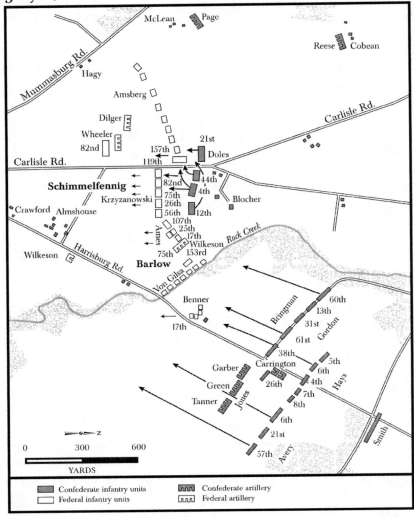

*Jones's cannon before targeting advancing Confederate infantry
as it drew within canister range.*[46]

*A half hour after Brady's four companies of the Seventeenth
Connecticut advanced, Ames moved to support Wilkeson's napoleons on Blocher's Knoll. Lieutenant Colonel Fowler instructed
his remaining six companies to leave their gear near the Almshouse, and, despite the warnings of his officers, he remained
mounted in order to inspire his men for the coming fight. Ames's
twelve hundred available men advanced and formed a line with
their right beyond Wilkeson's guns, extending behind the left of
the battery and then fronting northwest toward Doles's Georgians. The 17th Connecticut held the right, the 25th Ohio the
center, the 107th Ohio the left, and the 75th Ohio held in reserve.*[47]

*Ames's men came under heavy fire, especially due to their
proximity to Wilkeson's battery, and were targeted by both Rebel
infantry and artillery. Confederate fire killed Wilkeson's horse
and then destroyed the artillerist's right leg, forcing the young
lieutenant to apply a tourniquet made from a handkerchief and
amputate the dangling remains. Four of his cannoneers bore him
to the Almshouse, where he died that evening. Meanwhile, Fowler
tried to ease his men's nerves through humor, calling to his men,
"Dodge the big ones, boys," as Confederate shells crashed around
his line.*[48]

*Meanwhile, Schurz nervously monitored the growing pressure
on his right from the Hagy house near the left of the corps' line.
From its roof, the German general watched the gray lines in his
front getting stronger while also discovering that Barlow had
taken Blocher's Knoll. In so doing, Barlow had broken from his
assigned post on Schimmelfennig's right, and Schurz reluctantly
ordered Schimmelfennig to advance Colonel Wladimir Krzyzanowski's brigade and reconnect with Barlow's left. Schurz realized that this made his blue line stretch even thinner, however,
and he fired off several more requests to Howard on Cemetery*

---

[46] Pfanz, *Gettysburg—The First Day,* 232. OR, 27(1): 756, 757.

[47] Pfanz, *Gettysburg—The First Day,* 232. M. Browne to John Bachelder,
April 8, 1864, Ladd, *Bachelder Papers,* 1:148; Andrew L. Harris to J. B. Bachelder, Eaton, Ohio, March 14, 1881, in Ladd, *Bachelder Papers,* 2:743.

[48] Pfanz, *Gettysburg—The First Day,* 233–34. OR, 27(1): 748.

Hill, asking for the release of one of von Steinwehr's brigades to reinforce his right. Realizing the Confederates were about to attack his flank and potentially cut off the Eleventh corps and destroy it, he contemplated a withdrawal. Just as his worst fears materialized, Early's gray brigades swept forward.[49]

A native of Poland, Krzyzanowski understood that pressure was building on Barlow's front, and his face became "pale and distressed" upon receiving orders to advance his twelve hundred men. Upon reaching Barlow's left, Confederate troops appeared from the ravine of Blocher's Run, moving "firm and steady" with "banners bearing the blue Southern cross, flaunted impudently," "one line after the other in splendid array." Krzyzanowski barely had time to post his regiments east of Carlisle Road when Doles's brigade crashed into it, while Gordon's elite brigade of Georgians shattered von Gilsa's small force by hitting its exposed right flank. Historian Harry Pfanz aptly summed up the situation on the Federal right on July 1 at around 3:00 p.m.: "The numbers of attackers and defenders were approximately equal, but the position of the Eleventh Corps was poor, and most of its key commanders were new in the assignments. In contrast, the Confederates were veteran troops commanded by one of their army's best division commanders and by competent brigade commanders. As things stood, Early's division and Doles's brigade could strike Schurz's brigades one at a time with superior force. In retrospect, the result seems preordained."[50]

The four advanced companies of the Seventeenth Connecticut posted at the Benner house saw Brigadier Generals John Brown Gordon's and Harry T. Hays's brigades threaten to swallow them. Although composed of excellent marksmen and inflicting a toll on the approaching Rebels, the Connecticut men began retreating toward Gettysburg at Ames's order. Brady had difficulty getting one company to break from their position, "as they were so earnestly engaged and making such sad havoc among the rebels." Meanwhile, von Gilsa's nine hundred Federals, deployed

---

[49] Pfanz, *Gettysburg—The First Day*, 235–36. Schurz, "Battle of Gettysburg," 276. *OR*, 27(1): 727–29.

[50] Pfanz, *Gettysburg—The First Day*, 237–38. [Alfred E. Lee] A Company Officer, "Reminiscences of the Gettysburg Battle," *Lippincott's Magazine* (July 1883): 54–60: 56.

in skirmish line, faced twice as many Confederates. Shells from Wilkeson's battery passed so close over the head of Private Reuben Ruch of the 153rd that he felt the heat from them. Lieutenant Miller, commanding the two companies of the 153rd in von Gilsa's center, sent a corporal back to tell the remaining eight companies of his regiment in reserve that their shooting was hitting his sector. The corporal quickly rushed back to let Miller know the reserve was gone (von Gilsa ordered the eight remaining companies of the 153rd Pennsylvania to extend his brigade line) and that the bullets were from Confederate rifles in the Federal right rear. Gray lines were becoming visible in Miller's front as well, and he ordered a retreat in fear that his men would be surrounded and captured.[51]

In the words of one Confederate officer, the attack was "one of the most warlike and animated spectacles" he had ever witnessed, as the Confederates "charged across the plateau in their front, at double quick, sweeping everything before them, and scattering the extreme right of the enemy." Federal soldiers fell dead and wounded while Ruch observed a Confederate color-bearer cross Rock Creek "yelling like an Indian." Ruch nearly shot the man but thought better of it, deciding it would be more effective to shoot a Rebel with a rifle, and he drew his bead on one clambering over a fence thirty feet away. The Confederate fell wounded, and Ruch reloaded his piece only to realize that his fellow Union soldiers were falling back. He joined them and started running back from his position while noticing Federal casualties littering the ground and Wilkeson's cannon retreating from the knoll. One of Ruch's comrades in the 153rd Pennsylvania, Private John Trombeam, took cover by an oak tree and called out, "Come boys, let us give them what they deserve." A Confederate bullet struck his right shoulder, and Trombeam dropped his rifle but was determined to make a stand. Balancing the gun with his left shoulder, he took a shot. Captain Reeder remained behind as the Pennsylvanian regiment retreated, emptying the

---

[51] Brady's four companies had losses of only three killed, two wounded, and four prisoners. Pfanz, *Gettysburg—The First Day*, 240–41. OR, 27(1): 717. J. Miller to John Bachelder, Freemansburg, Pa., March 2, 1884, in Ladd, *Bachelder Papers*, 2:1026. Kiefer, *History of the One Hundred and Fifty-third Regiment*, 211–14.

cylinder of his pistol at Confederates less than fifteen feet away before running back to his company. Private John Rush, unable to raise his arms because both his shoulders had been shot, held his open cap box in one hand and his cartridge box in the other while a lieutenant loaded and fired his rifle. By the time Reuben Ruch reached the Almshouse and turned around, he could clearly see the brigades of Hays and Avery enveloping the Federal right and Union soldiers "dropping like flies." On foot, von Gilsa called for someone to catch a horse for him, and, upon obtaining one, he mounted and tried to rally his men in a line near the Almshouse barn, peppering his orders with German epithets.[52]

Ames had barely put his regiments into their advanced position before Confederate artillery began shelling his men and Doles's brigade, and Major Eugene Blackford's battalion advanced upon it. Barlow and Ames, as well as Ames's troops, observed on Gilsa's line break. William Warren watched as a "German regiment came back hallooing," while Colonel Andrew Harris of the Seventy-fifth Ohio noted that von Gilsa's brigade, "true to their natural instinct, being hard pressed by superior numbers, have way and thus left our Brigade, now equally engaged with the enemy in front and flank (and exposed) to an enfilading fired of the most terrible kind." Ames's line suffered confusion as some of von Gilsa's men ran through to get away from the oncoming Confederates. Yet, Barlow had no intention of ordering his men to withdraw and instead pushed Ames's small force forward to check the Confederate advance. Ames activated the Seventy-fifth Ohio from the reserve, ordering Harris's two hundred men to fix bayonets and advance between the Tenth and Twenty-fifth Ohio regiments to stop the Confederates. The Ohioans moved forward and, upon reaching a woods, fired at Doles's attacking Georgians and briefly halted the Rebel advance. Doles's men countered by maneuvering around the outnumbered and unreinforced Seventy-fifth's flanks. With four of his twelve officers and a quarter of his men dead or mortally wounded, and four more officers and half the rest of his regiment wounded, Harris ordered the

---

[52] George Campbell Brown, "My Confederate Experiences," typescript in the collections of Gettysburg National Military Park, quoted in Greene, "From Chancellorsville to Cemetery Hill," 78. Pfanz, *Gettysburg—The First Day*, 241–42. Kiefer, *History of the One Hundred and Fifty-third Regiment*, 211–15.

survivors of his regiment's stand to form a skirmish line and retreat.[53]

The Confederates handled Ames's other regiments as roughly. As Doles's men charged the 107th Ohio "yelling like Indians," Lieutenant Colonel Charles Mueller and Captain August Vignos were shot in their right arms, and Captain Barnet Steiner received a painful and mortal wound in his abdomen. Although the regiment took its position that afternoon with 434 men in line, only 171 remained that evening. The Twenty-fifth Ohio offered good initial resistance and at one point was so closely engaged with the Confederates that its color-bearer and his Southern counterpart struck each other with their flagstaffs. The Twenty-fifth began July 1 with 220 men, but only sixty rallied around its colors when night fell. On Ames's right, Lieutenant Colonel Fowler received the word to advance with excitement. Still mounted on a white charger, he called to his men, "Now, Seventeenth, do your duty! Forward, double quick! Charge bayonets!" His six companies hit a maelstrom of Confederate bullets, and a shell fragment shattered Fowler's skull, spraying some of his brains on Lieutenant H. Whitney Chatfield. Bullets also passed through Chatfield's hat and sleeve, snapped his sword's blade (which dated to the Revolutionary War), and killed his horse, while Mexican War veteran Captain James E. Moore took two bullets to the head. The night before, Moore had a premonition of his death and told a fellow officer he would soon be "at rest." [54]

Chatfield and a sergeant tried to bear Fowler's body off the field but had to abandon it. Private Warren of the Seventeenth recalled running for the Almshouse when "bullets were comeing [sic] in a shower, and, though thinking "I was spoke for, still kept moveing [sic] on and shortly I expect it was a piece of spent shell struck my right shoulder blade and almost knocked me

[53] Pfanz, *Gettysburg—The First Day*, 245–46. Hamblen, *Connecticut Yankees*, 23. OR, 27(1): 712, 715, 717. Andrew L. Harris to J. B. Bachelder, Eaton, Ohio, March 14, 1881, in Ladd, *Bachelder Papers*, 2:744.

[54] Pfanz, *Gettysburg—The First Day*, 246–47. Peter Young to J. B. Bachelder, Painesville, Ohio, August 12, 1867, in Ladd, *Bachelder Papers*, 1:310–11; Jeremiah Williams to J. B. Bachelder, Washington, D.C., June 18, 1880, in ibid., 1:668.

*over. . . . I ran across the field and everything before me looked
as white as a sheet." Only 241 of the Seventeenth's 386 men answered roll call the next morning, a casualty rate substantially
lowered by the fact that four of its companies served on detached
duty and missed the brigade's rout.*[55]

*Barlow tried to rally his shattered lines and oppose the Confed-
erate advance, but as he turned his horse, a bullet struck him
halfway between his left armpit and thigh. He clambered off his
horse and attempted to walk off the field, as two of his soldiers
stopped to assist him. In the process, one was shot, and then a
spent bullet bruised Barlow's back. Weakened from the loss of
blood, Barlow lay down as bullets continued whizzing about
him, one hitting his hat and another nicking his finger. Ames
assumed command of the division and tried in vain to rally a
line at the Almshouse. Schurz then ordered him to try to form a
line at the very northern edge of Gettysburg town, but the "whole
division was falling back with little or no regularity, regimental
organizations having become destroyed." Regiments lost officers
and direction quickly: with Ames in command of the division,
Colonel Andrew L. Harris of the Seventy-fifth Ohio assumed control of the brigade, while that regiment passed through the command of several captains as they fell killed or wounded in quick
succession. On the Rebel side, Major John W. Daniel excitedly
called to Early, "General, this day's work will win the Southern
Confederacy," though the division commander remained silent
on the issue and instead sent Daniel to find Gordon. During his
search for the brigadier, Daniel saw Barlow lying wounded
among his fallen men.*[56]

*After smashing Barlow's two brigades, Doles's and Early's men
turned their attention to Krzyzanowski's brigade and over-
whelmed it as well. Luckily for the Federals, Howard had finally
approved the release of one brigade from von Steinwehr's division, posted in reserve on Cemetery Hill, to assist Schurz. Colonel
Charles R. Coster's brigade took longer to reach the northern edge*

---

[55] Pfanz, *Gettysburg—The First Day,* 248. Diary of William H. Warren,
quoted in Hamblen, *Connecticut Yankees,* 25.

[56] Pfanz, *Gettysburg—The First Day,* 248–49. OR, 27(1): 712–13. Captain
M. Browne to J. B. Bachelder, Jacksonville, Fla., April 8, 1864, in Ladd, *Bachelder Papers,* 1:149.

of Gettysburg town than Schurz expected, doing so after Barlow's division had already been crushed. Upon its arrival, Schurz posted its nine hundred available men on the northeast edge of town to cover his two shattered divisions' retreat. Coster's brigade suffered horribly on July 1—as the Confederates smashed into its front and flank, over 550 men became casualties or prisoners, some of whom would suffer and die at Andersonville and Belle Isle prisons. They checked Hays's and Colonel Isaac Avery's pursuing brigades long enough, however, to allow Barlow's men to retreat through town.[57]

On the Federal left, the First corps' line had also broken under repeated assault from Major Generals Henry Heth's, Robert E. Rodes's, and William D. Pender's divisions. Men from both the First and Eleventh Corps streamed through Gettysburg town, unorganized and with men intermixed without regard to regimental designation, though troops of the Eleventh corps walked on one side of the street while those of the First used the other. They were not particularly panicked, and some joked as they walked back, but all semblance of military order dissolved. Upon reaching Cemetery Hill, Generals Howard and Doubleday worked to organize a new defensive Federal line. From the Eleventh corps, von Steinwehr's division held the stone walls west of the cemetery while Schimmelfennig's formed directly opposite the town. Ames, "cool and manly in appearance, though exhausted" formed the several hundred men who now comprised Barlow's division on the corps' right, to the east of the Baltimore Pike. The support of well-supplied Federal artillery helped make the Cemetery Hill line an imposing defensive position. All in all, it proved a rough day for a corps that had recently won the ignominious sobriquet of the "Running Half Moons" for what had happened at Chancellorsville.[58]

---

[57] Pfanz, *Gettysburg—The First Day*, 258–59, 261, 267–68. OR, 27(1): 729.

[58] Peter F. Young, an officer in the 107th Ohio, recalled that "such imperturbably coolness as Gen. Ames displayed in the trying hours of the first day under a most galling fire, I but seldom saw in my army experience; he has the highest admiration and regard of all under his command who ever fought under his guidance." Colonel Charles S. Wainwright likewise expressed a positive assessment of Ames's service at Gettysburg, both as a general and a man. Concerning July 2, Wainwright wrote, "Of Ames himself I saw a good deal; in fact, we were alongside each other pretty much all day. I found him the best

After the Confederates swept through the sector where Barlow lay wounded, it grew considerably safer and several assisted him. This generated one of the most enduring stories of the Civil War. According to John B. Gordon's postwar writings and speeches, the Southern brigadier rode forward with his men as they swept Barlow's bluecoats off the knoll. Coming across the badly wounded Northern general, Gordon dismounted, gave his Federal counterpart a drink, and had him moved into the shade. Barlow then asked the Rebel to remove Arabella's letters from his pocket and destroy them and to tell her, if they ever met, that her husband perished in the service of his country and that his final thoughts were of her. Gordon assured Barlow that he would do so and that he would grant Arabella, who was nearby, permission to cross through the Southern lines to find him. Convinced that Barlow was dying, Gordon rejoined his Georgians. Gordon was serving in the U.S. Senate fifteen years later when he received an invitation to dine with a New York congressman. Ignorant of their meeting on the fields north of Gettysburg, the congressman also invited Barlow, and Gordon asked, "General are you related to the Barlow who was killed at Gettysburg?" Barlow replied, "Why, I am the man, sir. Are you related to the Gordon who killed me? "I am the man, sir," retorted the Georgian, and the two engaged in a close friendship until Barlow's death.[59]

---

kind of a man to be associated with, cool and clear in his own judgment, gentlemanly, and without the smallest desire to interfere. We consulted together, but during the whole time we were here he never once attempted to pressure on his superior rank. Ames is a gentleman; and a strange thing in the army, I did not hear him utter an oath of any kind during the three days!" Butts, *Gallant Captain*, 78–79. Peter F. Young to J. B. Bachelder, Painesville, Ohio, August 12, 1867, in Ladd, *Bachelder Papers*, 1:312. Charles S. Wainwright diary entries, July 1, 1863; July 2, 1863, both in Allan Nevins, ed., *A Diary of Battle: The Personal Journals of Colonel Charles S. Wainwright 1861–1865* (1962; repr. Gettysburg: Stan Clark Military Books), 237, 242 (page citations are to repr. ed.). Culp, "Gettysburg." Pfanz, *Gettysburg—The First Day*, 324, 332–33. George Benson Fox to his father, Gettysburg, Pa., July 4, 1863, in William F. Howard, ed., "George Benson Fox's Letter to His Father Describes How His Regiment Became 'All Covered with Glory' at Gettysburg," in *Military History* 15 (December 1998): 10.

[59] John B. Gordon, *Reminiscences of the Civil War* (New York: Charles Scribner's Sons, 1903), 151–53. Ralph Lowell Eckert, *John Brown Gordon: Soldier Southerner American* (Baton Rouge: Louisiana State University Press, 1989),

Although it is a good story, Gordon probably embellished the battlefield meeting, if it occurred at all. Barlow never mentions the meeting in his letters immediately after Gettysburg, though he did relate with particular detail the aid he received from several Confederates (then again, some pages are missing from his first letter after Gettysburg). Barlow explicitly mentions destroying some letters he had on his person, and it seems strange that he would have needed Gordon to eliminate others. Furthermore, it seems doubtful that Gordon, who served his entire military career after Gettysburg fighting against the Army of the Potomac and achieved high rank and renown, never learned that Barlow survived and was an important division commander in the Federal Second corps. If anything, it is possible that Gordon encountered Barlow and ordered several nearby Confederates to assist the wounded officer. The anecdote illustrates, however, Gordon's larger postwar agenda of sectional reconciliation by showing virtue, honor, and valor on both sides of the Civil War.

In any event, on the evening of July 1, Arabella came onto the field in an ambulance and met Howard near the Cemetery gate, saying "Gen. Howard, my husband is wounded and left within the enemy's lines, I must go to him." Ames and von Fritsch also met her and described the location where they believed Barlow could be found. Despite rifle fire, the nurse rode through Gettysburg with a white flag in her hand, less a nurse at this moment than a wife searching for her beloved husband, not knowing whether or not he still lived.[60]

Because he seemed mortally wounded, the Confederates left Barlow in Gettysburg when they retreated in defeat.[61]

53–54, 315–16. William F. Hanna, "A Gettysburg Myth Exploded," *Civil War Times Illustrated* 24 (May 1985): 42–47. Pfanz, *Gettysburg: The First Day*, n. 23, 417–18. Hanna significantly discounts that this meeting happened, though Pfanz believes it largely to be true.

[60] Butts, *Gallant Captain*, 79–80. Oliver O. Howard, "After the Battle." Stephen Minot Weld, *War Diary and Letters of Stephen Minot Weld 1861–1865* (Boston: Massachusetts Historical Society, 1979), 233.

[61] Welsh, *Medical Histories of Union Generals*, 15.

> At a small house near Gettysburg Penn.
> 3 miles out on the Turnpike toward
> Baltimore Tuesday July 7th /63 1 P.M.

My Dear Mother

I will give you some account of my late experiences.

On last Wednesday morn of July 1st we left Emmitsburg to march to Gettysburg, a distance of 10 miles. The cavalry was in the advance, then the 1st Corps, and then the 11th. When we got about half way we were told by persons we met that the Cavalry were having a hard fight with the Enemies Cavalry + had been driven back somewhat.

On getting near the town we learned that the 1st Corps had engaged the enemies infantry + that Gen Reynolds was killed. Gen Howard was in command of both Corps + Gen Schurz in command of the 11th Corps. On arriving in the town Gen Schurz ordered me to go through the town, form on the right of the 3rd Division (which was just preceding us) + engage the enemy.

I went through + formed as directed, a battery of the 4th U.S. Artillery being sent to me. The enemy soon opened on us with his artillery. His number of guns was superior to mine + though another battery was promised me I never got it. The Capt. of my battery had one leg carried away one gun disabled + several horses killed, but still kept in position. The country was an open one for a long distance around + could be [letter ripped but a typescript copy at the Massachusetts Historical Society says "swept"] by our artillery. We could see their infantry make various attacks upon the other parts of the lines, or rather, _feel_ the lines. Finally, the 1st Corps, 3rd Division of the 11th Corps, + my Division were attacked simultaneously by the enemies infantry. A force came up against our front in line of battle with supports in the rear. We ought to have held the place easily, for I had my entire force at the very point where the attack was made. But the enemies skirmishers had hardly attacked us before my men began to run. No fight at all was made. Finding that they were going I started to get ahead of them to try to rally them + [letter ripped but most likely "form"] another line in the rear. Before I could turn my horse I was shot in the left side about halfway between the arm pit + the head of the thigh bone. I dismounted + tried to walk off the field. Every body was then running to the rear + the enemy were approaching rapidly. One man took hold of one shoulder + another on the other side to help me. One of them was soon shot + fell. I then got a spent ball in my back which has made <u>quite</u> a bruise. Soon, I got too faint to go any further + lay down. I lay in the midst of the fire some five minutes as the enemy were firing at our running men. I did not expect to get out alive. A ball went through my hat as I lay on the ground + another just grazed the fore finger of my right hand. Finally the enemy came up + were very kind. Major [A. L.] Pitzer, a staff officer of Gen. Early had me carried by some men into the woods + placed on a bed of leaves.[62] They put some water by me + then went on to the front again.

During this time the whole of our line had been driven back; both the 1st Corps + the 11th, the 3rd Division of this Corps (Schurz's) went at the same time and in the same way that we did. The 2nd Div. (Steinwehr's) was in reserve + I don't know what became of that except that it also was routed.

I lay in the woods sometime until the shells began to come in + then one of my own men who were prisoners carried me in a blanket to a house further off.[63] I was in considerable pain + bleeding a good deal. My trousers + vest + both shirts were saturated with blood.

They put me on a bed + about dark 3 Confederate surgeons came. They gave me chloroform + probed my wound. When I woke up they told me that a Minie ball had passed downward from where it entered, + through the peritoneum + lodged in the cavity of the pelvis + that there was very little chance for my life. They gave me some morphine + left me. Several Confederate officers passed the night at the house + were very kind + attentive. A brother of Alex. R. Boteler of Va. bathed my wound several times.[64]

---

[62] Pitzer was actually a lieutenant. *OR*, 27(2): 473.

[63] The Josiah Benner house. Welsh, *Medical Histories of Union Generals,* 15.

[64] Born in 1815, Alexander R. Boteler attended Princeton University before entering Virginia politics as a Whig. Elected to Congress in 1859, Boteler sought to prevent disunion during the crisis of 1860, but when Virginia seceded, he went with his state and represented the Old Dominion in the Confederate Congress. He was a volunteer on "Stonewall" Jackson's staff during the summer of 1862, and after that officer's death joined the staff of J. E. B.

We had been attacked (my Division) by Gordon's Brigade of Early's Division, of [Lieutenant Richard S.] Ewell's (late Jackson's) Corps.

In the morning one of our own captured Surgeons + the same Confederate Drs. came to see me + pronounced the same opinion as before. You will see that the danger to be expected was the same as from my former wound, this is peritonitis + that the bowels had been cut. But it is now evident that neither the peritoneum nor the bowels have been touched. The ball is probably imbedded in some of the muscles near my old would. It cannot be got out unless it works out itself, for the region is too dangerous for cutting. On Thursday morning, I moved up into another house just inside of the town where an elderly lady + her daughter were very kind to me.[65] I found some books there + passed Thursday + Friday very comfortably under morphine. I read + talked a good deal. I eat only some coffee + toast + cherries in these days. The ladies + some of our wounded in the house did what nursing I required. I saw some of our Surgeons + some of the enemies who said there was nothing to be done but to bathe the wound in cold water + wait. Some of the staff officers of Ewell + Early came to see me + I talked very freely with them. They were pleasant fellows. They despised our army + meant to fight to the last. [I] saw a good many of their men also + was much pleased with them. They are more heroic, more modest + more in earnest than we are. Their whole tone is much finer than ours. Except among those on our side who are fighting this war upon antislavery grounds, there is not much earnestness nor are there many noble feelings + sentiments involved. I heard the battles of Thursday + Friday close to me. The enemy had no doubt of capturing or utterly destroying our Army + I feared it would be so. Ewell + Early sent word that at the first flag of truce, they would

[remainder of letter is missing]

Stuart. He served in a number of appointed positions after the war and also painted such Confederates as Robert E. Lee, James Longstreet, Jefferson Davis, and George Pickett. *DAB*, 1:467–68.

[65] The John S. Crawford house. Welsh, *Medical Histories of Union Generals*, 15.

[First part of letter missing]

Edward staid two nights + a day here, but yesterday rode on after the Division to see about his leave of absence which had [sentence not finished] He was then going to strike directly for the Railroad + go North. I have not heard from him since he left. We shall have to leave our horses somewhere in the neighborhood + send for them. I have our coloured man Horace + one convalescent left here as a guard. The army has marched down into Maryland to overtake or intercept Lee + I have sent all my people back to the Division. This is the last of my connection with the Division. I would not accept it even if I did not get Dr. Howe's place. I would take a <u>Brigade</u> in preference to such a Division. <u>This is what I say about the fighting of the Division</u>. I wish you would mention only with the greatest care + remember the rascally publication of my Fair Oaks letter. I do not want to have anything to do with the disputes in which the Corps will probably indulge as after Chancellorsville. Gen. Ames behaved with great courage + coolness + also did some of his staff. Some of the German officers behaved well. Col. Von Gilsa I did not notice after the fight began. Probably he behaved well as he is personally brave. I sit up when I like + can hobble about easily but they think it dangerous. In a week I shall probably be dressed + about though it will be several weeks before I can exert myself at all. The wound is suppurating well. It was not nearly so severe a shock to the system as my former one + was dangerous only because it might have touched the peritoneum or bowels which it is now evident it has not. I have not had any pain or taken any morphine today.

I shall leave here on Friday + reach New York on Sat. I shall stay a day or two + then perhaps will come to Brattleboro if you are there. I wish you + I could go to the Dinsmore's for a visit. Your last letter said you were going to Brattleboro the next day. So we telegraphed there. This I send through R. I will write again before I leave. We have today an authentic announcement that

Vicksburg was taken on the 4th Inst.[66] So the enemy are hard pressed. I did not send you Mr Owens last letter saying that I should be nominated as the Negro Superintendent. As I lay in the field before the enemy reached me I remembered that I had two of these letters in my pocket + that the enemy might not be inclined to parole so important a functionary as the "Superintendent of the Freed Men throughout the U.S." So I destroyed the letters together with all others in my pocket.

I shall take the place as long as I am well enough.

I have written a long letter + am tired.

Goodbye—will write to R. just when I am coming.

E. will be in N.Y. in a day or two.

> Lovingly,
> Francis C. B.

I came via Baltimore

> 21 Franklin St.
> Baltimore Aug 5 /63

My dear Mr [Moses Blake] Williams

Mrs. Barlow wrote Aunt Mary some days ago of my wounding + my present condition. I should have written you before, but knew you had gone on your fishing expedition, beyond the region of letters. I do not know that you have even yet returned.

I am still on my back in Baltimore unable to be moved + suffering considerable from my wound which threatens to be more tedious than the former one in my groin.

As long as the ball was in me with its location unknown everything was uncertain + I could make but little progress. But now that the ball is extracted I presume I shall be well as soon as the hole which it made heals up.

How have you enjoyed your fishing excursion + has it been as

---

[66] Major General Ulysses S. Grant forced the surrender of Vicksburg and its defending army on July 4, 1863—a major victory for the North, especially when compounded with Lee's repulse from Pennsylvania.

usual? You never answered a letter which I wrote you shortly after I got a Brigade, proposing that Mo.[67] should come down + make me a visit + see how he liked the idea of becoming my Aide. Perhaps you did not want to agitate the subject with him again.

I recd your letter about Richardson a day or two after I had written about Mo.

I was very glad that I could comply with your wishes about him + the more so because I also liked him on his own account. As long as I kept the Brigade I retained him on my Staff + when I left it for a Division I applied to have him go with me but they would not let him leave the Brigade. As you know when I first returned to the Army I took a Brigade composed wholly of Americans + which I am confident would have fought. After Chancellorsville I was persuaded to give up my Brigade + take the Division which Gen. Devens had commanded + which was the first to begin the disgraceful performances at Chancellorsville. They gave me a first rate Gen. (Gen. Ames) under me + I thought we might bring the Dutchmen up by strict discipline. A Division command is so much more important than a Brigade command that it was quite an inducement to take it. But I am convinced that we can do nothing with these German Regts. They won't fight + the whole history of the war has shown it. I never will set foot in the 11th Corps again. I am glad to see by the papers that they talk of breaking it up or making some changes in it.

The Drs now promise I shall leave here on Friday. I shall come North slowly + join Mother at Brattleboro where she now is.

I hope to be about Boston a few days before I am fit for duty + shall then see you. My convalescence will be a short one compared to my last when I had the abcess to keep me down so long. I have never had a moments trouble from the old abcess. Has Mo. got out of his Military order + what is he doing.

I wish you would give me some account of your summers sporting. My address is care Richard D. Barlow Receiving Store, Navy Yard Brooklyn, New York

Truly
Francis C. Barlow

---

[67] This refers to his son, Moses E. Williams.

Soml New Jersey[68]
Aug. 12 /63

My dear Bob[69]

I have just recd your letter. I am shocked to hear of Sumner's death.[70] I had not heard of it as I have not seen any list of killed + wounded. It must be a great blow to your mother + I wish you would express to her my deepest sympathy.

I am glad he died so bravely. I have considered Charles [Paine] as dead for some time.[71] The papers so stated.

I was seduced into taking the Division. I did by the request of Gen Howard to see if I could introduce any discipline. It was composed partly of Dutch + partly of Ohio troops + was Devin's Division that behaved so badly at Chancellorsville.[72] They gave me a good Brigadier (Ames) to command one of my Brigades. But these Dutch won't fight. Their officers say so + they say so themselves + they ruin all with whom they come in contact. Where did you hear the nonsense about my going ahead of my skirmishers? How could you suppose I was such a damned fool?

---

[68] An abbreviation for Arabella Barlow's Somerville, New Jersey.

[69] This letter was written to classmate Robert Treat Paine. Born in 1835, Paine attended the Boston Latin School before studying at Harvard College, where he and Francis Barlow graduated at the top of their class of 1855. After studying at Harvard Law School, Paine became a member of the Massachusetts bar and invested the proceeds from his practice into railroad and mining endeavors. His quickly amassed wealth enabled him to turn from business to philanthropy, and he helped fund improved housing for laborers after the Civil War. Paine was also the founder of the Associated Charities of Boston, as well as its president from 1879 to 1907, and served as a director of the American Prison Association and Boston Children's Aid Society. *DAB*, 7:158–59.

[70] Born in Boston in 1845, Sumner Paine studied at the Boston Latin School before entering Harvard College in July 1861. His desire to participate in the war led him to join the Twentieth Massachusetts as a second lieutenant in May 1863, and he arrived in time to take command of his company when Captain Oliver Wendell Holmes Jr. went down wounded. He died while helping repulse Pickett's Charge at Gettysburg, his last words being "Isn't this glorious?" Higginson, *Harvard Memorial Biographies*, 2:477–80.

[71] In fact, Charles Paine survived the war. Crawford, *Famous Families of Massachusetts*, 2:18.

[72] The division had been the first one struck and routed by Jackson's corps at Chancellorsville on May 2, 1863.

It was not so. We had been under fire an hour before I was hit + it was not until the Division had fallen back. I staid to rally them as long as it was of any use + just as I turned my horse to go back I was hit, the fighting being about over.

I wish you would correct the impression that I went ahead of my skirmishers.

Your remarks about the Sanderson case have been sent me + I am glad you have so good an opinion of it. I am too sick + do not sufficiently remember the facts to make any suggestions now. But I am coming to Mass. as soon as I can probably in a fortnight + we can then talk of it. I was only able to be moved from Baltimore on Monday. My wound is healing + they have cut out the ball, but I have violent pains when I stand or sit + I am afraid there is something wrong inside. I shall see you soon my dear Bobus.

Give my compliments to Mrs Paine.

A letter sent care

> Richard D. Barlow
> Receiving Store
> Navy Yard
> Brooklyn New York

will always reach me.

> Yrs
> FCB

~

> Soml
> Friday Aug 14th 1863

Dear Mother

Your letter of Aug. 12th has just come + I am disappointed at what you say about our coming. I had arranged to go to New York on Monday + start for B. on Tuesday. I can get a servant if necessary but I now understand you to say that as long as I have to be on the stretcher + have everything brought to me, it would give too much trouble in the family.

In regard to my condition the wound has about entirely closed up + I have strength enough to sit up + walk about were it not for my other troubles. These are the pains of which I wrote in various letters. They are in my thigh bones + sometimes run across the lower part of the stomach, throbbing pains of a neuralgic character.

The Drs in Balt. attributed them partly to neuralgia + partly to flatulence. A week ago I could sit up + walk about + felt the pains only for a few moments on lying down again. Now I can't bear my weight on my legs or walk a step without having them severely. This has prevented me from trying to sit up any more. I am confined all day to the stretcher. And now they attack me even when I am lying perfectly still. Probably some nerve was cut + I must wait until it heals. I shall either go to town or get Dr. Hammond to come down here to see me. Were it not for these pains I should soon get about. As it is I can travel well enough by lying on the stretcher.

I will come on to Mass. + go to Newport or anywhere else. I don't care what the price of board is. If you can get rooms at Newport we had better go there. I think the Seashore would do us both good + you must not mind the price for I will pay it. I will come whenever you say. As soon as I can go about I will make the visit with you to the Dinsmores as you suggest, but I am not fit to visit now. Could we not get a place near you in Brattleboro.

Ask E. if he has my McClellan saddle in Balt? His came here on my horse. I have my horses at pasture at an expense of only $7 per month for both. It is better for them just now than living on grain as they are not used.

If the only objection to my staying at the Fields is the want of a servant I can easily get one.

Let me hear from you as soon as possible in this matter.

Affectionately
Francis

Sharon Springs, September 26, 1863

My Very Dear Charles [Dalton],

You must wonder at not hearing from me, but the truth is I have been so forlorn that I have not written to anybody.

Will you believe that on this, the 86th day of my wound, I am still lying on a stretcher and shouldn't dare to walk six rods? I have no suffering from my wound, which though it still dribbles a little is of no account, but for a long time I have been afflicted with neuralgia in the loins and legs. Sitting or standing is very painful and it attacks me even when lying still.

I am anxious to come to Boston and see Dr. Bigelow as soon as I can travel.[73] This week I was to have gone to the Howes at Newport but I can't travel, as my attacks have lately been worse than ever.

I left Brattleboro the last of August and spent ten days with a friend on the Hudson and then came here, where I have not improved, but am rather worse. But today I am freer from pains and if I continue so shall leave on Monday or Tuesday and after making my brother a visit in Brooklyn for a few days shall come to dear Massachusetts.

I hope you will be at Chelmsford where we can have a few days.

Don't you think I am an old cripple? For the last year I have been disabled by wounds nine months and on duty three.

I was well a fortnight ago that I ventured to New York for a day, but sitting up so long raised the devil with me.

I shall be very glad to see you. I should have written to you to come to Brattleboro, but we were to leave there a day or two after your letter came saying you would come.

I have heard nothing about my appointment as superintendent of the darkies. If they adopt Owen and Howes, etc., plan they will no doubt appoint me. The Secretary of War has as yet taken no action in the matter.

---

[73] Born in 1818, Henry Jacob Bigelow became a prominent surgeon in Boston. After studying at the Boston Latin School, he entered Harvard College at the age of fifteen and graduated in the class of 1837. Afterward, he studied medicine at Harvard and Dartmouth and became house surgeon at Massachusetts General Hospital in Boston. Bigelow played a key role in the early use of surgical anesthesia as well as other surgical advancements. *DAB*, 1:256–57.

Very affectionately,
Francis

As late as October 27, Barlow's wound continued discharging, and his health remained poor. He was well enough, however, to join other officers to lobby for Colonel Nelson Miles, future commander of the U.S. Army, to receive his first star. In late November, Barlow wrote Massachusetts Senator Henry Wilson:

> He is a man of untiring & sleepless energy who does not want to be told to do a thing, or when & how to do it, but who uses all means in his power to attain success without waiting to be urged or quickened by anyone. If you send him with a body of troops to accomplish a certain purpose you know that he will do all that under the circumstances skill, determination, & courage can do. To anyone who knows the habit of many military officers of fearing to take any responsibility & of sending at every step for orders & directions & of only doing just enough to escape censure or to obtain a reasonable degree of commendation, what I have said of Col. Miles will appear as high praise.
>
> He has also a remarkable talent for fighting battles. It is not only that he is very brave (for most officers are that) but he has that perfect coolness and self-possession in danger which is much more uncommon. The sound of cannon clears his head & strengthens his nerves.
>
> And his quickness of perception & skill in taking up positions & availing himself of advantages of & etc. in action I have not seen equalled. To all this he adds in an unusual degree the faculty of attracting men to him & arousing their pride & enthusiasm without relaxing discipline.
>
> In short I hardly know a military merit or quality (short of those higher powers of strategical combination whose presence he has yet had no opportunity to test or exhibit) which he does not possess. . . . I think he is an unusual instance of military ability which ought to be brought out & encouraged.[74]

---

[74] Surgeon's certificate dated October 27, 1863, in Barlow Papers NA. Francis C. Barlow to Henry Wilson, November 28, 1863, in the Miles/Cameron Papers in Library of Congress, quoted in Brian C. Pohanka, ed., *Nelson A Miles: A Documentary Biography of his Military Career 1861–1903* (Glendale, Calif.: Arthur H. Clark Company, 1985), 21.

On December 18, Barlow wrote Assistant Adjutant General Col. E. D. Townsend at the War Department to acknowledge an order directing that he assume command of the draftee depot at Springfield, Illinois. Barlow's troubling wound left him unable to mount a horse, however, and he informed Townsend that the "surgeons emphatically protest against my returning to duty at this time[.]" Barlow explained that he had conversed with a friend concerning his improving condition and that this friend must have repeated these comments "more strongly + without the qualifications with which I made them" in a subsequent interview with Secretary of War Stanton. Besides, Barlow noted, he wanted a command of troops in the field and had little desire to command a troop depot so far from action. A letter signed by two doctors accompanied Barlow's request and offered the medical opinion that Barlow's wound, healed for only about a week, would likely reopen under exertion. Additionally, the general continued to remain prostrate most of the time and was generally in too poor health to assume an active post. The doctors opined that resuming active duty in a period shorter than four or six weeks would expose Barlow to "the risque [sic] of permanent disability."[75]

Meanwhile, Winfield S. Hancock learned of Barlow's interest in a place in the Second Corps through Colonel Nelson Miles and was only too happy to bring him in as a division commander. In December, Hancock wrote Barlow in Boston to inform him that he had requested the change in assignment and assured that he would "always be pleased to have you in a command of mine."[76]

---

[75] Francis Barlow to Colonel E. D. Townsend, Boston, December 18, 1863; Report of Surgeon M. Dale, Boston, December 18, 1863, in Barlow papers, NA.

[76] Winfield S. Hancock to Francis C. Barlow, Washington, D.C., December 12, 1863, in Barlow collection, Massachusetts Historical Society, Boston, Massachusetts.

4

1864: "We have been in a most terrible whirl of marching + picket fighting"

In late January, Major General Winfield S. Hancock requested that Barlow be assigned to his Second corps and perform recruiting duty in New England until well enough to return to active duty. Realizing that he would not be able to personally visit New England on a recruiting tour that winter, Hancock urged the War Department to accept the "distinguished" Barlow's offer to assist efforts to obtain enlistees in that region. Simultaneously, Barlow informed the War Department of Hancock's opinion that the he could be of use on recruiting duty and requested assignment to Hancock, "leaving it to him to employ me in recruiting or in the field as he may think best." On January 26, Barlow once again became a member of the Second Corps and received orders to report, via letter, to Hancock at Harrisburg, Pennsylvania. He did so and began recruiting duties immediately, though he remained anxious to receive orders assigning him command of the Second corps' First division.[1]

On the first of April, Barlow formally assumed command of that division, composed of the Irish Brigade under Colonel Thomas Smyth and brigades under his friend Colonel Nelson Miles, Colonel John R. Brooke, and Colonel Paul Frank. On April 6 Barlow investigated his division's hospital, and a nurse, Cornelia Hancock, observed that the youthful general appeared barely twenty-five years of age (Barlow was, in fact, twenty-nine). She also noted Barlow's keen eye, that "there was not a

---

[1] Winfield S. Hancock to Colonel J. B. Fry, Philadelphia, January 22, 1864; Francis Barlow to Colonel E. D. Townsend, Boston, January 24, 1864; Special Orders No. 40, January 26, 1864; Barlow to Lieutenant Colonel C. H. Morgan, Boston, March 8, 1864, in Barlow's Generals Papers NA.

*spot in the hospital that he did not look into," and that ability
and presence, not age, were the prerequisites for having charge
in the service. She reported to her mother that, despite his age,
the young general had earned a reputation that his "commands
his Division."*[2]

April 9th /64
Saturday 8 p.m.

My dear Mother

I wrote a short letter last night. We had just recd orders for a
Review today by [Lieutenant] Gen. [Ulysses S.] Grant. But it has
rained violently all day + there has been no Review. I am glad
of it for now the mud will prevent it for several days after it clears
off + we shall be in better condition.

Today I have only been out over to the Camp of the 61st where
I dined with a party of the officers + Col. Miles. It was very
pleasant to see them again + talk over old times. There are quite
a number of the old officers remaining in the Regt, but very few
of the old men. No[w] + then I see one + always shake him by
the hand for I have a real affection for the old fellows. I am going
to get Braman at these Hd Qrs to take care of public horses. I
think Candler was right in what he said of this Div. It has a spirit
+ tone to it + a pride in its past successes which will always
make it fight well. It is rather loose in some matters of discipline
but it is improving every day + everyone is taking hold with the
best spirit. It has the misfortune of having a very large number
of new men but I hope the old ones will teach them how to fight
+ become good soldiers. The 61st is almost entirely a new Regt.
It has now some 250 men present for duty + some two hundred
recruits are yet to come.

Len has not been heard of + I am somewhat fearful of the
effects of this storm.

---

[2] General Orders No. 85, Headquarters First Division, Second Army Corps,
April 1, 1864, in Barlow's Generals Papers NA. Cornelia Hancock to her
Mother, April 6, 1864, in Henrietta Staratton Jaquette, ed., *South after Gettys-
burg: Letters of Cornelia Hancock 1863–1868* (New York: Thomas Y. Crowell
Company, 1956), 84–85.

I am very well satisfied with what has been accomplished since I came here. I think I have been successful in making a good impression. I have not lost my temper or spoken or acted hastily to anyone + though I am thought strict I think I am well liked.

Thanks for the brush + the recipe. I have just got some codine + will apply it. One of four men sentenced to be shot in the 15th has been pardoned by the Prest. I daresay the others will be before the time comes though I think it is a mistaken humanity to do so. 3 or 4 men per diem desert from the Division.

I have been busy all day as usual. I think it strange you have not recd my letters as I have written every day, with perhaps two exceptions, to some of you.

Give my best love to Mrs. Howe. I have not heard a word from anyone in Boston though some of them proposed to write.

With best love to all

Your affectionate son
Francis

Wednesday p.m.
April 13 /64

My dear Mother

Your letter of 9th April reached me this Evening. There is little for me to tell you. I suffer a good deal from the toothache, but as Dr. Harwood told me they were all right just before I started from Boston, I presume it is the process of acclimation that I am going through. I enclose letters from Clark + Livingston about coming on my Staff. I have applied for Clark. He has not had much experience but I find it very difficult to get a man for Aide that I am willing to take one green one for the sake of getting an educated man.

What a farce it is to order us to keep certain orders secret when Tom Dick + H. are allowed to publish them in the papers.

I have heard nothing from Len. He had not reached Washington on Monday. It is now 13 days since he sailed from New York + I have almost given him up.

I have just come in from a long ride to my picket line + my 4th Brigade which is camped 4 miles from here. I have not been out of my Division Camp or seen anyone since I wrote last.

Affectionately,
Francis

Barlow reviewed the Irish Brigade on April 15 and inspected its camp and hospital on April 17. Two days later, he hosted a reception after a review of his division by Meade and Hancock. Brigadier General Thomas Smyth, commander of the Irish Brigade, was present and proclaimed it a good time.[3]

April 19th /64
8.30 p.m.

My dear Mother
    Your letter of 14th + 15th + Edward's of 16th reached me last night. Bliss did not come—today recd a letter from him saying that business had called him suddenly back to New York. Today my Div. was reviewed. In the cleanliness of the men + the perfection of their equipment + the soldierly way of wearing their Knapsacks it was confessed by all to be superior to the others. We have more recruits than the rest of the Corps put together so did not so excel at marching but we were equal to any of them. It was a decided success. [Major] Gen. [George G.] Meade was there + after the Review Meade [Major General Winfield S.] Hancock, [Brigadier General John] Gibbon [Brigadier General Alexander] Webb [Brigadier General Joshua] Owen [Brigadier General Gershom] Mott + other Genls + many Colonels + staff officers came to my quarters where we gave them

---

[3] Thomas A. Smyth diary, April 15, 17, 19, 1864; typescript copy by Frank A Boyle.

a lunch with champaign &c.⁴ My Staff arranged all this lunch business. They staid sometime + all went off very well. T. Lyman was here + very jolly.⁵

Yesterday I went to the Review of the whole 6th Corps by Grant. None of the troops looked so well as mine though they are

---

⁴ Joshua Thomas Owen, nicknamed "Paddy" despite his birth in Wales, was brought to America at age nine. He became a teacher and then a lawyer in Pennsylvania, serving in that state's legislature from 1857 to 1859. He became colonel of a ninety-day regiment in the early days of the Civil War before assuming command of the Sixty-ninth Pennsylvania. He received a general's star on November 29, 1862, though this commission expired when the Senate failed to confirm the nomination. Owen's division commander John Gibbon preferred charges against him for disobedience of orders at Cold Harbor in June 1864, though the incident was closed with Owen's honorable discharge from the service a month later. Alexander S. Webb was born in New York City in 1835 and graduated from West Point in 1855. After fighting against Florida Seminoles, he returned to his alma mater as a mathematics instructor. Webb helped defend Fort Pickens when the Civil War erupted and he was an aide to the Army of the Potomac's chief of artillery, Brigadier General W. F. Barry, from July 1861 through the Peninsula campaign. On June 23, 1863, shortly before Gettysburg, Webb became brigadier general and took command of a brigade in the Second corps. On July 3 Webb and his brigade helped repulse Pickett's Charge, and he received a wound there (and, later, a Congressional Medal for his actions). Webb suffered a grievous wound at Spotsylvania and did not return to the Army of the Potomac until January 1865, at which time he became Meade's chief of staff. After the war, he taught at West Point until accepting the presidency of the College of the City of New York, an office he held for thirty-three years.

New Jersey businessman Gershom Mott became lieutenant colonel of the Fifth New Jersey Infantry. During the Peninsula campaign, Mott became colonel of the Sixth New Jersey and led it during Seven Pines and the Seven Days. After being wounded at Second Manassas, he was made brigadier general on September 7, 1862. He commanded a brigade in the Third corps during Chancellorsville, where he was again wounded, and in the spring 1864 he received command of a division in the Second corps. After Mott failed to adequately support an assault against the Confederate works at Spotsylvania on May 10, Meade consolidated Mott's division into a brigade. Although Mott disliked the arrangement, which effectively demoted him to brigade command, he regained a division command when Major General David Birney transferred to corps command in the Army of the James. Warner, *Generals in Blue*, 337–38, 353–54, 544–45.

⁵ Theodore Lyman was born into a wealthy household in Waltham, Massachusetts, on August 23, 1833. Barlow's classmate at Harvard, he graduated fourth in the class of 1855. A zoologist, he pursued his scientific work abroad until the Civil War erupted, though he did not hurry back to the United States to participate in it. A letter from Major General George G. Meade, however, whom Lyman had met on an expedition before the war, prompted the scientist to become a member of that officer's staff. As lieutenant colonel and aide to

mostly old men + have been under discipline all winter with good officers while this Div. has been running riot. I there saw Ned Dalton for a minute. He is coming over to spend some Sunday afternoon with me. In a day or two Gen. Grant will review the 2nd Corps all together.

As I wrote the horses are in fine condition. Len went home this morning.

I expect tomorrow a letter from Major [Louis H.] Pelouze about the papers for E. + R. + shall be very glad to see them.[6] I saw Capt Elliot this morning for a moment. He has just come back from leave + is coming over to see me. He enquired when the boys were coming. His Camp is very near mine. I am very well now + my cold is nearly gone. I <u>do</u> see the papers. The N.Y. Herald + Phila. Inquirer of the day before + the days Washington Chronicle. I hear no more of the Darkey Bureau + I have not heard from my application for Joe Clark nor again from him. I shall enjoy having a man of his stamp with me.

I am glad you enjoy Mrs Dana's. Give my best love to Mrs. Mason + tell her how short a time + how hurried I was in New York which prevented me from coming to see her.

With much love,
Francis

How about my clothes from Boston?

Hd Qrs 1st Div
2nd Corps 22nd April 1864

My dear Richard

Your letter of the 20th reached me tonight. I wrote E. last night + mother the day before. My letters for one of you must be con-

---

the commander of the Army of the Potomac, Lyman served through the entire 1864 campaign and until Appomattox. A collection of letters written to his wife are a font of useful information on this period of the war. After the war, Lyman became chair of the Fisheries Commission of Massachusetts and president of the American Fish Cultural Association. He was elected overseer of Harvard College in 1868 and also served a term in Congress. *DAB*, 6:519.

[6] Major Louis H. Pelouze was assistant adjutant general at the Department of War. *OR*, 37(2): 196.

sidered as addressed to all. It is impossible to tell when the Army will move. All that I can say is that I should not be surprised to get the order tonight + should not be surprised if it did not come for two weeks. I do not believe anyone short of Grant + Meade know. Everything is ready for a move.

You had better not come in uniform. Things are pretty strict here now + you could not wear uniform without having some official position. You could not be made a Volunteer Aide without a long + formal application + if you were you would have to do duty + be subject to military rules. It would not be pleasant for you + me for you to be here in any way that looks like a sham. The "Volunteer Aide" story will do very well at home as an excuse for your coming, but here you can be a visitor.

No answer yet from Major Pelouze. I have some fear that we shall find it hard to get a pass. Dr. Gardner had a good deal of trouble + I heard today that Charles Paine tried to get down but could get no pass. Fix the day of your coming long enough before hand for me to make application.

The Review of the 2nd Corps by Grant took place today. It was the best + most complete Review of so large a body of men that I ever saw + is so considered here. It beat the 6th Corps. There was perhaps not much to choose between the Divisions but certainly none of them surpassed mine. I was well satisfied which is a good deal for me. Dr Gardner was here + will call on mother + tell you about it. We all went to Hancocks Qrs. Afterwards + were introduced to Grant. Many Genls were there + we had very much the same sort of collation that we had at the Division Reviews. I saw [John R.] Adams the fighting parson of Miss Healeys who is a chaplain in the 6th Corps.[7] The 61st Regt. is on the extreme right of the whole Army + marches first at all Reviews &c. That is to say the 2nd Corps has the right of the line of Corps + the 1st Division the right in the Corps + Miles Brigade the right in the Div. + the 61st is the right Regt, in Miles Brigade. It is very desirable to march first at Reviews &c as everyone is fresh + gives more attention. I lead the Column today. I am very glad your vessels pay so well. Where is the bill of sale of my share of the Enchantress. I met Capt Elliot a moment today. He is coming over to see me.

---

[7] Barlow refers to John R. Adams, chaplain of the 121st New York Infantry.

I am very well but pretty tired tonight of all this Review &c.

With much love to all,
Francis

On side: I have not used your canvass yet as I have a straw bed.
Shall do so when we march.

Upon breaking winter quarters, the Army of the Potomac and Army of Northern Virginia engaged in almost constant maneuvering and combat for the next couple months. As commander in chief of all the Federal forces, Lieutenant General Ulysses S. Grant accompanied the Army of the Potomac and issued strategic orders to Meade. Grant proved a tenacious leader determined to crush Lee's army. Accordingly, he opened the spring campaign by crossing the Rapidan River with the intention of turning Lee's right flank and forcing the Confederates from their entrenchments and into an open battle, where superior Federal manpower and supplies would presumably prove decisive. Lee had other plans, however, and allowed the Federal army to cross the river so that his battle-hardened troops could unexpectedly hit them in the flank, in a dense wooded area known as the Wilderness.[8]

On May 3, the Army of the Potomac prepared to move but with a spirit of secrecy—division commanders were not informed of their march route until afternoon, and the Federal infantrymen were left unaware until shortly before the order to break camp. After dark, Hancock assembled the Second corps under a clear, starry sky, and by midnight his columns began moving from their winter encampment at Stevensburg to Ely's Ford across the Rapidan. Barlow's and Gibbon's divisions used the Culpeper-Fredericksburg Pike, and Hancock's other two divisions utilized a different road before uniting at Madden's Tavern and continuing on to Ely's Ford. Barlow's division reached it shortly before 5:30 a.m., just as a pontoon bridge was being completed, and his

---

[8] McPherson, *Battle Cry of Freedom*, 724.

men crossed—some using the bridge and others wading in the waist-high water. By 9:50 a.m., Hancock's forward regiments had reached their goal and began pitching camp just past Chancellorsville, where a battle had been fought exactly a year earlier and where signs of that clash, including skeletons, littered the ground. By 11:00, two of his divisions were in camp, and by 1:40, the entire Second corps had crossed. Meanwhile, the right wing of the Federal army, the Fifth and Sixth corps under Major General Gouverneur K. Warren and Major General John Sedgwick respectively, crossed the river at Germanna Ford and made for Wilderness Tavern.⁹

While the day's maneuver went smoothly for the Federal army, Lee had not been caught by surprise. As early as May 2, the Southern commander realized that Grant's advance was imminent and prepared the Army of Northern Virginia to move. On May 4, when it became clear that the Army of the Potomac had mobilized, Lee's gray columns responded accordingly.¹⁰

On May 5 Hancock's corps advanced toward Todd's Tavern via Catharpin Road, while Warren started from Wilderness Tavern, followed by Sedgwick's divisions. The Fifth corps marched for only a short while before Warren and his men encountered Lieutenant General Richard S. Ewell's Confederate corps. As more troops from both sides got funneled into the fight, it became clear that a quiet day's passage was no longer possible for the Army of the Potomac. A surging, full-blown battle erupted in woods so thick that troops often could not see the enemy, much less friendly units, and fires in the thicket burned wounded soldiers to death. The Federal army fought desperately to maintain control of the pike on which its advance relied, while one division deployed and struggled to maintain control of the intersection of the Brock and Orange Plank Roads on the Federal left. If this intersection fell to the Confederates, the Army of the Potomac would be split in two, with Hancock's corps perilously isolated

---

⁹ Gordon C. Rhea, *The Battle of the Wilderness May 5–6, 1864* (Baton Rouge: Louisiana State University Press, 1994), 61, 63–65, 69. William H. Green, "From the Wilderness to Spotsylvania," in *War Papers Read before the Commandery of the State of Maine, Military Order of the Loyal Legion of the United States,* 4 vols. (Portland, Maine: Thurston Print., 1898), 2:91–104: 92.

¹⁰ Rhea, *Battle of the Wilderness,* 78–81.

and unable to aid the other corps. Brigadier General George W. Getty's division of three brigades held the crossroads as Hancock marched his columns to its relief. The rough terrain and distance between Army headquarters and Hancock's corps, however, made communication between the two difficult, and Hancock did not receive Meade's orders to rejoin the other corps and attack the Rebels until later than anticipated. By 4:45, after a rough march, two of Hancock's divisions reinforced Getty as the struggle for the crossroads continued, and a third Second corps division entered the fight twenty minutes later. Barlow's marched last of the four.[11]

By evening of May 5, Hancock had four divisions, as well as Getty's tired men—a total of thirty-three thousand men—facing one Rebel division under Major General Henry Heth, though the terrain prevented either side from realizing the numbers each confronted. Furthermore, this struggle had even greater significance for Lee's battle plan. In reinforcing Getty, Hancock had left a key intersection at Todd's Tavern exposed. As long as Heth could keep the Federals occupied, Lieutenant General James Longstreet could advance his divisions from the Confederate right, march to Todd's Tavern, and smash an exposed Yankee flank.[12]

Several brigades from Major General Cadmus Wilcox's division reinforced Heth's right, but Barlow planned a strong attack against them. Although it was practically dark and all his troops were not yet up, Barlow deployed available portions of Colonels Miles's, Smyth's and Brooke's brigades and smashed into Brigadier General James Lane's North Carolinians. Under the intense attack, Lane's brigade broke, with the commander of the Seventh North Carolina and a large portion of that unit taken prisoner. Only nightfall put an end to the day's carnage around the wooded intersection, before Barlow's men could do any more damage.[13]

The next day, Grant planned for a concerted offensive with several corps, including the troops under Hancock's command.

---

[11] Ibid., 95, 108–144, 188–90, 197–200, 204, 206.
[12] Ibid., 206–8.
[13] Ibid., 235–39.

*Hancock ordered Barlow's division to hold a defensive position
on the corps' southern flank and placed Brigadier General John
Gibbon in overall command of that sector while the rest of the
Second corps advanced. A little before 5 a.m., the report of a
signal gun sent Hancock's assault force forward against the front
of Lieutenant General Ambrose P. Hill's position, not far from
the crossroads, while brigades under the command of Brigadier
General James Wadsworth struck Hill's northern flank. The Confederate defenses broke, and Hancock advanced in light of the
Southern collapse, excitedly exclaiming to Meade's aide Theodore Lyman, "We are driving them beautifully." Hancock's success soon turned, however, as Longstreet's corps deployed and
attacked his flank, taking him completely by surprise and driving his divisions back in disorder. By 8:00 a.m., the battle's mo-
mentum in Hancock's sector turned to the Southerners before
both sides settled down for a slogging match.*[14]

*During Longstreet's attack, Hancock recalled dispatching an
order to Gibbon to release Barlow's division and send it forward.
Only one of Barlow's brigades advanced, however, commanded
by Paul Frank, a mediocre but arrogant commander described
by one of Warren's staff as a "whiskey pickled, lately-arrived,
blusterous German." After the battle, Gibbon assured that he
only received a directive to release one brigade, and Barlow similarly affirmed that he never received any instruction from Hancock to advance his entire command. It seems that Hancock had,
perhaps mistakenly, only ordered the advance of one brigade, a
supposition supported by Gibbon's and Barlow's memories and
Hancock's notification to Army headquarters at 7:10 that "Barlow is putting in a brigade on the enemy's right flank, and I will
follow it up, if necessary, and have so directed." Had Barlow's
other three brigades come up, they could have hit Longstreet's
flank and perhaps repulsed his attack, inflicting serious damage
in the process.*[15]

---

[14] Ibid., 264, 269, 283–91, 308–13, 316. OR, 36(1): 326.

[15] Theodore Lyman judged Frank to be a "pleasant, talkative man, but one
who tried to make up for want of nerve by strong drink." He continued by
writing "Barlow was obliged to relieve him." Theodore Lyman, "Addenda to
the Paper by Brevet Lieutenant-Colonel W. W. Swan, U.S.A., on the Battle of
the Wilderness," in *Papers of the Military Historical Society of Massachusetts*,
14 vols. (Boston, 1881–1918), 4:65–73, 169. Rhea, *Battle of the Wilderness*,
333–34. OR, 36(1): 321; 36(2): 440–41.

By noon, Hancock's men had retreated to breastworks around the crossroads, and shortly thereafter, other Federal units reinforced the position. Eventually, Hancock cobbled together a defensive line with detachments of the Fifth and Sixth corps, in addition to his own. Barlow's division held Hancock's southern flank and helped fend off Confederate attacks until the battle in that sector ended. The Second corps lost nearly fifty-one hundred soldiers at the Wilderness; of them, nearly nine hundred came from Barlow's division.[16]

The next day, Grant determined to break the deadlock in the Wilderness by shifting his entire army, in a night march, to Spotsylvania Court House beyond Lee's right flank. Warren's brigades were to march down Brock Road followed by the Second corps so that the Fifth corps would reach Spotsylvania by morning just as Hancock's columns reached Todd's Tavern. Grant's remaining infantry was to march east to Chancellorsville before using Catharpin Road to reach the Spotsylvania area. In this way, Grant intended to keep his corps within closer supporting distance of each other, a mistake that had cost him dearly in the recent fighting. Each side felt out the opposing lines on May 7, trying to gain information and ascertain what the other army would do next. The Second corps' sector remained relatively quiet despite Barlow's belief that his division, holding Hancock's flank, would receive a daylight assault.[17]

At 8:30 that evening, Grant's subordinates tried to implement his marching orders, though darkness and traffic caused the march to proceed slower than anticipated. By May 8 the situation further changed, when Warren encountered and engaged Rebels at Laurel Hill, northwest of Spotsylvania. Hancock's corps remained guarding the Federal rear at Todd's Tavern, three miles north, with Barlow's men holding the field west of the tavern, Gibbon's brigades on his left, Mott's division on his right, and Birney in reserve around the tavern. Two forward regiments of Miles's brigade received the brunt of an attack by elements of two Confederate divisions before the Irish Brigade reinforced the

---

[16] Rhea, *Battle of the Wilderness*, 376–77, 390, 395, 436. OR, 36(1): 120–22.

[17] Gordon C. Rhea, *The Battles for Spotsylvania Court House and the Road to Yellow Tavern* (Baton Rouge: Louisiana State University Press, 1997), 14–15, 17–21.

*area and allowed them to withdraw. The 116th Pennsylvania
barely concluded a prayer service when their call to action came,
but they managed to finish it swiftly before rushing toward the
sound of rifle fire in their front.*[18]

*Lee had beaten Grant in the race to occupy Spotsylvania, and
on the night of May 8–9, the Confederates constructed an entrenched line near Laurel Hill, matched by the Federal Fifth and
Sixth corps. On the morning of May 9, reconnaissance from the
Second corps indicated that Confederates in its front had left,
but Hancock continued to expect an attack in that quarter, and
his divisions remained around Todd's Tavern. Meade's aide Theodore Lyman recalled Barlow's appearance at a meeting with
Hancock that day: "He looked like a highly independent
mounted newsboy; he was attired in a flannel checked shirt; a
threadbare pair of trousers, and an old blue kepi; frm his waist
hung a big cavalry sabre; his features wore a familiar sarcastic
smile." By 11:45 a.m., Hancock was satisfied that his sector was
secure, and that afternoon Grant ordered him to leave Mott's
two-brigade division at the Tavern and march the rest of his
command southeast, toward high ground overlooking the Po
River, and prepare to strike Lee's left.*[19]

*Between noon and two o'clock, three of Hancock's divisions
redeployed, with Barlow's marching down Brock Road before
forming in the fields west of the Tally house, with Birney's on his
right and Gibbon's on his left. As the Second corps swung into
position, Grant, Meade, and Hancock conferred near the Tally
house and watched as a Confederate wagon train—the rear of
Early's division—made its way to Spotsylvania Court House.
One aide proposed shelling the wagons, to which Meade retorted,
"Yes! And what good would you do? Scare a few niggers and old
mules?" Others urged opening with two nearby batteries, however, and once Meade agreed, their first salvo created a stampede
among the wagons. A Confederate battery under Major James
Thomson responded to the Federal cannon but was soon driven*

---

[18] Ibid., 44, 70–75, 78–80.

[19] Theodore Lyman to Elizabeth Lyman, May 20, 1864, in George R. Agassiz,
ed., *With Grant and Meade from the Wilderness to Appomattox* (1922; repr.
Lincoln: University of Nebraska Press, 1994), 107 (page citation is to repr. ed.).
Rhea, *Spotsylvania Court House,* 89–91, 101–3, 108–9.

out of range, and Meade ordered two regiments of Brooke's bri-
gade, the 145th and 148th Pennsylvania, to cross the Po River.
Most of the Pennsylvanians waded across, though some used a
log that had fallen, and they clambered up the steep embankment
to secure a lodgment on the river's southern bank. After the swift
erection of a pontoon bridge, the rest of Barlow's men crossed,
with Brooke's brigade in the lead, followed by Frank's, Miles's,
and then Smyth's. Thomson was surprised by the crossing, and
Brigadier General Ambrose Wright's Georgians, escorting the
wagon train, backtracked to cover Thomson's withdrawal and
contest Barlow's crossing until the train had gained a safe dis-
tance. By six o'clock, Barlow's entire force had crossed and re-
formed at Shady Grove Church Road.[20]

Grant perceived an opportunity slipping away and wanted to
attack the Southern left with Hancock's entire command. Bir-
ney's and Gibbon's brigades carried out orders to cross the river
in their respective fronts, and, despite some initial Confederate
resistance, the Rebels hastily withdrew once the Federals began
pushing forward. Some excitement came from Lieutenant Colo-
nel Richard McMichael of the Fifty-third Pennsylvania in
Brooke's brigade. He had skinned his nose on a tree while in a
drunken stupor and let everyone around him know that he was
the only man wounded in his regiment. McMichael pushed on
several hundred yards ahead of his troops, who later found him
striking his horse in punishment for sniffing conscripts earlier.
Understandably, Brooke swiftly relieved him from duty. By
seven, the Second corps had completely crossed the Po and
marched toward Block House Bridge and the Confederate left
flank. Barlow reached the bridge at nightfall but was disinclined
to cross the deep river in the evening darkness. Hancock also
hesitated, especially since he knew reinforced Confederates were
on the other side, and his troops remained where they were until
morning, eliminating the risk of a contested crossing and defeat
in piecemeal. His divisions held along Shady Grove Church
Road, with Barlow on the left nearest the Block House Bridge,
Gibbon on his right, followed by Birney.[21]

---

[20] Rhea, *Spotsylvania Court House,* 110–11. OR, 36(1): 330.
[21] Rhea, *Spotsylvania Court House,* 111–14, 125.

Lee realized the Second corps stood exposed and isolated from the rest of its army, and he set a trap to crush it. Further, a bend in the Po meant that a repulse of a Second corps attack would force it to cross the river twice, something that concerned Hancock and caused him to construct three pontoon bridges near the Pritchett house. Major General Harry Heth's division and a brigade of Major General William Mahone's division stealthily slipped from Spotsylvania Court House after midnight with instructions to cross the Po below Hancock and then pitch into the Second corps' flank, while the remainder of Mahone's brigades held Hancock's front. Meanwhile, as morning broke, Hancock and his subordinates assessed the situation in their front in light of Grant's orders to continue advancing against Lee's left. Confederate infantry and eleven cannon on the other side of the bridge made marching the corps across, in column of four soldiers abreast, impractical. As Meade nervously inquired as to Hancock's delay in moving, the corps commander threw out heavy reconnaissances to find other crossing areas, preferring to fight with his entire corps across especially in light of his Po River concerns. Brooke's brigade found a shallow spot a half mile below the bridge, and once its Sixty-sixth New York forded the river under heavy picket fire, Hancock planned to send the rest of the brigade, and then the entire Second corps, across.[22]

On the morning of May 10, Grant realized that he needed to alter his plan in light of Hancock's stalled advance across the Po and Warren's futile assaults with the Fifth corps against Laurel Hill. Mistaken reports from the Sixth corps' front that Confederates there seemed to be shifting over toward Hancock's sector also induced Grant's new plan. The Federal commander surmised that if he could continue Lee's belief that the Army of the Potomac's main advance would come from Hancock's front, the Confederate general would have troops massed around that area, with other portions of his line depleted. Grant proposed leaving one division—Barlow's—near the Block House Bridge while the rest of Second corps repositioned itself and joined the Fifth and Sixth corps in an all-out attack against Laurel Hill.[23]

---

[22] Ibid., 114, 123–27. OR, 36(1): 330, 331.

[23] The troops facing Hancock were, in fact, divisions taken from in front of Major General Ambrose E. Burnside's Ninth corps, not the Laurel Hill lines facing Fifth and Sixth corps. Rhea, *Spotsylvania Court House*, 130–33.

At eleven in the morning, Gibbon's and Birney's brigades pulled out of line to cross over the Po River pontoon bridges and began marching to participate in Grant's attack, ordered for 5:00. Barlow lined his regiments along Shady Grove Church Road and placed Miles's brigade on his left, near the bridge, followed by the Irish Brigade on Miles's right, then Brooke's brigade and Frank holding the division's west flank near Waite's Shop. Behind Miles and the Irish Brigade was a half mile of open land between the pontoon bridges in case of need to retreat, but behind Brooke and Frank was thick forest which would make for a difficult escape. Hancock warned Barlow of the division's precarious position, instructing him "Don't push your reconnaissances too far nor with large parties" and that no attack or crossing should be attempted without orders.[24]

Shortly after Hancock joined the rest of his corps, Heth's and Mahone's Rebels began probing Barlow's position and prepared to encircle and destroy his division. A messenger galloped to locate Meade and Hancock and, finding them together, informed them of Barlow's increasingly desperate situation, especially as Birney's and Gibbon's divisions had gotten too far away to assist their comrades. Meade anxiously ordered Hancock to go in person and save Barlow, and when the corps commander reached his lone division, he found it enfiladed by Confederate artillery while Southern infantry closed in on their prize. At about 2:30, Hancock and Barlow began extricating the bluecoats toward the cover of Federal artillery on the northern bank of the Po near the pontoon bridges, slowly and in stages. Repeated Confederate attacks took a heavy toll on Barlow's regiments, as Miles's and Smyth's brigades withdrew first followed by their comrades. Hancock recalled that the "enemy, in vastly superior numbers, flushed with the anticipation of an easy victory, appeared to be determined to crush the small force opposing them, and pressing forward with loud yells forced their way close up to our line, delivering a terrible musketry fire as they advanced." In addition to having to repulse Confederate advances, the bluecoats also had to contend with woods set afire from the heat of the contest. After the perilous withdrawal had concluded, the colonel

---

[24] Rhea, *Spotsylvania Court House*, 134.

of the 148th Pennsylvania took a long drink of whiskey offered him by an artillerist, the only such drink he took throughout the war. By 5:00, after the Second corps artillery stopped Heth's and Mahone's powerful advances, and barely, Barlow's troops had reached safety.[25]

Elsewhere, Federal troops attacked Lee's line, but despite making several significant initial gains, the Confederate line held. On the afternoon of May 11, Grant ordered the Second corps to position itself behind the Fifth and Sixth corps and prepare for a major attack against the Confederate line at four in the morning of the following day. While Hancock met with Barlow, Birney, and Gibbon at corps headquarters, the soldiers of the Second corps quietly prepared to march and got under way at ten o'clock that evening. Barlow took the lead followed by Gibbon and Birney, and all headed for the Brown house opposite their morning objective: a large, fortified salient in the Rebel line known as the Mule Shoe manned by Major General Edward Johnson's division. Although Barlow's men had to move only three miles, it proved a treacherous and tense march, as the rainy night was dark, and the exhausted men crossed through forests, streams, and swampy terrain. A soldier in the ranks remembered that it was "so black that you could not see your file leader, and only knew that he was there when you ran up against him" and that the trees and brush were "dripping with moisture, the ground slippery from the rains[.]" One of Barlow's staff officers, Captain John D. Black, recalled that the "movement was necessarily slow with frequent halts, at which time the men, worn out by loss of sleep and the terrible nervous and physical strain they had endured during the past eight days, would drop down for a moment's rest, and be asleep almost as soon as they touched the ground."[26]

---

[25] Ibid., 135–41. *OR,* 36(1): 331–23.

[26] Rhea, *Spotsylvania Court House,* 221–23. John D. Black, "Reminiscences of the Bloody Angle," in *Glimpses of the Nation's Struggle: Papers Read before the Commandery of the State of Minnesota, Military Order of the Loyal Legion of the United States, 1892–1897* (Saint Paul, Minn., 1898), 420–36: 421. Edward C. Jackson, "The Bloody Angle," in *Civil War Sketches and Incidents: Papers Read by Companions of the Command of the State of Nebraska, Military Order of the Loyal Legion of the United States* (Omaha: Commandery, 1902), 258–62: 259. Green, "From the Wilderness to Spotsylvania," 97. *OR,* 36(1): 334–35.

Barlow rode at the head of the column with the inspector general of the Second corps, Lieutenant Colonel Charles Morgan, engineer Lieutenant Colonel G. H. Mendell, and two of his brigade commanders, Miles and Brooke. Along the way, Barlow asked Morgan and Mendell for information about the attack and the terrain over which it would pass but could not get any. After the war, Barlow recalled the "ludicrousness of the scene. . . . As we staggered and stumbled along in the mud and intense darkness, and I vainly sought for information, the absurdity of our position—that we were proceeding to attack the enemy when no one even knew his direction, and we could hardly keep on our own legs—appealed to me very strongly as I listened to the conversation of Colonel Morgan (who was what might be called a profane swearer) and his criticisms on the 'conduct of the war.'" After laughing at some of Morgan's comments, Barlow pleaded to him, "For Heaven's sake, at least, face us in the right direction, so that we shall not march away from the enemy, and have to go round the world and come up in their rear." Soon, Miles weighed in with his complaints and grew so heated that Barlow had to "tell him to be quiet."[27]

At 12:30 Barlow's men reached the Brown house, and when Birney and an aide entered the building at two o'clock, they found Hancock lying on a couch, Gibbon watching the fire, and Barlow asleep on the floor. Hancock briefly conferred with Birney before taking a quick nap, and then Birney and Gibbon sat by the fire and talked. When he awoke, Hancock held a council of war with his division commanders to plan the morning's attack, though no one present had made a thorough reconnaissance of the ground over which the assault was to be made or had examined the Rebel works. As Barlow's division was to lead the charge, its commander was a vocal participant in the discussion:

"What is the nature of the ground over which I have to pass?" The reply was "We do not know." "How far is it to the enemy's line?" "Something less than a mile." "What obstructions am I to meet with, if any?" "We do not know." "Well, have I a gulch a thousand feet deep to cross?" And still the answer "We do not know."

---

[27] Francis C. Barlow, "Capture of the Salient, May 12, 1864," in *Papers of the Military Historical Society of Massachusetts*, 14 vols. (Boston: Historical Society of Massachusetts, 1881–1918), 4:245–62: 246–47.

Barlow then proposed to form his division in two columns, though other members of the council objected on account that this would make them an easy target for Rebel artillery. Barlow retorted, "If I am to lead this assault I propose to have men enough, when I reach the objective point, to charge through Hell itself and capture all the artillery they can mass in my front." After a brief debate, Barlow prevailed: his brigades would lead the attack, supported by Birney's and Mott's divisions, and Gibbon in reserve.[28]

The normally aggressive Barlow had doubts about the charge's overall chance for success as well as his own personal safety. His aide recalled,

> *I never remember seeing General Barlow so depressed as he was on leaving Hancock's headquarters that night; he acted as if it was indeed a forlorn hope he was to lead. His voice was subdued and tender as he issued his orders to the staff, for the formation of the command; very different from the brusque and decided manner usual for him, accompanied by the remark we had heard so many times on similar occasions, "Make your peace with God and mount, gentlemen; I have a hot place picked out for some of you today"; or the consoling remark that would sometimes follow, after hearing of some general officer who had particularly distinguished himself and had certain of his staff killed or wounded, "Well, gentlemen, it beats Hell that none of my staff get killed or wounded."*[29]

Before four o'clock in the morning, Barlow's regiments formed in two columns with regiments doubled on the center, five paces between regiments, and ten between brigade. Miles's and Brooke's men took position in the front followed by Smyth's and Colonel Hiram Brown's regiments (Brown replaced Frank upon that officer's relief for drunkenness). Skirmishers received instructions not to fire but rather surprise the Rebel pickets and capture them so that the Confederate main line would hear no alarm. At 4:35, as a faint glimmer of sunlight began to lighten the sky, the Rebels' forward pickets were disposed of, and the division swiftly advanced half a mile. Upon reaching a ridge, the

---

[28] Black, "Reminiscences of the Bloody Angle," 422–23.
[29] Ibid., 423–24.

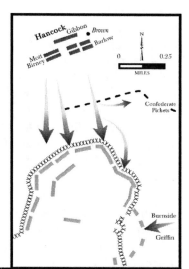

Attack of Hancock's Second Corps at the Mule Shoe, Spotsylvania, morning of May 12, 1864

Map at left illustrates Federal approach to Confederate pickets; below, the assault on the "Bloody Angle."

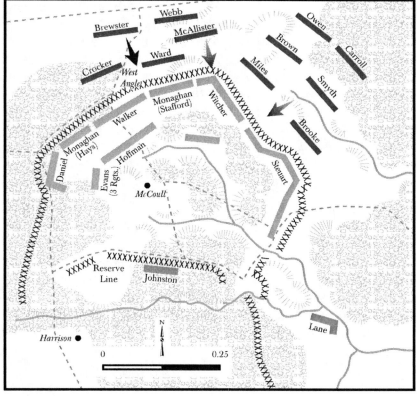

*men broke their silence and charged with a loud yell, only to
realize that the Confederate works were two hundred yards farther. A Southern volley issued from behind the breastworks, but,
luckily for the bluecoats, most of the projectiles passed overhead.
Barlow ordered, "Forward! Double-quick! Charge!" and the division dashed forward with cheers, with Miles's and Brooke's men
tearing away abatis in their path and springing over the Rebel
works and with Barlow following shortly behind. Before the Confederates could even react, Barlow's men had torn from the foggy
mist and breached the right side of the Mule Shoe salient, while
Birney's brigades slammed into its front left side. All was confusion inside the salient, as officers tried to rouse their surprised
men and Johnson limped through his lines, swinging a walking
stick at oncoming Federals and using it to ward off bayonets.
Quickly, four thousand Southerners of Johnson's division, including Johnson himself and Brigadier General George H. Steuart, along with twenty cannon and over thirty stand of colors,
fell into Federal hands.*[30]

*Brown's and Smyth's brigades went forward to pursue some
fleeing Confederate elements but struck Confederate entrenchments at the base of the Mule Shoe and were repulsed with Colonel Brown captured. The rest of the day, Federal and Southern
troops struggled for control of the salient, as the Rebels mounted
continual counterattacks and the area turned into what one officer later described as a "boiling, bubbling and hissing cauldron
of death." The air filled with deadly missiles so that a red oak
tree nearly two feet in diameter was cut down by minie balls. A
heavy rain began to pour around one o'clock; everywhere were
pools of red, bloody water. After the battle, Captain Black joined
Major Church of the Twenty-sixth Michigan in trying to find the
body of a wealthy comrade who had fallen on the Rebel works.
The soldier had asked Church to retrieve his elegant gold watch
and send it to his parents should he fall, and the major wanted
to honor his promise. Black recalled the macabre scene when
they did find the body: "Had it not been for some of his comrades
who had seen him fall and identified the place, we would never*

---

[30] Ibid., 425–26. Barlow, "Capture of the Salient," 252. Jackson, "Bloody
Angle," 260. Rhea, *Spotsylvania Court House,* 235, 238. OR, 36(1): 335–36.

*have recognized it as having been a soldier. There was no sem-
blance of humanity about the mass that was lying before us. The
only thing I could liken it to was a sponge, I presume five thousand bullets had passed through it; and after a careful search the
largest piece we could find was three links of the chain, not to
exceed one-quarter of an inch in length; the watch was entirely
shot away." Starting from the moment of the Second corps' attack, the Mule Shoe would be known by a new name: the Bloody
Angle.[31]*

*Barlow sent Captain Black to Hancock for reinforcements to
guard the division's left flank, and the aide found the Second
corps' victorious general meeting with Johnson and Steuart.
Hancock extended his hand to Johnson and, in a "graceful and
courtly manner," said, "General Johnson, I am glad to see you."
Johnson shook his hand but in tears movingly replied, "General
Hancock, this is worse then death for me." With that, the Northern general assured, "This is the fate of war, general, and you
must not forget that you are a soldier." Hancock's exchange with
Steuart was less cordial, however, and when he extended his
hand to the brigadier, the Southerner defiantly insisted, "Under
existing circumstances, Sir, I cannot take your hand." Without
hesitation, Hancock shot back, "Under any other circumstances,
Sir, it would not have been offered." Shortly afterward, Black
conferred with Hancock, who praised Barlow, promised reinforcements, and instructed Black to "direct him to give my compliments to Miles and Brooke and assure them that they may
consider themselves brigadier-generals from to-day." At another
point, Barlow found Hancock to suggest to him that too many
fresh men were being poured into the Angle, disrupting Barlow's
efforts to restore order among his lines. Excitedly, Barlow called
out, "For God's sake, Hancock, do not send any more troops in
here," the first and last time that he omitted the "General" before
his commander's name.[32]*

---

[31] Black, "Reminiscences of the Bloody Angle," 426–27, 432–33. Robert S.
Robertson, "From the Wilderness to Spotsylvania," in *Sketches of War History,
1861–1865: Papers Read before the Ohio Commandery of the Military Order of
the Loyal Legion of the United States* (Cincinnati, Ohio, 1883), 1:252–92: 283.

[32] For good measure, on May 13, Barlow also recommended that Brooke and
Miles be promoted to brigadier general. *OR*, 36(2): 710. Black, "Reminiscences
of the Bloody Angle," 428–31. Barlow, "Capture of the Salient," 254–55.

By late morning, Lee decided against trying to reestablish his line at the salient, and he used the troops fighting there to buy enough time to construct a line of earthworks at the Mule Shoe's base. By two o'clock, the fighting had reached a deadlock while Southerners feverishly labored to construct their new line, chopping trees and forming breastworks under fire. Finally, at three in the morning, a courier quietly told the Rebels near the salient to carefully retreat to the new position, and their withdrawal went unopposed. Barlow had over fourteen hundred killed, missing, and wounded in an assault he judged to be "the most brilliant thing of its kind of the war," but also one he admitted to be largely "a lucky accident," especially in light of how it got under way. "It was an accident," Barlow opined after the war:

> *that we struck this angle, always a weak point in a line; an accident that the morning was misty to an unusual degree; an accident that we found a space for our rush so free from obstacles; an accident that we do escaped the observation of the enemy's outposts and pickets, that we were upon them before they could make any substantial resistance. That we were in that solid formation which was practically irresistible was of course designed, but that such a formation was practicable was because at the last minute it was found that the nature of the ground permitted it.*

It was a bloody culmination to a week which saw the Second corps lose forty percent of its troops, starting from twenty-seven thousand effectives on May 5 and ending with but sixteen thousand men in line on May 13.[33]

The next several days passed relatively quietly for the Second corps, while casualties and the expiration of the term of service for several units in Mott's division led Hancock to consolidate it into a brigade and assign it to Birney's division. On May 17, Hancock received orders for his corps to attack the Southern line the following morning, with the Sixth corps to push forward simultaneously on his right. At four in the morning of May 18, Barlow's and Gibbon's divisions advanced into a storm of Confederate cannon and rifle fire, while rough terrain and thick aba-

---

[33] Barlow, "Capture of the Salient," 251, 256. Rhea, *Spotsylvania Court House,* 290, 294, 306–7, 319.

tis further impeded their advance. By 10 a.m., Hancock realized the futility of their attack and ordered his men to withdraw.[34]

> Wed. May 18th /64
> 3.45 p.m.[35]

My dear Mother

We attacked the enemy this morning at day light. The 2nd + 6th Corps. We struck upon an abbattis + were stopped. Our loss was not very heavy. I sent Joe Clark to the front line with a message + have not heard from his since. We have searched for him without success. An officer thought he saw him struck in the shoulder or arm + go to the rear. He may turn up wounded. I hope to find him this evening. I can't find him in the Hospitals up to this time.

We have been at it now 15 days + it has become rather tedious. Hancock has recommended me for Major Genl. Miles + Brooke are to be made Brig Genls.

Arabella is at Fredericksburg 10 miles off but I have not + cannot see her. All is hurry + confusion so I cannot write more than a line now + then. Do not be alarmed about me. I am very well.

> Lovingly
> Francis

While her husband commanded on the front lines, Arabella was not far behind, and the couple sent messages carried back and forth by ambulance drivers. She worked at the hospitals at Fredericksburg, where she witnessed firsthand the terrible privations that wounded soldiers had to endure. Nurse Cornelia Hancock

---

[34] *OR*, 36(1): 337–38.

[35] Barlow wrote this letter on patriotic stationery. It bears a fasces in the upper left-hand corner; in front of it is a sword crossed with a scabbard with a liberty cap on its tip, a shield bearing stars and stripes, and a banner wrapped around it reading "North South In Union There is Strength."

*reported to her sister that it was "an awful time" in Fredericks-
burg, with limited supplies and "no end to the wounded." Many
of the wounded were quartered in the city's houses, and as "one
vast hospital," Hancock noted, "the groans go up from every
building" in Fredericksburg. Another observer depicted the town
"full of badly wounded," with injured men everywhere, even in
"filthy shops, old shoe stores, old blacksmiths' rooms, men lying
on the floor without even straw under them, and with their heads
on old bits of cast iron." Into this desperate situation, the Sanitary Commission sent a "large corps of volunteer nurses" working under the surgeons and providing supplies and food for the
hurt soldiers and those ministering to them. Some began calling
Arabella "the Raider," as she procured a small cart and scoured
the area for any provisions or supplies that might improve the
comfort of the wounded. For example, when more straw was
needed one day, Arabella cheerfully said she would find some; a
half hour later, she returned with some loaded onto her wagon.[36]*

*Meanwhile, on the evening of the eighteenth, Barlow's division
joined most of Hancock's corps in relocating to Anderson's Mill
on the Ny River. Early on the twentieth, the corps moved to Mil-
ford and Bowling Green to take possession of the right bank of
the Mattapony River.[37]*

May 20 /64 11.45 a.m.

My dear Edward
I have recd your letter of the 14th inst. In the hurry + confusion here it is impossible to write at any length. All our leisure
time has to be spent in eating + sleeping. We have had no fighting in this Div. since that of the 18th of which I wrote you. Tonight I suppose we shall move somewhere.
I am well as usual. I wish R could get to Fredericksburg as he

---

[36] Georgeanna Muirson Bacon to Jane Eliza Woolsey, Fredericksburg, Va.,
May 15, 1864, in Eliza Woolsey Howland, ed., *Letters of a Family during the
War for the Union 1861–1865,* 2 vols. (privately printed, 1899), 2:588–89. Cor-
nelia Hancock to her sister, Fredericksburg, Va., May 20, 1864, in Jaquette,
South after Gettysburg, 95–96. Lauter, "'Once upon a Time in the East,'" 20.
[37] *OR,* 36(1): 338, 340–41.

could then probably get up here. Joe Clark has not been heard of + I cannot find him in the Hospital near here. But he could hardly have been killed for we should have found his body + I think he must have gone off wounded. I only wonder that he does not send me word. I have written to Mrs Clark. I hear from Arabella but have not seen her.

I heard that I was made a Major Genl but don't believe it.

I long for this damned Campaign to be over that I may see you all again.

With much love
Francis

The Second corps remained near the Mattapony River until the morning of the 23rd, at which time it marched to the heights near the North Anna River. Once there, Barlow's men occupied the center, while Gibbon's line stretched across the Fredericksburg and Richmond Railroad tracks on Barlow's left and Birney took possession of the Telegraph Road on Barlow's right. On the morning of the 24th, it became clear that the Rebels had abandoned their line on the North Anna's southern bank and Hancock ordered his corps across the river.[38]

Headquarters, 1st Division, 2nd Corps,
May 24th, '64

My Dear Charles [Dalton]

What is the state of the Darkey Bureau question? Will the bill pass and whom will they put at the head of the Bureau?

When this Campaign is over I think I should like it unless I can get an independent command. I am not much delighted with the performances here, though this is in the strictest confidence.

We are across the North Anna near Hanover Junction where the enemy are in force. I think they will make a great effort and

---

[38] Ibid.: 341–42.

attack us as they did in 1862 and I always doubt the result of
these great battles.

What is the news with you? Why don't you write to me?

My kindest regards to Mrs. Dalton and Julia. Where are you
going to live this summer?

I am looking for a wound but it has not come. My health is
splendid. I have seen Pen once or twice since we started.

Truly,
Francis C. B.

*The Second corps remained on the southern bank of the river
until ordered to return to the northern bank on the evening of
May 26. At ten the next morning, the corps began a march to the
Pamunkey River, where it bivouacked at ten that night. At 5:30
a.m. on the twenty-eighth, the corps found itself again on the
march, crossing the Pamunkey four miles above Hanovertown
and swinging into position on the left of the Sixth corps. The
next day, Barlow's division made a reconnaissance in force in
its sector, engaging the Rebels in a lively skirmish.[39]*

*Further maneuvering brought the Second corps to Cold Har-
bor, where Barlow's and Gibbon's divisions assaulted the Confederate works, with Birney's men in support, on June 3. Barlow
formed his men in two lines, with Miles and Brooke in the first
followed by Colonel Richard Byrnes's Irish brigade and Colonel
Clinton MacDougall's regiments in the second. Barlow advanced
at the appointed time and drove the Rebels from their position
along a sunken road, capturing three hundred prisoners and
three cannon in the process, before Southern artillery enfiladed
his line and a counterattack pushed his men back. Brooke suffered a severe wound in the assault, just as his men broke
through the Rebel works. On Barlow's right, Gibbon met with
even less success, and Hancock called off further attack. In less
than an hour, the two divisions had lost over three thousand
men. That night, Captain Augustus C. Brown reported to Bar-*

---

[39] Ibid.: 342–43.

low's headquarters with a detachment of the Fourth New York Heavy Artillery, ordered to help build an artillery redoubt on the division's front. Barlow's headquarters "consisted of a wall tent with a sentry and a Division flag in front of it," and inside Brown found Barlow "curled up in the corner of his tent examining a map with a candle[.]" Barlow ordered a staff officer to show Brown the way to the planned redoubt, and the New Yorkers constructed the little fort under fire. During the night, Barlow inspected the position, having to crawl in on his hands and knees to avoid the Rebel projectiles. On June 6, Barlow identified that the attrition suffered as a result of the army's recent campaigning was sapping its ability to effectively carry out attacks. "The men feel just at present a great horror and dread of attacking earthworks again," Barlow warned, "and the unusual loss of officers, which leave regiments in command of lieutenants, and brigades in command of inexperienced officers, leaves us in a very unfavorable condition for such enterprises. . . . I think the men are so wearied and worn out by the harassing labors of the past week that they are wanting in the spirit and dash necessary for successful assaults." Barlow's superiors realized this as well, and the Second corps remained in position and conducted siege operations until it relocated to a new and shorter line covering Cold Harbor on June 12.[40]

Meanwhile, Arabella continued alleviating the suffering of the Federal troops at the hospitals around Fredericksburg. In one instance, she bent over "a young and perhaps reckless boy, who was about to die," when she "heard him singing the song 'Possum up a gum tree.'" The boy's voice "became every moment more feeble, when a member of the Christian Commission rushed up to her saying, 'Madam, did you catch his last words?'" One onlooker described the look of "the horror-stricken missionary when she repeated them." In early June, she summoned Cornelia Hancock to the front lines and conferred with her regarding the possibility of establishing a station where wounded soldiers could receive food while on their way from front line hospitals to

---

[40] Ibid.: 344–46, 369. Francis C. Barlow to Lieutenant Colonel Francis A. Walker, June 6, 1864, in *OR*, 36(3): 646–47. Augustus Cleveland Brown diary entry for June 3, 1864, in Augustus Cleveland Brown, *The Diary of a Line Officer* (privately printed, 1906), 63–64.

those in the rear area. Hancock reported that while the two shared the ambulance from Barlow's headquarters, they came "as near Richmond as any lady in the Army." Afterward, Arabella took advantage of a lull in the fighting on June 7 to visit her husband.[41]

On June 13, the Second corps began moving toward the James River, and Barlow had his soldiers move at a rapid pace. Theodore Lyman recounted,

> We kept on, on the flank of the column, admiring its excellent marching, a result partly due to the good spirits of the men, partly to the terror in which stragglers stand of Barlow. His provost guard is a study. They follow the column, with their bayonets fixed, and drive up the loiterers, with small ceremony. Of course their tempers do not improve with heat and hard marching. There was one thin, hard-featured fellow who was a perfect scourge. "Blank you!—you—" (here insert any profane and extremely abusive expression, varied to suit the peculiar case) "get up, will you? By blank, I'll kill you if you don't go on, double quick!" And he looked so much like carrying out his threat that the hitherto utterly prostrate party would skip like the young lamb. . . . The column marched so fast that I was sent forward to tell General Barlow to go more gently. I found that eccentric officer divested of his coat and seated in a cherry tree. "By Jove!" said a voice from the branches, "I knew I should not be here long before Meade's Staff would be up. How do you do, Theodore, won't you come up and take a few cherries?

Unfortunately for Lyman, his other duties prevented him from enjoying the snack. By four o'clock in the morning on the fifteenth, all but one regiment and four batteries of the Second corps had stopped near Wind-Mill Point. General Hancock had been promised that sixty thousand rations would be waiting for his troops there, but despite the corps commander's efforts, they never arrived. Later that morning, the corps began marching for Petersburg, an important rail hub and city south of Richmond.

---

[41] Abigail Hopper Gibbons to Sydney Howard Gay, Washington, D.C., May 31, 1864, in Sarah Hopper Emerson, ed., *Life of Abby Hopper Gibbons: Told Chiefly through Her Correspondence*, 2 vols. (New York: G. P. Putnam's Sons, 1896), 1:93. Cornelia Hancock to her Mother, Hospital 1st Div. 2nd Corps, Va., June 7, 1864, in Jaquette, *South after Gettysburg*, 106–7.

Due to the delay in waiting for the rations that never came, however, the Second corps was unable to arrive in time to participate in the day's attacks on the strategic city. Only on the sixteenth, when they occupied works in front of Petersburg, did the famished men of the Second corps finally receive their rations.[42]

All day, sharp skirmishing and heavy artillery fire marked the Second corps' front. At around six o'clock in the evening, Hancock's divisions, supported by two brigades each from the Ninth and Eighteenth corps, assaulted the Confederate line in front and to the left of the Hare house. After a sharp fight, they pushed the enemy back and held against several Rebel counterattacks, while the Irish Brigade lost its commander, Colonel Byrnes. On the morning of June seventeenth, Barlow and some of the Ninth corps again attacked, while Birney's and Gibbon's divisions pushed the Southerners off the hill around the Hare house and held it against counterattacks. Despite local successes, however, the Rebels maintained control of Petersburg, and the Second corps settled in for a long period of siege operations against that town. From June 27 to July 26, the Federals erected earthworks and then inched their trenches closer to those of the Confederates, all the while under artillery and sharpshooter fire. Barlow's division lost nearly twenty three hundred men from June 13 to July 26.[43]

June 19th /64 10 p.m.
Sunday

My very dear Mother

Your letter enclosing Mrs Clark's came last night. I wish you would send all letters you think of interest which you receive + I will do the same—though I get very few. You speak of not having recd any letters but very short ones from me. I have written two quite long + full ones June 3rd which do not seem to have reached you. R. starts for home tomorrow + he will tell you how

---

[42] Theodore Lyman to Elizabeth Lyman, June 13, 1864, in Agassiz, *With Grant and Meade*, 157–58. OR, 40(1): 303–5.

[43] OR, 40(1): 306–7.

impossible it is for me to write on a great many of the days. Sometimes for two or three days we do nothing but march + shift our lines from one place to another + fight at intervals + every minute I can get has to be devoted to sleep. When we have a day of leisure I always write, but you do not seem to have recd any of the long ones. By this time you are in Boston where I wish I was. Of course you will see Mrs Howe + I hope Mrs Bell. I am afraid R. is rather disgusted with the life of the soldier. He is covered with flea bites + says he is very dirty, but as I am so much dirtier I don't appreciate his filthiness. Has Mrs Clark heard any more of Joe? I asked Lyman, who went over with another flag of truce today to make enquiries of him. We arrived before Petersburg on the 15th + have been attacking at various times since + have driven back the enemies lines some distance but they still have other works + we have not reached the City yet. R. will have a good deal to tell you of things here. When he gets through some of his other visiting + settles down with you for the summer I shall look forward to E's coming down for a visit. R. thinks he can arrange to get him a passage in one of McCready's vessels if it can be done in no other way. Do you receive the Commonwealth which I ordered sent to you? I enclosed a note for Mary Gardner in my last letter. I wish you could give my love to her. Are you going to [illegible word] this summer?

Your affectionate Son
Francis

June 23rd /64
7 30 p.m.

My very dear Mother + brother

Your letters of 16th + 18th came today + were most welcome I assure you. Now we have a mail regularly every day + I shall get yours + you will get mine. I have written much oftener than you gave me credit for. R. went home on Monday as I wrote before. I have hardly had time to miss him for we have been in a most terrible whirl of marching + picket fighting &c ever since all of which has accomplished nothing. Things do not look very bright. You say very little of your visit to Boston. I infer you saw nothing of my more intimate friends, or you would have mentioned it. I am as fully resolved as one can be of anything in the future to resign when this active Campaign is over. I think I can easily get some public place of importance + if not can make an advantageous business partnership (as a lawyer). I would not say this now or have it said, so be careful. I wish you could go to Conway where such pleasant people as the Gardners + Miss Wilby are + I believe you will go there yet. I fully explained in my former letters that I had not been nominated as Maj. Gen. There are no vacancies now + the Senate are very strict in only confirming to fill vacancies. R. will explain fully what occurred. I think they will make no promotions anymore until they see whether the Campaign is successful. I see the Herald + Washington Chronicle pretty regularly. They do say a good deal about me, but it is mostly nonsense. You speak of Mary Williams + I infer you saw her in Brookline. Was it not? Who did you see? I did receive Mary Gardner's letter + have enclosed an answer to you. Did you receive it? Why does not Miss Rotch write to me? She promised to do so. I wish you could have got a place to board in Milton. I have had two staff officers (Capt Bird, Pioneer Officer, + Lt. Black, Aide) wounded lately, but not dangerously. Yesterday three (Capt Derickson, Ordnance Officer, + Lts Alexander + Brady Aides) were captured—whether wounded or not I don't know. The line of the whole Corps had to fall back rapidly, by reason of the Enemy appearing on our flank + these officers, who had been sent with riders were probably gobbled by the rebs in the confusion. I merely heard by flag of truce that Clark had got into the enemies lines by mistake + was a prisoner. Lyman merely heard it incidentally. He was dismounted when he was captured I believe. If not he was on a public horse which I furnished him. I left his pocket book with one of my officers the night before, because we thought we were going into a desperate fight with the whole Div. (which we did not). Sent it home by R. I am well, though, everyone + everything is somewhat dilapidated. We captured a reb Colonel who had a fine (for the Army) white mare which I shall buy. He wanted to give it to me, but I refused. I went to sleep at 11 last night + got up at 3 this morning + have been about all day. So I must go to sleep. I opened your letter to R. Don't mind expense in your summer arrangements.

Lovingly
Francis

In this letter, Barlow mentions a famous photograph for which Hancock and his division commanders posed. Barlow's Harvard classmate James Kendall Hosmer noted that in the photograph, Barlow stood "just as he looked in college," with his nonchalant attitude and few trappings of rank.[44]

July 2nd 1864
3.30 p.m.

My dear Edward

Your letter of June 28th was recd last night. I envy you Brattleboro, stupid as it is. Nothing can be worse than the life here for the last week. It seems to get hotter each day + we <u>imagine</u> we have hotter weather than has ever been seen before.

At any rate it is bad enough. I sit in my tent with only my shirt + drawers on.

Going out is not to be thought of except in the cool of the Evening. The troops are kept as quiet as possible + no military movements are going on. They say they are besieging Petersburg further to our right but we hear little firing. You will have seen an account in the papers telegraphed from Boston putting the whole blame of the disaster of the 22nd on this Div. It is an unmitigated lie + I have written to contradict it. Gibbon was attacked in his own front independently of us + must bear his

---

[44] Hosmer, *Last Leaf,* 63.

own burdens. He was more than ½ mile from my line. The affair was not at all serious to us.[45]

We lost only some 240 prisoners + no guns or colors + no regimental organizations. Is not the proposed picture in Harpers disgusting? Have you seen the one that Brady took of Hancock myself &c?

I perfectly long to get home but it is hard to see when I shall be able to do it. No one would be allowed to resign now or to leave the Army on any pretence. Arabella is sick in Washington + I fear seriously. She is all run down with a fever.

I keep wonderfully well. Miles had an attack of vertigo or some such thing the other day + fell flat down when I was talking to him but is now all right again. It only lasted a few minutes. I see Col Prescott is dead.

I enclose a letter from Fletcher. He has singular ideas to suppose that he would be allowed to go about at large at the North + then return to the South. I shall write him to this effect.

You affectionate brother
Francis

Did you get the money for Dinsmore for the lost clothing

Theodore Lyman visited Barlow on July 7 and found the general sweltering in the heat but "lying in his tent, neatly attired in his shirt and drawers, and listening to his band, that was playing without." Barlow indicated to Lyman that he was ready to personally lead an assault against the Confederates, as he "wanted no more trifling" but instead, and in character, desired swift

---

[45] On June 22, the Second corps swung toward the Petersburg and Weldon Railroad, and closer to Confederate lines on Petersburg's south side. Mahone's Rebel division countered by attacking Barlow's division, on the corps' right, and, after it pushed Barlow's brigades back, took Gibbon's division in flank. The Second corps had losses of 650 killed and over 1,700 captured, though Gibbon blamed the corps' poor performance on the massive casualties, especially among its officers, suffered in the previous two months' campaigning. Noah Andre Trudeau, *The Last Citadel: Petersburg, Virginia June 1864–April 1865* (Boston: Little, Brown and Company, 1991), 68–79.

and vigorous pursuit of victory. A few days later, Lyman met Barlow again at Hancock's headquarters, wearing a "checked shirt and old blue trousers, with a huge sabre, which he says he likes, because when he hits a straggler he wants to hurt him."[46]

On July 13, Hancock sent Seth Williams a letter he had written two days earlier, urging Barlow's promotion to major general "for distinguished conduct" during Spotsylvania and "for gallant and meritorious conduct during the Whole Campaign." After briefly recounting Barlow's military career—and taking care to note that his brigade had supported the Thirds corps during Chancellorsville and was absent during the Eleventh corps' rout of May 2, 1863—Hancock noted that "General Barlow is brave, vigilant and ambitious to wide renown. His command is under strict discipline and is well cared for in every respect. I know of no officer more deserving of promotion."[47]

Nonetheless, as can be seen from the letter below, Barlow's morale began to sink low around this time. Constant combat proved both physically and mentally exhausting, and the prospects for Federal victory seemed, to him, to be slipping away. Furthermore, personal matters weighed on Barlow's mind, as Arabella had fallen ill. She first became sick while working at the hospital at City Point but partially recovered in the care of friends at Washington, D.C. On July 6, she returned to the front and visited her husband's headquarters but still appeared frail from typhus fever. They both agreed that she should return to the Northern capital to fully recuperate, where Barlow took Arabella to his division's hospital. Doctor Robert Potter escorted her to a steamer at City Point that brought her to Washington. It was the last time Barlow saw Arabella alive.[48]

---

[46] Theodore Lyman to Elizabeth Lyman, July 7, 1864; July 12, 1864 in Agassiz, *With Grant and Meade*, 186, 189.

[47] Winfield S. Hancock to Brigadier General Seth Williams, near Petersburg, Va., July 11; July 13, 1864, both in Barlow Papers NA.

[48] Lauter, " 'Once upon a Time in the East,' " 21–22.

July 15 /64
8.30 p.m.

My dear Mother,

I have recd nothing from you or E. since yours enclosing Mrs. Ames letter. Neither have I written for a few days past as the communications are so uncertain. Until the news came last night that the rebs were retreating we did not suppose indeed that we should ever see any of you again. We supposed that you would all be carried South with the rest of the plunder. Is not this last raid the most disgraceful thing that has happened in the war? No[t] a gun seems to have been fired until the 6th Corps reached W. except the disgraceful affair at the Monocacy.[49] If the cowards of the North choose to let what now proves to have been a very small force, march through this Country at will I am only sorry that they did not destroy every man + thing in Maryland + Pennsylvania.

We do not think ourselves safe in sending <u>less</u> than 5000 or 6000 men to cut the Railroads in this Country where every able bodied man is away from home + yet some 500 Cavalry of the enemy penetrate as far into the thickly populated Country of Maryland as Gunpowder Creek. Not one man from Harpers Ferry to Washington seems to have had the sense to count the enemy as they passed his front door + let the authorities know how many of them there were. We could not march a mile into the South without the Confederate Govt knowing just what force we have.

I am utterly disgusted with the craven spirit of our people. I wish the enemy had burned Baltimore + Washington + hope they will yet.

We have been drawn a good ways back from the front + are now in reserve. We are nowhere near the enemy, but we do not

[49] On July 6, a Confederate force of 15,000 men under Lieutenant General Jubal Early crossed the Potomac and, after pushing aside a hastily assembled opposition at Monocacy, marched toward Washington. The Rebels reached five miles north of the White House by July 11, causing great panic for the safety of the capital, and Grant dispatched the Sixth corps to bolster Washington's defenses. The corps arrived just in time, and Early retreated rather than making an assault. McPherson, *Battle Cry of Freedom,* 756–57.

gain much rest thus far as the whole Div. has been engaged in
digging on Earthworks ever since last night.

I have been quite busy for a day or two past in acting as council
for Capt Elliot who is being Court Martialed for attempting to
defraud the Govt. by crediting himself with certain rations which
were not issued + by overcharging in sales to officers. I think he
has been careless in not looking closer after his business, but do
not think he has been guilty of any fraud. The result is somewhat
doubtful.

I have not heard further from Forbes about the darkey Corps.
A letter of similar purport came from Judge Russell. I see that a
party of Cavalry commanded by Major Forbes was nearly all
killed or captured by Mosby + I presume Major Forbes was lost
also.[50] Higginson writes that he is detained in N.Y. by illness but
will join me very soon. Tell E. I met [Brigadier General Adelbert]
Ames + had a long talk with him today. He says [Major General
Quincy A.] Gilmore is a Jackass.[51] He seems just the same as

---

[50] On July 6, 1864, as 150 troopers from the Thirteenth New York and Second Massachusetts Cavalry regiments, under the command of Major William
H. Forbes of the Bay State regiment, were reconnoitering in the vicinity of
Leesburg, Virginia. Forbes allowed his men an hour's break in the fields around
the farmhouse of Samuel Skinner and deployed a few pickets a mile and a half
to the west to warn of any Confederate attack. Suddenly, the feared Rangers
under John S. Mosby appeared. The Yankee sentinels warned the main body
by opening fire, and Forbes deployed his men in two ranks, but the Rangers
moved too quickly for his men and swarmed around his position. Forbes tried
to rally his men, but the Yankees broke when his horse was shot and pinned
him to the ground. Some escaped from the field only to be pursued by Mosby's
men, while Forbes and forty-four others were captured. Mosby sustained seven
casualties (one killed, six wounded) in the engagement, while Forbes had
losses of twelve killed and thirty-seven wounded, not including those taken
prisoner. Jeffry D. Wert, *Mosby's Rangers* (New York: Simon and Schuster,
1990), 173–76.

[51] Quincy A. Gillmore graduated first in his West Point class of 1849 and
became an instructor at the Military Academy. In 1861–62, he served as chief
engineer of the Port Royal expedition on the Carolina coast and successfully
planned the reduction of Fort Pulaski near Savannah, Georgia. He was promoted to major general to date from July 10, 1863, and placed in command of
the Department of the South and of the Tenth corps operating to capture Fort
Sumter and Charleston, South Carolina. In May 1864, he and his corps were
transferred to the Army of the James, and during Confederate General Jubal
Early's raid on Washington in July, Gillmore led two divisions of the Nineteenth
corps. In February 1865, Gillmore once again took command of the Department of the South and held that post through the end of the war. Warner,
Generals in Blue, 176–77.

ever. Capt [John M.] Brown became Lt. Col. of the 32nd Maine + was lately wounded.[52]

We are pushing siege operations here but no fire has been opened on the enemy from the trenches yet. I should think that Grant would strike while part of Lees Army is absent, but he does not.

I do not believe we shall starve out the rebel Army by cutting the railroads even if we could keep them cut. The inhabitants of Richmond + Petersburg may suffer, but I believe they have enough rations there to subsist their Army all summer.

No mail has come tonight. Arabella has been seriously ill, but the fever is broken + in time she will be well again. The Smiths + Mishets have taken care of her.

I have just seen the picture taken by Brady of Hancock myself &c. I do not think mine is good.

The box sent by R. has not arrived + I fear it is lost. He had better write about it.

> Write often to you aff Son
> Francis

> July 19th /64
> 9 p.m.

My dear Mother + brother,

I was very glad to receive mother's letter of the 11th giving an a/c of the visit to G.T. Davis + enclosing J. Russell's oration + Edward's of the 14th enclosing letter from the Tribune + C. Dehais card. I do not believe any were lost in the captured mail though some of mine may have been. It was many days however before I recd any of your letters.

---

[52] Formerly a member of the Twentieth Maine, John M. Brown served on the staffs of Brigadier General Romeyn Ayres and Brigadier General Adelbert Ames. He later mustered in as lieutenant colonel of the Thirty-second Maine, suffered a gunshot wound to his left arm and side near Petersburg on June 19, 1864, and had to resign the following September on account of the injury. Henry C. Houston, *The Thirty-second Maine Regiment of Infantry Volunteers,* 2 vols. (Portland, Maine: Press of Southworth Brothers, 1903), 2:460.

I had seen J. R's oration before—both he + C. Dalton had sent me a copy. I shall get to be a great <u>newspaper</u> here bye + bye.

I have seen Brady's Photographs. The one where all the staff was taken do not amount to much but the one of four figures is good they say though I do not like mine. I presume no one likes their own. I should like 4 or 5 of both kinds if they can be sent me in any portable form—without the large cards on which they usually come.

We have been very quiet since I last wrote. Every few days the Div. goes out to dig in the fortifications but nothing more. Tomorrow I am going to City Point. I shall go + see + dine with Ned Dalton + see Miss Eilson + C. Dana. I want to see the letter about the darkey Corps + show him John Forbes last letter + ask him about the best way of getting detailed for the work + doing it. I will send you Forbes letter or soon as I have answered them. I believe I told you I had a letter for Forbes written on the 10th in which he goes into a calculation of the large numbers of darkeys he is going to get out of the bush in the different localities + asks me how to go to work to get me detailed. I want to ask Dana on the last point. I have not written Forbes again until I can find out on these subjects. I see that R. is planning various marine + other excursions. Do you think you will change your base? If I go into the nigger business I ought to get a few days at home. I think E had better come down as soon as he can. Let me know the time + I will get him a pass. Can't E. find someplace in the Qr. Masters Dept or some such place in New York. They are easy places + I think I could get him one if he could find out just what was a good one.

Tell R. that I can no doubt get C. Miles a place in the Commissary Dept as clerk but he must agree to come + say when. The Court Martial on Capt Elliott ended today but we do not know the result. I have been at home excepting visit to Gen Ames + Lyman on Sunday. C. Adams came over to see

[remainder of letter missing]

On July 26, Hancock's command left its camps and proceeded to Deep Bottom, where it crossed the James River on a pontoon

bridge at two o'clock in the morning on the 27th. As soon as day broke, Barlow's division led the corps' advance as it attacked the Rebel line in that sector and prevented Confederates from harassing two divisions of Federal cavalry that crossed the James to maneuver closer to Richmond.[53]

That same day, Arabella succumbed to the typhus fever contracted during her nursing duties. Harper's Weekly *announced her death in Washington, D.C., and deemed her "amiable, accomplished, admired, beloved" and as "among the most eminent of the many heroines in this war whose names are not loudly mentioned but whose memory will be forever fresh in the grateful heart of their friends and country." Meanwhile, George Templeton Strong lamented that "she did great service" and was a "very noble woman[.]" Maria Daly grieved, "Poor Belle, how little I ever thought of so short a life for one so full of energy, so untiring," while after the war, Oliver O. Howard fondly remembered a personal encounter with her, in which her "stimulating, encouraging words . . . brightened my own life under circumstances of great sorrow and depression." On July 29, a devastated Barlow left the front on a fifteen-day leave of absence to accompany her remains to Somerville, New Jersey. He arrived there on July 30, and Arabella was buried the next day in the Old Somerville Cemetery.*[54]

Barlow returned to duty on the morning of August 13, but he continued to mourn. Furthermore, he had grown weak, having suffered from diarrhea since the beginning of July. He resumed command of his division on August 13 and participated in the Second corps' maneuvers that day, but by August 17, he relinquished command to Miles and proceeded to the hospital at City Point. On August 24, Barlow began a twenty-day leave in order to try to recuperate from his sorrows, illness, and combat exhaustion. During Barlow's absence, Hancock recommended his subordinate and friend to receive his second star, to date from May 12—the day of the triumphant attack on the Bloody Angle.

---

[53] *OR*, 40(1): 308–9, 330–31.

[54] *Harper's Weekly*, August 13, 1864. Strong diary, July 30, 1864, in Nevins, *Diary of the Civil War*, 467–68. Maria L. Daly diary, March 26, 1865, in Hammond, *Diary of a Union Lady*, 345. Howard, "After the Battle." Lauter, "'Once upon a Time in the East,'" 22. *OR*, 40(1): 331. *OR*, 42(2): 148.

*By September, Barlow hoped he might be able to return to ser-
vice, and he wrote as such to Hancock. Hancock quickly replied,
sending his wish for a speedy convalescence and telling his subordinate that he could have used him in recent combat.*[55]

*A letter written to him by his friend Charles Russell Lowell
indicates Barlow's poor condition, however. Lowell cautioned,*

Take care of yourself, old fellow. Just get your mother to take you
to some quiet place and make much of you—don't think too much
of campaigns and of elections. This isn't the end of the world,
though it is so important for us. Don't mind Lincoln's shortcomings too much: we know that he has not the first military spark in
his composition, not a sense probably by which he could get the
notion of what makes or unmakes an Army, but he is certainly
much the best candidate for the permanency of our republican
institutions, and that is the main thing. I don't think even he can
make the people tire of the war. What you want is rest and care;
don't be foolish, my dear fellow, and neglect to take them. Unless
you give yourself some time now, you will never half complete
your career. What the devil difference does it make where a man
passes the next six months, if the war is to last six years? If it is
to be ended in one year, you have done and suffered your share
in it.

There are better things to be done in the Country, Barlow, than
fighting, and you must save yourself for them too. I remember we
said to each other six months ago, that the man who wasn't in the
coming campaign might as well count out. Bah! It hasn't proved.
There are as many campaigns for a fellow as there are half years
to his life.[56]

*Trying to recover in Massachusetts, Barlow required more
time to recuperate from the various shocks he suffered, both
physical and mental. He obtained twenty-day extensions of his*

---

[55] *OR*, 40(1): 331. *OR*, 42(1): 247–29. *OR*, 42(2): 148, 594. Abbott, "Francis
Channing Barlow," 529. Barlow to Lieutenant Colonel Francis A. Walker,
Headquarters First Division Second Corps, August 17, 1864; Barlow to Lieutenant Colonel Francis A. Walker, Headquarters First Division Second Corps,
August 24, 1864; Special Orders No. 228 Army of the Potomac, August 24,
1864, in Barlow's Generals Papers NA. Winfield S. Hancock to Francis C. Barlow, Headquarters Second Army Corps, September 10, 1864, in Barlow collection, Massachusetts Historical Society, Boston, Massachusetts.

[56] Charles R. Lowell to Francis C. Barlow, Ripon, Va., September 10, 1864,
in Emerson, *Life and Letters of Charles Russell Lowell*, 343–44.

leave on September 12 and October 3, though the October 22 extension indicated that his condition had actually worsened: Barlow suffered from dysentery following the diarrhea and remained confined to bed.[57]

Meanwhile, New York Senator Edwin Morgan wrote an emphatic letter to Secretary of War Stanton:

> I would be very glad to have you make Brig Genl Barlow a Major General by brevet to date from the battle of Spottsylvania [sic] Court House. He is worthy of it. It will gratify many friends, among them,
>
> Your very obt svt
E.D. Morgan[58]

In November, Hancock wrote with information from the front as well as wishes that Barlow's health would "soon be restored." Others among Barlow's friends realized that he needed more time away from the service in order to recover. On October 29, Barlow applied for leave of absence until April 1, 1865, with permission to visit Europe in order to cure himself. The general noted in support of his petition that if not abroad, he would be spending the next several months on sick leave anyway and away from active duty. Barlow also enclosed a surgeon's letter offering a medical opinion that Barlow's sickness, resulting from "fatigue and exposure in a malarious climate while in the line of his duty," required several months' recuperation and that "a sea voyage and change of climate are absolutely necessary to ensure his recovery." Charles Sumner personally submitted Barlow's entire application with an accompanying endorsement. In his own letter, the powerful Massachusetts senator assured, "I have seen the General + find him very feeble + weak." After noting that both "the medical authorities + his friends are very anxious in regard to his condition," Sumner observed that Barlow had friends leaving for Europe on November 9 and requested that the general receive permission by then in order to join them. On November 3, Henry Halleck wrote on Sumner's letter, "So far as

---

[57] Surgeon's Certificates dated September 12; October 3; October 22, 1864, all in Barlow's Generals Papers NA.

[58] E. D. Morgan to Edwin M. Stanton, New York, September 26, 1864, in Barlow Papers NA.

I am aware applications of officers for leave to visit Europe during the war have been uniformly rejected. If an exception is made in this case it must be by the authority of the Secty of War." On November 5, the War Department gave Barlow his requested leave of absence. E. D. Townsend's telegram with the news noted that "*although such indulgence is unusual the Secretary of War considering your distinguished services has granted you leave of absence till April first, eighteen sixty five (1865) with permission to visit Europe, on account of ill health. Order goes by mail today. Acknowledge receipt."* On November 7, Massachusetts Governor John A. Andrew personally acknowledged receipt and informed Townsend that Barlow had been notified. That Andrew went on to thank Townsend for his kindness indicated that the governor had likely earlier urged acceptance of Barlow's application as well. Barlow took advantage of the news and planned his journey to Europe.[59]

Before his trip, however, Barlow faced another tragic loss. Although he had not seen his father since childhood, he learned through friends in Philadelphia that the elder Barlow, now in poor health and having sight only in one eye, worked in a hospital near Haddington, Pennsylvania. Unsure of what reaction his father would have to an overture, the general asked a Harvard friend, Phillips Brooks, to make first contact and offer his father some financial support if necessary. On November 29, Brooks met David Barlow at Haddington Hospital. Barlow declined his son's offer of assistance except if he lost sight in his other eye, and Brooks later reported that his quarters at the hospital were sufficient. During their conversation, however, the elder Barlow asked Brooks for information about his son and appealed for him to visit so that the two could, at long last, meet again. After this

[59] Francis Barlow to Brigadier General Lorenzo Thomas, Boston, October 29, 1864; Letter of Anson P. Hooker, M.D., Boston, October 29, 1864; Letter of Charles Sumner, Boston, October 29, 1864, and endorsement of Henry Halleck on it, dated November 3, 1864; telegram of E. D. Townsend to Francis Barlow, November 5, 1865; telegram of John A. Andrew to Colonel E. D. Townsend, November 7, 1864, all in Barlow Papers NA. Special orders No. 384, War Department, November 5, 1864, in Barlow's Generals Papers NA. Winfield S. Hancock to Francis C. Barlow, Headquarters Second Army Corps, November 3, 1864, in Barlow collection, Massachusetts Historical Society, Boston, Massachusetts. Abbott, "Francis Channing Barlow," 529.

meeting, David Barlow took a walk into Haddington, and while returning, a shocking crime took place. Brooks, no doubt already aware of his friend's fragile condition, had to inform Barlow that his father had "received [a] blow which resulted in his immediate death" from an unknown assailant. With an even heavier heart, Barlow left the United States for Europe on his quest to reestablish himself and recover senses shattered by war, illness, and loss.[60]

---

[60] Phillips Brooks to Barlow, October 12, 1864; November 31, 1864, both in Francis G. Shaw Papers, Massachusetts Historical Society, Boston; these letters have been quoted in Richard F. Welch, *The Boy General: The Life and Careers of Francis Channing Barlow* (Madison, N.J.: Fairleigh Dickinson University Press, 2003), 196–97; they are also mentioned as being located in the "David Barlow" folder in this same collection in Thomas B. Buell, *The Combat Generals* (New York: Crown Publishers, 1997), 466. Extensive searches at the Massachusetts Historical Society, however, were unable to locate the original letters.

CONCLUSION

Barlow returned from Europe healthier than when he left, though during a visit with Judge and Mrs. Daly in New York in late March 1865, he still wore Arabella's ring on his finger. He rejoined the Army of the Potomac on April 6, 1865, just in time to see it victorious at Appomattox, but he resigned from the military soon afterward. He had volunteered for the service as a young attorney unschooled in military matters, but he left it a battlefield commander, with a honed sense of authority after having proven his abilities to himself. Brimming with untried potential in 1861, Barlow grew into a confident and vigorous man of action, tested and tempered by the experience of combat, the growth involved in becoming a field general, and the loss of his wife. Barlow would go on to face new challenges between various governmental posts as well as his remarriage and raising of a family, but the Civil War remained the transformative event of his life. Through it, Barlow's latent talent became invigorated as he seized the opportunity to have an impact on his country's history, both during the great struggle between North and South and beyond.[1]

Barlow accepted promotion to major general of volunteers on May 25, 1865, though he declined a commission in the regular army as he pondered his future career.[2] Barlow considered remaining in the military as well as simultaneously serving in the Freedmen's Bureau. In late July, he wrote his friend and Freedmen's Bureau commissioner Oliver O. Howard from Brookline:

---

[1] Maria Daly, diary entry of March 26, 1865, in Hammond, *Diary of a Union Lady*, 345.

[2] New York Monuments Commission, *In Memoriam: Francis Channing Barlow*, 130. Francis Barlow to Edwin H. Abbot, June 20, 1880, in Harvard College, *Report of the Class of 1855 in Harvard College: Prepared for the Twenty-fifth Anniversary of Its Graduation* (Cambridge, Mass.: J. Wilson and Son, 1880), 17.

I do not know whether the newspapers give a correct account of affairs in the Southern States but if they speak the truth some of the military commanders do not believe much in the "darkey" + do not give your Bureau much assistance.

You know the interest I have always taken in these Freedmen[']s affairs + I have just written to the Secretary of War asking him to assign me to a command in the Southern States + suggesting that at the same time I might be made Superintendent of Freedmen in my District. If you think of any way in which I can help your general plans by holding a military command or otherwise will you let me know or see the Secretary on the subject. I should prefer being assigned to South Carolina or Georgia.[3]

In September, Barlow again wrote Howard to introduce Major Henry Lee Higginson and Lieutenant Colonel C. F. Morse, two former Federal officers who intended to go "into the Southern States with a view to buying or hiring land of your Bureau + raising cotton &c." Barlow noted that they were "both good officers + good fellows" and added that they "are with sound Massachusetts principles + are just the people whom it is for our good to settle in the South." Although he had come to respect the Southern spirit in the course of the war, Barlow viewed the Federal victory as an opportunity to transform the former Confederacy by implanting solidly Northern principles and values. Furthermore, he reiterated that he wanted to participate in this process. Barlow reminded Howard that "sometime ago I wrote you saying that I wished to get assigned to a command in the South + to be made Superintendent of Freedmen in the District where I had command" and asked, "Do you think this would be possible?"[4]

Barlow won election as secretary of state for New York that same month, however, a victory that precluded his taking a position in the Freedmen's Bureau. He opposed another former comrade from the Army of the Potomac, Democratic nominee Major General Henry W. Slocum, and defeated him by 27,491 votes. Barlow's resignation from the U.S. Volunteer Forces was

---

[3] Francis C. Barlow to Oliver O. Howard, Brookline, Mass., July 24, 1865, in Howard Papers.

[4] Francis C. Barlow to Oliver O. Howard, Brookline, Mass., September 17, 1865, in ibid.

accepted on November 17, 1865, to date from the preceding day. As secretary of state, Barlow had a seat on New York's Canal Board, was a commissioner of its Canal Fund, and served as a commissioner of the Land Office in charge of supervising public lands.[5]

War service had transformed Barlow and solidified the taciturn nature of his personality. He joined other members of his Harvard class at a ten-year reunion at the Parker House, and though the class of 1855 had produced many distinguished men, Barlow proved to be the celebrated figure among them. At the reunion, Theodore Lyman recounted Barlow's achievements, which culminated in calling for nine cheers for the general who had captured the Bloody Angle. One classmate recounted, however, that "Barlow was the only man in the room who showed not the slightest emotion. He stood impassive, his face wearing his queer smile. Other men might have been abashed at the tumultuous warmth of such a reception from his old mates; a natural utterance at such a time would have been an expression of joy that the war was over and that the country had been saved, coupled with modest satisfaction that he had borne some part in the great vindication, but that was not Barlow's way. He laughed it off lightly, as if it had been a huge joke."[6]

Similarly, when he dined with his friends, the Dalys, in November 1865, Maria Daly recounted:

> What a thoroughly practical New England character! He seems to look upon his military career now as only a good advertisement for him as a lawyer. . . . I esteem him and respect his bravery, but I do not know why it is that I feel so little sympathy with him. I think he looks as though he had a very sensuous temperament and might become a very hard, money-making, selfish man as he grows older. Although very courageous, he is neither romantic nor has he any sympathy with either the poetical or the philosophical. He very frankly confessed that he had read very little except Shakespeare.[7]

---

[5] Special Orders No. 605, War Department, November 17, 1865, in Barlow's Generals Papers NA. New York Monuments Commission, *In Memoriam: Francis Channing Barlow*, 130–31. Francis Barlow to Edwin H. Abbot, June 20, 1880, in Harvard College, *Report of the Class of 1855*, 17.

[6] Hosmer, *Last Leaf*, 64–65.

[7] Maria Daly, diary entry of November 25, 1865, in Hammond, *Diary of a Union Lady*, 379.

Of course, this opinion must be considered in light of its author, who was frequently very critical of those in her company. Furthermore, considering that Barlow graduated first in his Harvard class, he undoubtedly read works by authors other than Shakespeare.

Meanwhile, in 1866, Winslow Homer commemorated his friend in the oil painting *Prisoners from the Front,* now held in the Metropolitan Museum of Art in New York City. The painting appears as if a moment captured in time, yet addresses grander themes of both the war and reconstruction, a simple narrative fraught with deeper meaning. Before the well-dressed Federal officer, clearly Barlow, three types of Confederates stand—one defiantly but tragically with hand on hip, an elderly Southerner with ragged uniform and suppliant with hat in hand, and a young boy. Barlow looks at the trio with a sensitive expression; while he has power over them, he does not abuse it. Homer has captured Barlow's characteristic sense of authority as well as the Southern spirit, but has done so in a painting depicting a decidedly commonplace wartime event, lacking the heroic tone of a desperate charge or a resolute repulse. Having Barlow face the Confederates as defeated but equal, Homer comments on the postwar healing between North and South, as a nation rent apart began the long process of mending wounds.[8]

Barlow did not have to remain in Albany full time to fulfill the demands of his office, and he added to his public duties by resuming the practice of law, opening an office in New York City on May 15, 1866. Shortly afterward, he became counsel to the National Park Bank, one of the largest banks in the United States at the time and a lucrative client Barlow retained through his future law career. He also remarried in October 1867, wedding Ellen Shaw, the sister of his former pupil Robert Gould Shaw as well as sister of the wives of Charles Russell Lowell and George William Curtis. Barlow had two sons with her—Robert Shaw Barlow, born on July 4, 1869, and Charles Lowell Barlow, born

---

[8] Julian Grossman, *Echo of a Distant Drum: Winslow Homer and the Civil War* (New York: Harry N. Abrams Publishers, 1974). Lucretia H. Giese, "Prisoners from the Front: An American History Painting," in *Winslow Homer Paintings of the Civil War,* ed. Marc Simpson, et al. (San Francisco: Fine Arts Museums of San Francisco, 1988), 65–81: 65–67.

on October 10, 1871—and both later attended Harvard and became attorneys like their father. His daughter, Louisa, born on July 27, 1873, later married Pierre Jay of New York and had four children of her own.[9]

The Republican Party declined to renominate Barlow for another term, and he devoted himself fully to his law practice. Barlow soon served in another public capacity when Attorney General Ebenezer R. Hoar successfully urged President Grant to appoint him U.S. marshal for the southern district of New York in May 1869. Barlow only held the position for half a year, but rooted out corruption within the area with vigor and energy. Within his first week in the position, he cashiered everyone in his office and replaced them with men known to him to be honest, angering those who wished Barlow to play under the traditional rules governing patronage at the time.[10]

Other excitement during his tenure as marshal came in his quashing an attempt by filibusters to send soldiers and equipment to aid an insurrection in Cuba. Grant authorized his former subordinate special powers of command over the military, naval, and revenue forces of New England, New York, and New Jersey under an act dating to 1818. Through this, the president empowered Barlow to do what was necessary to prevent the filibusters' expedition and, with it, certain war with Spain. Barlow captured a vessel in New York City filled with Cuban rebels and laden with arms before it left the harbor, and thus put an end to the endeavor. Barlow found the yearly salary of six thousand dollars accompanying his position inadequate, however, and its duties too great to allow him sufficient time to practice enough law to support himself in a lifestyle he deemed adequate. As soon as he resolved the Cuban crisis, Barlow resigned as U.S. marshal.[11]

Barlow returned to the full-time practice of law, with Effin-

---

[9] New York Monuments Commission, *In Memoriam: Francis Channing Barlow*, 132, 136. Francis Barlow to Edwin H. Abbott, June 20, 1880, in Harvard College, *Report of the Class of 1855*, 18, 23.

[10] Abbott, "Francis Channing Barlow," 538. New York Monuments Commission, *In Memoriam: Francis Channing Barlow*, 132.

[11] Abbott, "Francis Channing Barlow," 538. New York Monuments Commission, *In Memoriam: Francis Channing Barlow*, 132–33. Francis Barlow to Edwin H. Abbott, June 20, 1880, in Harvard College, *Report of the Class of 1855*, 18.

gham T. Hyatt and Peter B. Olney, at the law office of Barlow, Hyatt & Olney at No. 21 Park Row in New York City. During the last week of November 1870, Oliver O. Howard called on Barlow twice at the law office, but, unaware that his former commander was in town, Barlow missed Howard both times. Barlow immediately expressed his regret and invited Howard to dinner next time he was in town, offering that he "should like so much to have a good talk" with his former Corps commander.[12]

In the early 1870s, Barlow helped found the Association of the Bar of the City of New York. After the Civil War, New York's courts were racked by scandalous behavior and its government imbued with corrupt dealings. The situation eventually got so bad that George Templeton Strong confided to his diary, "The New Yorker belongs to a community worse governed by lower and baser blackguard scum than any city in Western Christendom, or in the world." The law, along with the attorneys and judges who administered it, seemed irreversibly plummeting into disrepute. Finally, the *New York Times* called for attorneys to organize, and soon afterward a short letter circulated among members of New York City's legal community. The document asserted that "the organized action and influence of the Legal Profession, properly exerted, would lead to the creation of more intimate relations between its members," "sustain the profession in its proper position in the community," and thereby "enable it . . . to promote the interests of the public[.]" Within a few weeks, over two hundred attorneys endorsed the circular and organized into the Association of the Bar of the City of New York. Barlow became one of its Committee of Seventy, specially commissioned to take action to oust "Boss" William Marcy Tweed and attempt to recover money his ring had embezzled from the city. Barlow later served as chair of the Association's Law Committee and one of four paid counsel.[13]

---

[12] Francis C. Barlow to Oliver O. Howard, New York City, November 26, 1870, in Oliver O. Howard Papers, Special Collections & Archives, Bowdoin College Library, Brunswick, Maine.

[13] George Templeton Strong, diary entry April 9, 1868, quoted in George Martin, *Causes and Conflicts: The Centennial History of the Bar of the City of New York 1870–1970* (New York: Fordham University Press, 1997), 3, 11, 15, 65. New York Monuments Commission, *In Memoriam: Francis Channing Barlow*, 133. Francis Barlow to Edwin H. Abbott, June 20, 1880, in Harvard College, *Report of the Class of 1855*, 20.

Around this time, Barlow was elected for a two-year term as attorney general of New York. Hailed by the *New York Times* as an active warrior against corruption, he held that office from November 7, 1871, to November 3, 1873. During this tenure, Barlow prosecuted the Tammany Ring and overthrew Boss Tweed, and he also began proceedings against judicial and governmental corruption later continued to completion by Charles O'Conor and Samuel J. Tilden.[14] In so doing, Barlow took an active lead in the fight for clean and honest government, and Secretary of Treasury Charles S. Fairchild recalled:

His devotion to public duty, his bravery and aggressiveness therein, and disregard of selfish considerations or of consequences to himself, filled me with admiration and enthusiasm, and, I see, as I recall it now, set me a standard of public duty that has influenced all my life since. I believe that, if it had not been for General Barlow's zealous work, it would never have come to Mr. Tilden to take the position that he did upon canal matters, a position to which Mr. Tilden owed the immediate prestige that compelled his nomination for the presidency in 1876. Tilden but took up and carried on the work that General Barlow had begun, and begun under circumstances of great difficulty and great danger to himself, for he was all alone. Not another State officer dared stand with him at the beginning of the fight. Before that time he had so pursued and pointed out the judicial wrongs that surrounded the Erie and other litigations that his work was one of the chief contributions to what culminated in the impeachment of the judges. I believe that the State owes General Barlow more than she does any single man for results without which the life of an honest man would have been intolerable in this State.[15]

Despite service that earned him praise from some quarters, however, Barlow's attack on corrupt but powerful men and his open voicing of opinions led others to resent him, and the Republican Party declined to renominate him for office. Some also continued to begrudge something he did while still serving as U.S. marshal. The Republican committee assessed Barlow for an expected donation based on the income supposed to be available

---

[14] Abbott, "Francis Channing Barlow," 539.
[15] Charles S. Fairchild, quoted in Abbott, "Francis Channing Barlow," 539–40.

to a U.S. marshal, though that figure was often based on "supplementary" income rooted in corrupt dealings. Barlow refused to pay an assessment based on that figure and not his honest salary, and he did so in a letter read by the public and which embarrassed party leaders.[16]

Despite a return to private life, Barlow continued to play a public role and circulate among the leading figures of the nation. For the centennial of the beginning of the American Revolution, Barlow returned to Concord for the great celebration that town held to commemorate the events of April 19, 1775, and to dedicate a bronze statue of a farmer-soldier. Ralph W. Emerson excitedly helped organize the ceremony, in which former attorney general Ebenezer Hoar presided, George W. Curtis (who had helped Almira Barlow find lodging in Concord in the first place) delivered a speech, and Barlow served as marshal. As early as April 5, Barlow examined the site for the event and planned where female observers should watch the ceremonies and where the spectator's tent should be placed. On April 19, 1875, President Grant led the list of luminaries, which included cabinet members, congressmen, governors, and business magnates, all of whom attended the proceedings.[17]

The next year, Republicans once again called upon Barlow to perform public service, but his scrupulous honesty over partisan interest in the mission ensured that he would never receive another nomination for political office again. During the disputed election of 1876, his party dispatched Barlow to help investigate ballot counting in the disputed state of Florida. Barlow received assignment to examine Alachua County, a mostly African American area where it was expected the Republicans would gather evidence in support of Rutherford B. Hayes's victory. Barlow explored rumors, however, that Republicans in one precinct cast hundreds of fraudulent ballots, and when he announced his

---

[16] Abbott, "Francis Channing Barlow," 540.

[17] Ralph W. Emerson to George Bancroft, Concord, Mass., March 12, 1875; Ralph W. Emerson to George B. Emerson, Concord, Mass., April 6, 1875; Ralph W. Emerson to John M. Forbes, Concord, Mass., April 10, 1875, both in Rusk and Tilton, *Letters of Ralph Waldo Emerson*, 10:156, 158–59. Townsend Scudder, *Concord: American Town* (Boston: Little, Brown and Company, 1947), 265–76.

finding that Democratic claims to the state's electoral votes had merit, he was recalled and replaced. On December 6, 1876, Florida's electors were declared for Hayes, but in the process, Barlow continued to voice his concerns that the Democrats might be entitled to the Floridian vote, and this open statement of his findings alienated members of his party. One Republican remarked, "Think of a lawyer confessing he had no case in the presence of the jury," and though Barlow later offered to draw up a statement showing that "there were questions before the B.[oard] as to which men might fairly differ, & people will see that there was not the wholesale fraud which the Democrats pretend," his report embarrassed Republicans who proved slow to forget and publicly attacked Barlow for his independence of thought. In recounting Barlow's life, Edwin H. Abbott, contended that Barlow "was never forgiven for telling the whole story, as he did" about the election in Florida, and Barlow never received another nomination for the rest of his life.[18]

The remainder of Barlow's professional life focused on the private practice of law, and he also spent time with his family, likely wanting to be a more involved father than his own was. In January 1882 Barlow wrote his friend Oliver O. Howard to express regret that the two had not spent more time together during a visit to West Point, and he mentioned wanting to bring his sons up some warm Saturday to see the Military Academy. A couple of years later, Barlow wrote Howard to intervene on behalf of his sons' alma mater, the Cutler School in New York City. Its boys often played football on Governor's Island, and when this privilege seemed in jeopardy, Barlow became involved in the dispute. He did this not only to assist his sons' former school but also because of his continuing belief in the value of the strenuous, active life learned during the Civil War. "Football makes the boys vigorous + hardy," Barlow argued, "and I am sure that so distinguished a Second Corps man as you are will be glad to encourage these qualities." Nonetheless, Howard seems to have denied

---

[18] Keith Ian Polakoff, *The Politics of Inertia: The Election of 1876 and the End of Reconstruction* (Baton Rouge: Louisiana State University Press, 1973), 216–18. Francis C. Barlow to William E. Chandler, December 11, 1876, quoted in Polakoff, *Politics of Inertia*, 217. Abbott, "Francis Channing Barlow," 540.

permission to continue playing on the property. Barlow thanked him for a response a week later but stated, "the interests of the Government + the service are of course the most important things." Barlow involved himself in various veterans' events, attending meetings of the Sixty-first New York's organization, visiting the Gettysburg battlefield with friends in June 1888, and accepting the presidency of the Second Corps Club in July of that year. In keeping with his active lifestyle, Barlow also went on a seven-week hunting expedition on Nantucket, Massachusetts, in the summer of 1889.[19]

Barlow expended considerable energy to promote the military career of his friend and former subordinate, Nelson C. Miles. He also, however, opposed a movement sponsored by the Grand Army of the Republic to expand the definition of those eligible for a government pension. The proposal called for pensions for any veteran who served ninety or more days' service and had become disabled, regardless of whether the disability was related to military service. Barlow responded with a written statement conceding that those who had been disabled by military service, as well as wives and children of those killed, were entitled to assistance, but not regardless of whether they bravely did their duty or were a shirker seeking advantage. The letter went on to claim that soldiers should not seek further recompense but instead realize that "a soldier of our army always has and always will have especial honor from his fellow citizens" and that "this and his own approving conscience is a soldier's surplus reward over and above that the government agree to pay him."[20]

Barlow's health began to fail in the mid-1890s, and he died at his home at 39 East Thirty-first Street in New York City on January 11, 1896, of chronic Bright's disease and endarteritis (inflammation inside the artery). Two days later, a funeral service was held at the Church of the Incarnation on Madison Avenue and Thirty-fifth Street before his body was returned to Brookline,

[19] Francis C. Barlow to J. B. Bachelder, Nantucket, Mass., September 2, 1889, in Ladd and Ladd, *Bachelder Papers,* 3:1963. Welch, *Boy General,* 241. Francis C. Barlow to Oliver O. Howard, New York, January 21, 1882; October 22, 1894; October 24, 1894; October 29, 1894, all in Howard Papers.

[20] Welch, *Boy General,* 241–42. Barlow to E. L. Godkin, August 9, 1890, *New York Evening Post,* quoted in Welch, *Boy General,* 243–45.

Massachusetts, and interred in the Penniman family tomb in the Walnut Street Cemetery, where his mother, brothers, and other family members rest.[21]

Upon Barlow's death, some recalled his courage. According to classmate Edwin H. Abbott, "Barlow was not merely brave. His courage was more than ignorant insensibility to risk and the consequence of exposure to danger, for he was twice grievously hurt. He seemed throughout life, in civil as well as military affairs, literally incapable of fearing anything in any form. Fear was not in him." Similarly, Theodore Lyman recounted an anecdote in which Barlow and General Humphreys "rode toward the enemy on a reconnaissance. Neither of them was willing to face about, and they nearly went over the rebel skirmish line, when a shower of bullets persuaded them to retreat, both laughing heartily as the peril."[22]

Another classmate, James Kendall Hosmer, eulogized, "No other Harvard soldier reached Barlow's eminence, and probably in the whole Army of the Potomac there were few abler champions. He was a strange, gifted, most picturesque personality, no doubt a better man under his cynical exterior than he would ever suffer it to be thought. His service was great, and the memory of him is an interesting and precious possession to those who knew him in boyhood and were in touch with him to the end." And, his friend and comrade in arms Miles summed up Barlow's life and personality aptly, writing

> Under the most depressing circumstances he never was without hope and fortitude. He was apparently utterly devoid of the sensation of fear, constantly aggressive, and intensely earnest in the discharge of all duties. His integrity of purpose, independence of character, and sterling honesty in the assertion of what he believed to be right and just, made him a marked man among public men. He abhorred a coward; had a perfect contempt for a demagogue, and despised a hypocrite. He believed in the administration of public affairs with the most rigid integrity, and did not hesitate

[21] Welch, *Boy General*, 247.

[22] Welsh, *Medical Histories of Union Generals*, 16. New York Monuments Commission, *In Memoriam: Francis Channing Barlow*, 136. Abbott, "Francis Channing Barlow," 529–30.

to denounce wrong as he believed it to exist, and maintain what he believed to be right under all circumstances.[23]

New York State dedicated a monument to Barlow on "Barlow's Knoll" on the Gettysburg battlefield on June 6, 1922, in the presence of Barlow's widow, three children, and two grandchildren, one of whom unveiled the statue. Harvard's class of 1855, however, found the most fitting way to honor their most famous member. After the Civil War, alumni raised funds for the construction of Memorial Hall, dedicated in 1874 to honor Harvard veterans who fought for the North during the Civil War. Barlow's class decided to donate a stained-glass window for Memorial Hall, and while meeting to decide what famous warrior from the past it should portray, many of Barlow's classmates voiced their opinion that his face should provide the model for the figure. Barlow laughed off the suggestion, and when someone else suggested that Alcibiades should be depicted, he asked who would provide the model for the Greek warrior's famous dog. All gathered burst out in peals of laughter, though Barlow's attempt to use humor to distract attention from himself failed. After his death, despite a previous rule that only someone dead for at least a century should appear as a likeness on any of Memorial Hall's windows, Barlow's face was selected as the model for Godefroy. A German knight who conquered Jerusalem in 1099, Godefroy is depicted wearing a white tunic over his armor, and wields a sword in his right hand and the red-crossed white banner of a crusader in his right. Perhaps this is the most appropriate metaphor for Francis C. Barlow, who entered the Civil War as a reluctant intellectual and became transformed into an engaged and commanding warrior for the North and, afterward, for clean government. Perhaps Barlow's classmates realized that Barlow had been a crusader in their midst, one who wielded both his sword and his mind in support of the principles he risked his life to uphold.[24]

---

[23] Hosmer, *Last Leaf,* 66. Nelson Miles, quoted in Abbott, "Francis Channing Barlow," 535–36.

[24] Hosmer, *Last Leaf,* 65. Abbott, "Francis Channing Barlow," 541.

WORKS CITED

Unpublished Sources

Bowdoin College Library, Special Collections & Archives, Brunswick, Maine.
Oliver Otis Howard Papers.
Massachusetts Historical Society, Boston, Massachusetts.
Francis C. Barlow papers.
National Archives, Washington, D.C.
Francis C. Barlow papers, M-1064 microfilm roll 241 (Barlow Papers NA).
Francis C. Barlow's Generals Papers, RG 94-9W4/6/10/A, Box 2 (Barlow's Generals Papers NA).
Francis C. Barlow File, Field and Staff Officers Papers, Sixty-first New York Volunteer Infantry (Barlow Field and Staff Officers Papers NA).
Thomas A. Smyth diary, typescript copy provided by Frank A Boyle.

Published Sources

Abbot, Richard H. *Cobbler in Congress*. Lexington: University Press of Kentucky, 1972.
Abbott, Edwin H. "Francis Channing Barlow." *Harvard Graduates' Magazine* 4, no. 16 (June 1896): 526–42.
Agassiz, George R., ed. *With Grant and Meade from the Wilderness to Appomattox*. 1922; repr. Lincoln, Nebr.: University of Nebraska Press, 1994.
Ames, Blanche Butler, ed. *Chronicles from the Nineteenth Century: Family Letters of Blanche Butler and Adelbert Ames*. 2 vols. Privately published, 1957.
Bailyn, Bernard. "Why Kirkland Failed." In *Glimpses of the Harvard Past*, edited by Bernard Bailyn, et al., 19–44. Cambridge, Mass.: Harvard University Press, 1986.

Barlow, Francis C., to E. L. Godkin, August 9, 1890, *New York Evening Post.*

Barlow, Francis C. "Capture of the Salient, May 12, 1864." In *Papers of the Military Historical Society of Massachusetts.* 14 vols., 4:245–62. Boston: Historical Society of Massachusetts, 1881–1918.

Bates, Samuel P. *History of Pennsylvania Volunteers, 1861–65.* 5 vols. Harrisburg, Pa.: D. Singerly, State Printer, 1869.

Benson, Henry King. *The Public Career of Adelbert Ames, 1861–1976.* Ph.D. diss., University of Virginia, Charlottesville, 1975.

Black, John D. "Reminiscences of the Bloody Angle." In *Glimpses of the Nation's Struggle: Papers Read before the Commandery of the State of Minnesota, Military Order of the Loyal Legion of the United States, 1892–1897,* 420–36. Saint Paul, Minn., 1898.

Brown, Augustus Cleveland. *The Diary of a Line Officer.* Privately printed, 1906.

Buell, Thomas B. *The Combat Generals.* New York: Crown Publishers, 1997.

Butterfield, Julia Lorrilard. *A Biographical Memorial of General Daniel Butterfield.* New York: Grafton Press, 1904.

Butts, Joseph Tyler, ed. *A Gallant Captain of the Civil War: Being the Record of the Extraordinary Adventures of Frederick Otto Baron von Fritsch.* New York: F. Tennyson Neely, 1902.

Clifford, Deborah Pickman. *Mine Eyes Have Seen the Glory: Julia Ward Howe.* Boston: Little, Brown, and Company, 1978.

Conyngham, David P. *The Irish Brigade and Its Campaigns.* 1867; repr. New York: Fordham University Press, 1994.

Crawford, Mary Carolina. *Famous Families of Massachusetts.* 2 vols. Boston: Little, Brown, and Company, 1930.

Culp, E. C. "Gettysburg: Reminiscences of the Great Fight by a Participant." *National Tribune,* March 19, 1885.

Current, Richard N. *Three Carpetbag Governors.* Baton Rouge: Louisiana State University Press, 1967.

Curtis, Edith Roelker. *A Season in Utopia: The Story of Brook Farm.* 1961; repr. New York: Russell & Russell, 1971.

"Charles Henry Dalton Papers." In *Proceedings of the Massachusetts Historical Society, October 1922–June 1923,* 56: 354–495. Boston: Massachusetts Historical Society, 1923.

Davis, William C. *Battle at Bull Run*. Baton Rouge: Louisiana State University Press, 1977.

Duncan, Russell, ed. *Blue-Eyed Child of Fortune: The Civil War Letters of Colonel Robert Gould Shaw*. Athens: University of Georgia Press, 1992.

Dyer, Frederick H. *A Compendium of the War of the Rebellion*. 3 vols. Des Moines: Dyer Publishing Company, 1908.

Eckert, Ralph Lowell. *John Brown Gordon: Soldier Southerner American*. Baton Rouge: Louisiana State University Press, 1989.

Emerson, Edward W., ed. *Life and Letters of Charles Russell Lowell*. Boston: Houghton, Mifflin, and Company, 1907.

Emerson, Sarah Hopper, ed. *Life of Abby Hopper Gibbons: Told Chiefly through Her Correspondence*. 2 vols. New York: G. P. Putnam's Sons, 1896.

Ferguson, Ernest B. *Chancellorsville 1863: The Souls of the Brave*. New York: Alfred A. Knopf, 1992.

Frederickson, George M. *The Inner Civil War: Northern Intellectuals and the Crisis of the Union*. 1965; repr. Chicago: University of Illinois Press, 1993.

Fuller, Charles A. *Personal Recollections of the War of 1861*. Sherburne, N.Y.: News Job Printing House, 1906.

Giese, Lucretia H. "Prisoners from the Front: An American History Painting." In *Winslow Homer Paintings of the Civil War*, edited by Marc Simpson, et al., 65–82. San Francisco: Fine Arts Museums of San Francisco, 1988.

Grossman, Julian. *Echo of a Distant Drum: Winslow Homer and the Civil War*. New York: Harry N. Abrams Publishers, 1974.

Gordon, John B. *Reminiscences of the Civil War*. New York: Charles Scribner's Sons, 1903.

Green, William H. "From the Wilderness to Spotsylvania." In *War Papers Read before the Commandery of the State of Maine, Military Order of the Loyal Legion of the United States*. 4 vols., 2:91–104. Portland, Maine: Thurston Print., 1898.

Greene, A. Wilson. "From Chancellorsville to Cemetery Hill: O. O. Howard and Eleventh Corps Leadership." In *The First Day at Gettysburg: Essays on Confederate and Union Leadership*, edited by Gary W. Gallagher, 57–91. Kent, Ohio: Kent State University Press, 1992.

Hamblen, Charles P. *Connecticut Yankees at Gettysburg*. Kent, Ohio: Kent State University Press, 1993.

Hammond, Harold Earl. *Diary of a Union Lady 1861–1865*. New York: Funk & Wagnalls Company, 1962.

———. *A Commoner's Judge: The Life and Times of Charles Patrick Daly*. Boston: Christopher Publishing House, 1954.

Handlin, Oscar. "Making Men of the Boys." In *Glimpses of the Harvard Past*, edited by Bernard Bailyn, et al., 45–62. Cambridge, Mass.: Harvard University Press, 1986.

Hanna, William F. "A Gettysburg Myth Exploded." *Civil War Times Illustrated* 24 (May 1985): 42–47.

Harvard College. *Report of the Class of 1855 in Harvard College: Prepared for the Twenty-fifth Anniversary of its Graduation*. Cambridge, Mass.: J. Wilson and Son, 1880.

Harper's Weekly, August 13, 1864.

Hennessy, John J. *Return to Bull Run: The Campaign and Battle of Second Manassas*. New York: Simon and Schuster, 1993.

Higginson, Thomas Wentworth. *Harvard Memorial Biographies*. 2 vols. Cambridge, Mass.: Sever and Francis, 1866.

Hosmer, James Kendall. *The Last Leaf: Observations, during Seventy-five Years, of Men and Events in America and Europe*. New York: G. P. Putnam's Sons, 1912.

Houston, Henry C. *The Thirty-second Maine Regiment of Infantry Volunteers*. 2 vols. Portland, Maine: Press of Southworth Brothers, 1903.

Howard, Charles H. "The First Day at Gettysburg." In *The Gettysburg Papers*, edited by Ken Bandy and Florence Freeland. 2 vols. Vol. 1, 309–36. Dayton, Ohio: Morningside, 1986.

Howard, Oliver O. "After the Battle." *National Tribune*, December 31, 1885.

Howard, William F. ed. "George Benson Fox's Letter to His Father Describes How His Regiment Became 'All Covered with Glory' at Gettysburg." *Military History* 15 (December 1998): 10–14.

Howland, Eliza Woolsey, ed. *Letters of a Family during the War for the Union 1861–1865*. 2 vols. Privately published, 1899.

Jackson, Edward C. "The Bloody Angle." In *Civil War Sketches and Incidents: Papers Read by Companions of the Command of the State of Nebraska, Military Order of the Loyal Legion of the United States,* 258–62. Omaha: Commandery, 1902.

Jaquette, Henrietta Staratton, ed. *South after Gettysburg: Letters of Cornelia Hancock 1863–1868.* New York: Thomas Y. Crowell Company, 1956.

Kiefer, W. R. *History of the One Hundred and Fifty-third Regiment Pennsylvania Volunteers Infantry.* Easton, Pa.: Chemical Publishing, 1909.

Ladd, David L. and Audrey J. Ladd, eds. *The Bachelder Papers.* 3 vols. Dayton, Ohio: Morningside, 1994–95.

Lauter, Don Richard. "'Once upon a Time in the East': Arabella Wharton Griffith Barlow." *The Journal of Women's Civil War History* 1 (2001): 8–25.

[Lee, Alfred E.] A Company Officer, "Reminiscences of the Gettysburg Battle." *Lippincott's Magazine* (July 1883): 54–60.

Leech, Margaret. *Reveille in Washington 1860–1865.* 1941; repr. Alexandria, Va.: Time-Life Books, 1980.

Leopold, Richard. *Robert Dale Owen.* Cambridge, Mass.: Harvard University Press, 1940.

Lipset, Seymour Martin, and David Riesman. *Education and Politics at Harvard.* New York: McGraw-Hill Book Company, 1975.

Long, E. B. *The Civil War Day by Day.* Garden City, N.Y.: Doubleday & Company, 1971.

Lyman, Theodore. "Addenda to the Paper by Brevet Lieutenant-Colonel W. W. Swan, U.S.A., on the Battle of the Wilderness." In *Papers of the Military Historical Society of Massachusetts.* 14 vols., 4:165–73. Boston, 1881–1918.

Malone, Dumas, ed. *Dictionary of American Biography.* 10 vols. New York: Charles Scribner's Sons, 1927–1936.

Marcus, Edward, ed. *A New Canaan Private in the Civil War: Letters of Justus M. Silliman, 17th Connecticut Volunteers.* New Canaan, Conn.: New Canaan Historical Society, 1984.

Martin, George. *Causes and Conflicts: The Centennial History of the Bar of the City of New York 1870–1970.* New York: Fordham University Press, 1997.

McPherson, James M. *Battle Cry of Freedom: The Civil War Era.* New York: Oxford University Press, 1988.

Mills, Sally. "A Chronology of Homer's Early Career, 1859–

1866." In *Winslow Homer Paintings of the Civil War,* edited by Marc Simpson, 16–24. San Francisco: Bedford Arts, Publishers, 1988.

Milne, Gordon. *George William Curtis and the Genteel Tradition.* Bloomington: Indiana University Press, 1956.

Moore, Frank. *Women of the War.* Hartford, Conn.: S. S. Scranton, 1866.

Nevins, Allan, ed. *Diary of the Civil War 1860–1865: George Templeton Strong.* New York: Macmillan Company, 1962.

———, ed. *A Diary of Battle: The Personal Journals of Colonel Charles S. Wainwright 1861–1865.* 1962; repr. Gettysburg: Stan Clark Military Books.

New York Monuments Commission. *In Memoriam: Francis Channing Barlow 1834–1896.* Albany, N.Y.: J. B. Lyon Company: 1923.

Ostrander, Gilman M. *Republic of Letters: The American Intellectual Community, 1776–1865.* Madison, Wis.: Madison House Publishers, 1999.

Pfanz, Harry W. *Gettysburg—The First Day.* Chapel Hill: University of North Carolina Press, 2001.

———. *Gettysburg: Culp's Hill & Cemetery Hill.* Chapel Hill: University of North Carolina Press, 1993.

Phisterer, Frederick. *New York in the War of the Rebellion 1861 to 1865.* 3 vols. Albany, N.Y.: J. B. Lyon Company, 1912.

Pohanka, Brian C., ed. *Nelson A Miles: A Documentary Biography of his Military Career 1861–1903.* Glendale, Calif.: Arthur H. Clark Company, 1985.

Polakoff, Keith Ian. *The Politics of Inertia: The Election of 1876 and the End of Reconstruction.* Baton Rouge: Louisiana State University Press, 1973.

Porter, David D. *Naval History of the Civil War.* New York: Sherman Publishing Company, 1886.

Pride, Mike, and Mark Travis. *My Brave Boys: To War with Colonel Cross and the Fighting Fifth.* Hanover, N.H.: University Press of New England, 2001.

Priest, John Michael, ed. *John T. McMahon's Diary of the 136th New York 1861–1864.* Shippensburg, Pa.: White Mane Publishing Company, 1993.

Quint, Alonzo H. *The Record of the Second Massachusetts Infantry*. Boston: James P. Walker, 1867.

Rhea, Gordon C. *The Battles for Spotsylvania Court House and the Road to Yellow Tavern*. Baton Rouge: Louisiana State University Press, 1997.

———. *The Battle of the Wilderness May 5–6, 1864*. Baton Rouge: Louisiana State University Press, 1994.

Robertson, Robert S. "From the Wilderness to Spotsylvania." In *Sketches of War History, 1861–1865: Papers Read before the Ohio Commandery of the Military Order of the Loyal Legion of the United States*, 1:252–92. Cincinnati, Ohio, 1883.

Rusk, Ralph L., and Eleanor M. Tilton, eds. *The Letters of Ralph Waldo Emerson*. 10 vols. New York: Columbia University Press, 1939–95.

Schurz, Carl. *Reminiscences*. 3 vols. New York: McClure and Company, 1907–8.

———. "The Battle of Gettysburg." *McClure's Magazine* (July 1907): 272–82.

Scudder, Townsend. *Concord: American Town*. Boston: Little, Brown and Company, 1947.

Sears, John van der Zee. *My Friends at Brook Farm*. New York: Desmond Fitz-Gerald, 1912.

Sears, Stephen M. *To the Gates of Richmond: The Peninsula Campaign*. New York: Ticknor & Fields, 1992.

Sears, Stephen W. *George B. McClellan: The Young Napoleon*. New York: Ticknor & Fields, 1988.

———. *Landscape Turned Red: The Battle of Antietam*. New York: Ticknor & Fields, 1983.

Simmers, William. *The Volunteers Manual*. Easton, Pa.: D. H. Neiman, 1863.

Swanberg, W. A. *Sickles the Incredible*. 1956; repr. Gettysburg, Pa.: Stan Clark Military Books, 1991.

Trudeau, Noah Andre. *The Last Citadel: Petersburg, Virginia June 1864–April 1865*. Boston: Little, Brown and Company, 1991.

U.S. Government. *Biographical Directory of the United States Congress 1774–1989*. Washington, D.C.: Government Printing Office, 1989.

———. *The War of the Rebellion: A Compilation of the Official*

Records of the Union and Confederate Armies. 128 vols. Washington, D.C.: Government Printing Office, 1880–1901.

Warner, Ezra J. *Generals in Blue.* Baton Rouge: Louisiana State University Press, 1964.

Weld, Stephen Minot. *War Diary and Letters of Stephen Minot Weld 1861–1865.* Boston: Massachusetts Historical Society, 1979.

Welch, Richard F. *The Boy General: The Life and Careers of Francis Channing Barlow.* Madison, N.J.: Fairleigh Dickinson University Press, 2003.

Welsh, Jack D. *Medical Histories of Union Generals.* Kent, Ohio: Kent State University Press, 1996.

Wert, Jeffry D. *Mosby's Rangers.* New York: Simon and Schuster, 1990.

Wheeler, Ruth R. *Concord: Climate for Freedom.* Concord, Mass.: Concord Antiquarian Society, 1967.

Wilson, Christopher Kent. "Marks of Honor and Death: Sharpshooter and the Peninsular Campaign of 1862." In *Winslow Homer Paintings of the Civil War,* edited by Marc Simpson, 25–46. San Francisco: Bedford Arts, Publishers, 1988.

Wormeley, Katharine Prescott. *The Other Side of War with the Army of the Potomac: Letters from the Headquarters of the United States Sanitary Commission during the Peninsula Campaign in Virginia in 1862.* Boston: Ticknor & Company, 1889.

INDEX

THE NORTH'S CIVIL WAR SERIES
Paul A. Cimbala, series editor

20. Paul A. Cimbala and Randall M. Miller, eds., *An Uncommon Time: The Civil War and the Northern Home Front.*
21. John Y. Simon and Harold Holzer, eds., *The Lincoln Forum: Rediscovering Abraham Lincoln.*
22. Thomas F. Curran, *Soldiers of Peace: Civil War Pacifism and the Postwar Radical Peace Movement.*
23. Kyle S. Sinisi, *Sacred Debts: State Civil War Claims and American Federalism, 1861–1880.*
24. Russell Johnson, *Warriors into Workers: The Civil War and the Formation of Urban-Industrial Society in a Northern City.*
25. Peter J. Parish, *The North and the Nation in the Era of the Civil War.* Edited by Adam L. P. Smith and Susan-Mary Grant.
26. Patricia Richard. *Busy Hands: Images of the Family in the Northern Civil War Effort.*
27. Michael Green. *Freedom, Union, and Power: The Mind of the Republican Party During the Civil War.*